KEYHOLE

INN-SIGHTS:
An Uninhibited
Peek Into the Hotel
World  *By*

C. DE WITT COFFMAN
and
JOHN KEASLER

Cartoons by Don Wright

PRENTICE-HALL, INC., *Englewood Cliffs, N.J.*

To the Hotel World . . .
Its Transient Guests
and Its Permanent Inmates . . .

KEYHOLE
Inn-Sights: An Uninhibited Peek Into the Hotel World
by C. DeWitt Coffman and John Keasler
Copyright © 1972 by C. DeWitt Coffman and John Keasler
Illustrations © 1972 by Prentice-Hall, Inc.
Printed in the United States of America   3
Prentice-Hall International, Inc., London
Prentice-Hall of Australia, Pty. Ltd., North Sydney
Prentice-Hall of Canada, Ltd., Toronto
Prentice-Hall of India Private Ltd., New Delhi
Prentice-Hall of Japan, Inc., Tokyo

●

Library of Congress Cataloging in Publication Data

Coffman, Charles DeWitt.
    Keyhole: inn-sights.

    1. Hotels, taverns, etc.—Anecdotes, facetiae,
satire.   I. Keasler, John, joint author.   II. Title.
PN6231.H7C6   818'.5'407   74-37517
ISBN 0-13-514836-7

TABLE OF CONTENTS

ABOUT THIS BOOK

Keyhole is written to tell you the light side of the paying guest industry and to offer a picture of its traditions, secrets, and outlook.

It's a strange business; the inn is a home for strangers, and strangers can get fairly strange. It's also a business wise in the ways of humans, and it has its way of sizing up its single commodity—you, the guest. It might be entertaining, and could well be advantageous, for you to size up this unique industry.

The hotel is changing fast and always has. It's been only a flicker in time since a man named Statler, in 1908, added an available bath to every room. ("A Room and a Bath for a Dollar and a Half.") It's been even less time since alert ears cocked to the clank-clank of autos from a newfangled assembly line. And hotels were flattened out on acreage, with stall space for the Lizzie—an "m" nudged the "h" over and the motel was born, and prospered.

The change goes on.

Called hotels, motels, motor hotels, inns, now sometimes called boatels . . . the business sells what it always sold: hospitality and comfort of the guest. That's an ancient art, back to the times of currycombs and welcoming flagons for the wayfaring stranger.

Now a quick stirrup-cup . . . one for the road of time . . . and we lift into the future. Who will adapt the moon cave?

Meantime, this book toasts the most grandly untrammeled period of them all—hotels of the right-now.

What is a hotel? Adventure, glamor, sex, humor, multistoried memories, and the unexpected. And, for most of us, a hotel is a break in routine. Many guests not only break routine—they shatter it past recognition, and this book deals with such memorable anecdotes.

A hotel is one of the few places where we can feel pampered . . . taken care of . . . relieved of some of the prosaic sameness of life.

A hotel is a tingle of excitement, where you never really know what may happen around the turn of any corridor. We need that. Computers may get hotels some day . . . but, oh, computers have a fight on their hands! How do you program a business where the exception *is* the rule?

We may computerize the business but who predicts the guests?

Each hotel grows its own personality. It takes a little from each guest. You leave a little of yourself at a good hotel and it gives you in return a memory, and both sides get the best of the swap . . .

A hotel is an individual. Think of all the hotels musing in the night: old and tired hotels, passed by the Freeway of Progress; prim little hotels, tsk-tsking at all the change; hot-shot big-city hotels, playing at the knowing smirk of sophistication. All these hotels say one thing.

If I could only talk, hotels say in the night. People

are born here, people die here, and the things people do in between: these are what I would tell of, hotels say, if I could only talk.

Go ahead and talk, hotels. We're listening.

ABOUT THE AUTHORS

C. DeWitt Coffman is president of Treadway Inns and Resorts, a chain of some forty inns, resorts, motor hotels, and conference centers. His varied experience, which as president of International Hotel Management Company included hotel troubleshooting in this and other countries, goes back to starting in the business as a hawker of hotel accommodations. That last was back when it was no field for shy violets.

His career covers both fact and theory. He has written two other books: *The Full House* and *Marketing,* both published by Cornell University. They are now the prime textbooks for the fifteen major universities which give hotel management degrees. He also writes a monthly column called "Management" for *Hospitality,* one of the trade's leading journals.

He has built an outstanding reputation as a convention and promotion expert. He headed Philadelphia's Convention Bureau; has headed special studies for various cities wishing to attract convention business; was regional supervisor for the Schine chain; was general manager of other large hotels; and at one point supervised putting together a chain of twenty-four hotels and motels for the Futterman Corporation. He is also past international president of the Hotel Sales Management Association.

When Coffman was running International Hotel Management the Miami *News* said, "C. DeWitt Coffman is the Lone Ranger of the hotel management field—he's the rescuer of beleaguered hotel properties."

He collected these documented anecdotes in the hotel business, and the bemusing signs which precede each chapter, over years of travel.

He's putting them in this book form partly just for fun and also to show the adventurous and interesting side of the business to young people. He said:

"We need young talent in the hotel business and one lure is too often neglected, and that is that this business is, among other things, a hell of a lot of fun."

Coffman is a frequent speaker at hotelmen's conventions and he says, "In hotels, every day brings its own oddball absurdity. That's what a hotel is—a series of unexpected and wacky acts by guests and staff alike. This book takes you backstage where the goofiness is."

John Keasler writes two nationally syndicated humor columns for more than one hundred newspapers and is a short story writer and novelist. His humor, fiction, and articles have appeared in many leading national magazines; he has written three other books; and he himself has been the subject of articles in *Time, Newsweek, Life, True,* and other publications.

He has worked on papers from his native Florida to California and back and is now a staffer on the Miami *News.*

Hotels have always fascinated him. Once when working for Hearst papers in San Francisco he lived a week, and very well, at hotel conventions where he had absolutely no business. His only credential was a blue ribbon (which said nothing) on his lapel.

"I was accepted, lived like a prince on caviar and good gin, and would be there yet if it weren't for my wife and the city editor who made me go back to work," he said. He is now writing a musical based on hotel conventions; lives on Key Biscayne with his wife Margery, herself a writer, and their six children.

"In this book, Witt and I disagreed on only one thing," Keasler said. "Each of us insisted he was in the craziest business in the world—Witt in hotels, me in newspapering. We've got a dead heat. I had just been looking at hotels from a guest's point of view, and that's funny enough. But from the inside, it really gets wild."

Don Wright, Pulitizer Prize winning cartoonist for the Miami *News,* has, while still in his thirties, walked off with the heaviest prizes in the tough-minded world of editorial cartooning. They include the Overseas Press Club Award, the Grenville Clark Editorial Page Award, and others.

His work regularly illustrates *Time, Newsweek, The New York Times,* the Washington *Post* and his five-a-week output of cartoons is distributed nationally by the Washington *Star* syndicate. His first book, *Wright On!* has received enthusiastic reviews. Even frequent targets, including President Nixon, have asked for his original work. Spiro Agnew hasn't yet, but Barry Goldwater did—along with a host of other high-ranking victims. (But Spiro was in the cartoon President Nixon asked for. He was getting all the attention while the president was ignored.)

Which is to say that Wright, a too-rare throwback to

the badly missed days of hard-knuckle opinion before they started calling newspapers media, is known more for using his pen as a sword than as a feather but the hotel world tickled him into it. With his sense of humor he understands perfectly and, with his sense of class, he pictorially says it all.

Prologue

The First Inn

The hotel business started shortly after a nonconformist Neanderthal named Ogg invented something called *Inside*. Ogg invented *inside* by moving into a cave, simultaneously getting in out of the rain and adding a new dimension to life. Prior to that time, everything had been *outside*.

Ogg was delighted to find that not only was it nice and dry in this new place called *inside,* but you could even roll a stone up and block the entrance. This eliminated the probability of a saber-toothed tiger using you for a midnight snack, a widespread cause of nervous tension at the time.

Ogg, of course, was at first considered eccentric by his tribesmen. Eventually, however, the idea of *inside* began to catch on. Caves became very *In*. Ogg, in fact, gained a certain status and respect as the pioneer of *inside* and, had he let well enough alone, he could have lived out his life an unharried **man**.

But one night he was sitting around *inside* when he heard a stranger shouting in terror and alarm. Night had fallen and trapped the stranger in the outside. Ogg cracked his stone and peered out. The stranger, who had been en route to his own home in a distant tree, was afraid of the demons of the dark. It's always something.

All the other cavemen had slammed their stones in the face of the stranger, and this was Ogg's first instinct. (In those benighted days, men tended to be distrustful of strangers, particularly treemen, who had a lot of nutty ideas.)

However, as we have seen, Ogg was an innovator; an original thinker; a man not afraid of the untried. Furthermore—and this is pertinent—Ogg noticed that the itinerant treeman was carrying several fresh, lean mastodon chops . . .

Immediately, Ogg quoted both his overnight and weekly rates and showed the treeman inside to his corner, first taking two mastodon chops in advance, as the treeman had no luggage.

The first hotel had been invented.

The treeman, history's *first paying guest,* promptly clubbed a nearby cavewoman and dragged her to his corner; demanded that fresh clean skins be put on his rented ground; complained about the *inside* temperature; cooked in his corner; disturbed everyone by singing far into the night; burnt a hole in his bedclothing, or groundclothing as it was called in those days; slept two hours past check-out time, and left, swiping Ogg's flint fire sparker for a souvenir.

"You know what?" Ogg said to his wife the day after the night he invented the first hotel. "I must have been out of my mind to get into this crazy business."

He at that point became history's first hotel manager.

Even as he groused, he waited eagerly for more paying

Immediately, Ogg quoted both his overnight and weekly rates and showed the treeman inside to his corner, first taking two mastodon chops in advance, as the treeman had no luggage. *The first hotel had been invented.*

guests. Sure enough, that night another transient treeman came into Cave City at nightfall at a dead run, hurrying to get in out of the demons.

"Checking in, sir?" Ogg asked, rubbing his hands.

"Yeah," said the treeman, moving right along, "but not here. I'm registering at the brand-new Wogg Arms across the clearing. It just opened this afternoon, has a swimming puddle, and features free breakfast in your corner."

"*$$*$!" Ogg cursed in Neanderthal, and gritted to his wife: "What does that stupid Wogg know about runing a hotel? I'll tell you one thing—*hotels sure don't have the class they did in the old days!*"

His wife said nothing. She helped him remodel to meet the growing competition. They filled in sinkholes in the cave floor and advertised wall-to-wall ground; later painted abstract bison on the wall. Mrs. Ogg knew he was hooked in the hotel business—and he was.

"Anybody who would get into the hotel business," Ogg would shout, "doesn't have enough damn sense not to come in out of the rain!"

But he stayed in the hotel business all the days of his life. Once you know the *inside* stuff, everything outside is dull.

1

As a Rule, There Are Only Exceptions

NO DANCING IN THE BATHROOMS

> (*Sign in each room of a hotel on the Gaspé Peninsula*)

BECAUSE OF THE IMPROPRIETY OF ENTERTAIN-
ING GUESTS OF THE OPPOSITE SEX IN THE BED-
ROOMS, IT IS SUGGESTED THE LOBBY BE USED
FOR THIS PURPOSE

> (*Sign in Hotel Washington, Colon, Panama Canal Zone*)

THE OCEAN IS CLOSED!

> (*Notice posted at a Miami Beach hotel when lifeguard is off duty*)

Signs, signs, signs. They are a hotelman's attempt to control, or at least guide, his hotel's destiny. Deep down, of course, he knows signs won't do it—but he tries.

In the hotel business, transgressions outstrip policy, rules alone never quite do it, signs fall behind the times, rule-makers come unglued and signs won't cover it. Anyhow, people sometimes steal the signs. What does a hotelman do, then, in his daily—and, notably, nightly—effort to impose some appearance of order on his houseful of unpredictable humans?

To be quite simplistic, he does the very damn best he can. And, somehow, in an ad-lib industry dealing largely with the unexpected, his best averages out quite good.

What is a hotel? Put a sign in your front yard that says "C'mon In, World!" Then you will get an idea.

But you will not use a rulebook long or your rulebook will be taller than your hotel. You will be dealing with the most unpredictable form of life in the known universe—*any given person away from home*. Your commodity is the oldest known explosive: the rental bed. Whole religions have been composed about that.

The good hotelman plays it by ear, not by regulation, and he must come up with instant solutions to unprecedented problems. Each day rings in with a new ding-a-ling and tolls out with a goofy gong.

Some day a neat little computer will be placed in every room and it will be shockproof, waterproof, magnetic-proof, and capable of solving every emergency. The guest in 1810 will break it trying to turn the central air conditioning down, and 1412 will pack it and take it home with the towels, soap, and showerhead.

A hotelman is director of the wildest show in town. In Miami Beach so many middle-class tourists flock into swank hotels to gawk at the rich tourists that managers seriously discuss putting on a cover charge—and that's just for the show in the lobby.

A hotel manager is psychologist, counselor, half hard-nose businessman and half mystic and, above all, fast on his wits. It's a tough, everchanging business and he adapts and stays afloat on a surging sea of ego and surprise or he sinks in the Red Ink Sea.

Would you like to know about the hotel business?

Consider one sign alone. NO DANCING IN THE BATH-ROOMS.

How many people, do you suppose, danced in bath-rooms on the Gaspé Peninsula to warrant such a blanket warning? How many people dance in bathrooms on the Gaspé Peninsula now? Probably a great many, once this rule is posted to remind them. For the basic fact is this:

People act differently away from home. People *are* different in hotels. Don't try to explain it. Accept it. Did you ever hear a joke about a nontraveling salesman?

And the thing about the hotel business is the guests keep changing the rules on you.

Stop to consider the "flagpole."

"I can't figure out how to hang my flagpole out the window," a guest called downstairs at the Deauville Hotel. "And, anyhow, I can't find the flag. Where do you keep the flag?"

This is a bemusing question to get in a hotel which doesn't furnish individual room flagpoles. Investigation showed it wasn't a flagpole. It was a pole vaulting pole somebody else had left behind and that the maid had somehow missed.

The basic point is not how do you forget a pole vault-ing pole. It is not how does a maid not see it. It is not even why the next guest complains he has no flag for his nice flagpole.

It's that you can never anticipate anything, not in the hotel business.

(Left-behind items in that same hotel during that same season included arch supports, false teeth, an incredible number of foam rubber inserts for bras, an artificial leg (who knows?), a vaccine syringe of the type used for doping race horses, and six hockey pucks.)

NO UNNECESSARY LOUD SCREAMING says one sign in a Georgia hotel. This will tell you much about the hotel business, if you care to dwell upon it. What is *unnecessary* loud screaming?

Perhaps "No Screaming" the sign composer felt, cast too much of a pall on his hopefully gala atmosphere. Perhaps. Perhaps unnecessary loud screaming is what, eventually, any hotelman does who tries to run the joint strictly by inflexible rules. . . .

At the Sheraton Cadillac in Detroit, a guest was so enraged the operator put him straight through to the big boss, Mark Schmidt, general manager.

"I've been robbed!" the guest was squalling. "Everything stolen! My suitcase, even my clothes!"

"We'll be right up," said Schmidt.

He followed procedure and took a look at the guest's folio. This tells a lot more than your name and address. To experienced eyes what you've charged, how much, and your number of phone calls add up to a quick picture. For instance, no contact at all with the outside world could—not necessarily does—mean anything from oddball to suicide; huge charges of outside goods to a hotel bill are often the sign of a bill skipper; three solid days of gin fizzes and no solid nourishment except two aspirin say something else.

At any rate, any good hotelman follows procedure. This particular guest seemed okay, but when Schmidt arrived at the room he found one mad—and naked—individual.

"I put everything in my closet when I came in last night," the guest raged. "I mean, yeah, I had a couple of drinks, but I distinctly remember putting everything in the closet."

Schmidt thought it a peculiar robbery. The guest's wallet, keys, and change were still on the dresser.

"Everything else is gone," the guest was hollering. "What the hell kind of place is this where burglars come in the room of a law-abiding citizen?"

The manager called downstairs and a bellhop brought up the guest's suitcase, shoes, socks, shorts, shirt, suit, and necktie. The house detective had found them in the corridor the previous night. You don't go knocking on doors asking who lost their pants, so the house officer turned them in.

"Aha!" shouted the guest, grabbing his belongings. "Who stole them? You catch him?"

He quieted as the truth was explained to him. It must have been pretty good bourbon he had been drinking. He had weaved in, undressed, foggily opened what he thought was a closet door, and thrown everything out into the corridor.

What do you do? Post a sign on the inside room door saying "Not the Closet"? (DO NOT THROW YOUR PANTS INTO THE CORRIDOR.) No—you laugh the guest out of his embarrassment, make a friend of him, and send up a Bloody Mary for breakfast, on the house.

At the Augusta Town House Motor Inn in Augusta, Ga.,

He was sitting nervously watching a horror movie when a man crashed through the third floor window.

a quiet little man was in his room on the third floor watching TV. He sat nervously on the edge of the chair, his eyes bugging out at a horror movie. A man crashed through the picture window and landed on the rug on all fours, scaring the guest no end. Gotcha!

"Help, help!" the guest screeched, falling backward out of his chair. The man who had crashed through the window moved toward him to help, reinforcing the little man's definite impression that Dracula was fixing to have him for supper. He yowled twice as loud and the manager came running.

'Sorry," said the intruder, who didn't represent the Forces of Evil after all. "I just decided to climb up the building and see if I couldn't swing over to the overhang." He pondered this sadly and added, "I guess since I retired I'm out of shape."

He was a senior citizen with five martinis under his belt who had suddenly been seized with the impulse to try his old trade once more.

He was a retired human fly.

See how nice it is to have a nice normal guest like you in the place? Of course, appearances can't be trusted. What looked like an award-winning (for cozy normalcy) All-American family checked into the Manger Windsor Hotel in New York. This hotel is popular with family groups, not only because of its large rooms but because good family hotels have a feeling that parents sense.

And this family was what is always described as lovely. A lovely couple with three lovely children. And lots of good, solid, middle-class luggage . . . which says a bit to hotelmen.

A manager's dream? A manager's nightmare. When

they checked out they took not only the towels, wash cloths, sheets, pillows, blankets, and bedspreads, but the shower curtains, the pictures off the wall—and the television set.

All that nice respectable luggage had been empty. At least when they checked in . . .

That's why pictures are bolted to the walls and television sets and radios secured. It's not that management doesn't trust you. It doesn't trust anybody. (We assume you didn't already *know* the pictures were bolted to the walls.)

Some thefts defy logic. Police were called to one hotel where a man was filling his suitcase with *telephones*. Hotels may be the only business where management spends a lot of money to protect its customers from being robbed while some of the customers are busy robbing them.

Tradition has it that hotelmen don't like to talk about pilferage to folks outside the trade, particularly reporters and writers. The idea—it may have some validity—is that publicizing thievery may remind more guests to steal. However, no accurate picture of the hotel business can be given without showing that facet. People *do* steal— people who ordinarily wouldn't dream of stealing. It's part of the away-from-home syndrome . . . as we said, people are different in hotels. At the Sans Souci, somebody stole the stone statues out of the lobby—and they weighed eight hundred pounds each. We don't think pilferage is a well-kept secret.

"We come for the rugs," briskly said one of the overalled men who with two helpers walked into New York City's Gotham Hotel.

Employees even helped them roll up the expensive oriental rugs, under the impression the rugs were going to the cleaners. The hotel was going to the cleaners—the trio were of a bold breed known in the trade as "comfers," as in: "We come for the fire extinguishers." And—at the Manger Vanderbilt—they got what they come for: dozens of extinguishers, exchangeable for upwards of fifteen dollars each (for the brass) to any fence.

"I wish they had left just one extinguisher," moaned the assistant manager. "The manager almost burned me up when he found out."

Oddly, in the business where much effort is devoted to making off with hotel property, other guests leave immensely valuable things behind—expensive jewelry, trophies, fur coats. One guest some years ago checked out of Atlanta's Henry Grady and flew home forgetting his car.

Parents have left their children in the lobby and taken a cab to the airport. A man and his mother-in-law left a hotel while arguing so heatedly, reports Miami hotelman Gene Hogan, that they were airborne toward Detroit before remembering they had left his wife at the hotel.

Hogan, of the Deauville, is a master publicist who immediately turns all such incidents to good use: in his view it happened because the wife couldn't bear to leave.

One tip from the trade. If you do forget something, don't wait for the hotel to send it to you—unless you write or call and ask for it. Hotels these days are, usually, too smart to stick their foot in your mouth. The trade is full of unhappy incidents resulting from letters like this:

Dear Mr. and Mrs. Wilfrawp:
   We trust you enjoyed your stay at the Naive-Arms and will return again. We are returning the blue lace

negligee and bottle of Unconditional Surrender perfume
left by Mrs. Wilfrawp, along with Mr. Wilfrawp's Elk's
tooth with his social security number engraved on it.
Cordially, the Management, Naive-Arms.

Sad experience has shown this doesn't make a lasting
friend of Mr. Wilfrawp if it develops the real Mrs. Wilfrawp had been at home with her sinus all the time. So it's
worth knowing that you should write for what you've left.
Many things about hotels are worth knowing—to the
guest.

And what's a guest? He's a member of the world's
biggest family: nomads seeking shelter, protection, fun,
and the magic of change . . . wanderers with a thousand motivations, moving through our restless land. Sometimes, in fact, they're real nomads. George De Kornfeld,
vice-president of London's Carlton Towers, remembers a
group of Arabs from the oil-rich Middle East—they rented
a whole floor, but complained about the beds. Nothing
was wrong with the beds as such: they just hated sleeping
in beds.

"They put their tents in the corridors and slept in them,"
said De Kornfeld. "We didn't object, of course. One must
make the guest feel quite at home, you know."

Maybe not *quite* at home, always . . . the hotel man
is always a step away from chaos, and he must keep rela-
tive order in the house.

A good hotel has to maintain a balance between being
a ho-ho-hotel and a no-no-hotel. Nobody likes to check
into a disciplinary camp. On the other hand the bed-
rental business produces much hanky-panky. This requires handling.

Hotelmen can handle it, although on some occasions guests come up with answers which are hard to top.

When Frank Bennett was night manager of the Cleveland Statler he made the standard call, after reports of shenanigans, and asked, "Are you entertaining a lady in your room?"

"Yeah," the man growled. "What do you think I am? A fag?"

And another time when Bennett called with the rhetorical question—when hotelmen call to ask, they already know—he asked this guest if he had a lady in his room.

"I'll be damned if I know," came the reply. "Hang on— I'll ask her."

A guest, to put it one way, is the flip side of us all. We're different out of town. Where is Life, with its capital L—the glamor and screwball excitement of it all? You remember—it was in the hotel, in a distant town.

Hotels are a different world because no matter where they are . . . everybody is from out of town. And, oh, this makes the difference.

Fifty-three percent of Americans have never spent a night in a hotel or motel. In some ways it seems a shame. On the other hand, when you stop to think of what the other forty-seven percent have been up to . . .

Not you, of course.

This book is about the other guests.

There were two places left in this modern, hurried world where a person could be totally, beautifully alone —as opposed to lonely.

One was the passenger train, but it is vanishing. You could be alone on a train. Complete isolation. No phones.

No immediate demands for a little while. Freedom. Freedom from . . . not responsibility, exactly, a furlough, a few hours away from the chaos of little things. Now the train is leaving us, trailing its mournful whistle of deep-toned memory; highballing into the past.

The other place—the only other place for most of us—is a hotel or motel room. What feeling matches it?

You've tipped the bellhop; the door closes; you're out of your mental button-down collar, or the girdle is on the floor. It's a time of contemplation, a time to flop back onto a beautifully strange and comfortable bed on an island of promise. There is a strange glamor in a hotel, regardless of the price of your room.

Enchantment lives in hotels. The farm boy feels it the first time he goes to Little Rock or Phoenix or St. Paul. The tycoon feels it at the Waldorf. It's the same feeling. It's a rare breath of *alone* before a look at a world with something new in it.

A weekend in a hotel turns a wife back into a bride. Something about a hotel makes a man surge with adventure. All kids think that heaven has a swimming pool and an ice machine down the Pearly Corridor. Of all the things an inn sells, the basic thing is magic.

Something's going to happen. Something new and different. That is the aura of promise.

And something usually does.

2

Checking In?

TO EXPEDITE EGRESS, PLEASE LEAVE IRRE-
SPECTIVE OF SEX

> (*Elevator sign in a San Francisco hotel*)

THE DIRECTORS HAVE THE RIGHT TO REFUSE
ADMISSION TO ANY LADY THEY THINK PROPER

> (*Behind the front desk of a London hotel*)

It takes some special kind of mentality to be a hotel room clerk. To the guest, he represents management—consequently he catches hell. To management, he represents something less than top echelon rank—as his paycheck tells him every week—and he catches hell from that end, too.

But, oh, the passing parade he sees.

It's tradition that you can't rattle a good room clerk. Like some of the better traditions, that one even has some truth in it.

One "resort hotel" offered free golf in its national advertising. A guest who had just checked in came back down happily as soon as he could change, carrying his golf bag, and asked the clerk, "Where's the course?"

"Actually," said the clerk, "the, ah, larger golf course isn't what you might say on the premises."

In was, in fact, $7.50 away as the cab meter ticks.

"Where's the smaller course?" growled the guest.

Mutely, the clerk pointed out the back door. A putting green about eighteen yards long was in the cabana area.

The guest was a true golfer, all right. He exploded.

"Your ad said FREE golf. By God!" he shouted, "and I'm going to *get* free golf!"

As the clerk ducked behind the desk the guest whipped out his driver, pounded the desk until he bent the shaft, and then got out his putter. Black marble slivers began flying from the desk top and striking the wall.

"What's happening?" shouted the manager, sticking his head out of his office into range of marble shrapnel.

From beneath the front desk came the room clerk's reply: "Fore!"

A room clerk must, above all, be adaptable. Every manager dreams of hiring a clerk-psychologist like the one who used to work at the Emerson Hotel in Baltimore. He was on duty when two very apparent male homosexuals half-skipped across the lobby, swished up to the front desk, and asked coyly for a room.

"Sorry," said the clerk. "If you don't have a reservation, we're all filled."

A room clerk has to make instant judgments and the "all filled-up" line is one of the few weapons in his slim arsenal.

"Filled? Oh, that's nothing but a *fib!*" shrilled one of the pair.

"You're discriminating against us," the other shouted, stamping his dainty foot.

People in the lobby were turning to look.

"Sorry," said the clerk, putting on his remote look and playing robot. "Without a res—"

"Bigot, bigot, *bigot!*" shrieked one of the pair.

"And a meanie, too!" piped the soprano.

The tantrum was picking up steam. Then, suddenly, the clerk stamped *his* foot furiously, put his hands on *his* hips and shrilled right back, "Don't you *dare* to talk to me like that or I'll scratch your bitchy eyes right *out!*"

The lovers shot him one startled look through faint mascara and took off at a fast mince.

The clerk looked solemnly at another man waiting to register. The clerk said in a voice about as effeminate as a longshoreman's, "Don't jump to conclusions, sir. I just had to speak to them in their native language!"

That's good thinking—a lot better than management actually deserves in the room clerk situation, generally. Hotel brass—the money boys—can be uncannily shrewd in many matters. In the clerk situation, however, management sometimes seems to have a short circuit in its mental wiring. The average clerk's pay just isn't in accordance with the importance of the job.

To the guest, a clerk *is* management. Perhaps the doorman gives an important first impression of a hotel, maybe the bellmen contribute to that impression. But it's the

clerk alone who makes the arriving guest feel important
or, too often, feel furious. Why invest a huge sum in the
swankest, most luxurious hotel possible—then make the
man who is your official greeter rank somewhat lower
than employees nobody even sees?

Newer thinking tends to rank him in relationship to the
importance of his job.

It's not so bad for the clerk. If he's good he'll advance.
If he's not, he won't survive. While he's there, he has a
fascinating time.

It's inevitable at least in larger hotels, that the old-
fashioned idea of clerk will change. He *is* management to
guests—it's obvious he will have to become management
to management, too. The future "clerk" may actually be
an executive, overseeing pretty young ladies, ideally, or
computers, less ideally.

Meanwhile, he goes about his somewhat split-person-
ality job with aplomb and, more often than not, has a ball
in the process—if he learns, first of all, to be immune to
abuse.

"That clerk is so stuck-up he should be fired!" a dowager
told the assistant manager at a Seattle hotel. "Where's the
nice clerk who always smiled at me and joked a lot when
I saw him last year?"

"That's him," the assistant manager said. "He's changed,
since you complained last year about him being so fresh."

At the Mayflower in Washington, D.C., the Century
Plaza in Los Angeles, the Regency in New York, and
other hotels frequented by celebrities, famous faces and
names are commonplace. Real big-timers, as a general
rule, don't throw their weight around. Only the bush
leaguers are rude. The biggest pains are the newly arrived pan-flash show-business types. They're furious if

their "privacy" is violated—but they go right up the wall if they're ignored or unrecognized.

One of these egotistical hambos arrived at the Mayflower so incognito that people were staring from all over the lobby. He had a loud scarf around his neck and chin, his hat was pulled low, and he was wearing huge sunglasses. He looked like Claude Raines playing the *Invisible Man*. When he registered, the clerk couldn't read his handwriting.

"Don't you know who I am?" shouted the self-styled star, whipping off his glasses and scarf and turning his good side. The clerk had never laid eyes on him, but he said, "Gee! Can I have your autograph?"

Ego intact, carefully signing his autograph, this gift to the acting art strode away. The clerk later said, "I could make out his name on the autograph, and just copied it right on the register."

For one of the most distinguished publishers of hotel trade journals, the following episode will always sum up room clerk personality—and unflappability.

The publisher was staying at a hotel and had celebrated something or other a bit too freely. He would take a drink, despite association with the teetotaling trades of journalism and hotels. On one occasion, in fact, he took more than one drink—his story exemplifies two fascinating things: the strange logic of a drunk and the perhaps stranger suaveness of a good clerk.

Let Mr. Smith tell it, starting immediately after a blackout binge we shall not try to trace, as it is, probably, irrelevant.

"All I remember," muses Mr. Smith, "is that when I came to I was standing in the corridor. In my pajamas. Bare-footed. It must have been about 2 A.M. To this day

I do not know where I had been, which may be fortunate or unfortunate, depending on circumstances.

"Anyhow, drunks *do* think and reason. They really do. It would be better if they didn't, but they do. I realized I was standing outside my own room. The door was locked. So, I reasoned, if the door was locked, I must already be in there asleep. I knocked to wake me up to let me in.

"Eventually I reasoned that I had probably had so much to drink I wasn't about to hear me knocking, so I did the next logical thing. I took the elevator to the lobby and weaved up to the clerk, barefooted, as I say, and in my rather fetching purple pajamas.

"My intention was to ask him for a spare key, explaining I couldn't get into my room as I was already in bed sound asleep, or, if the truth were known, probably stoned as an owl. My thinking was perfectly clear but my tongue kept getting caught on various obstacles—my teeth, the roof of my mouth, and so on—and I couldn't pronounce a single word, including my own name.

"The clerk chose not to believe a purple drunk was there at all, waving dumbly and making faces at him. He went on about his business. 'Mmmmpf ithhhppp,' I would state. He never raised his eyes from his tabulating work.

"At long, long last he looked up with that complete deadpan the good ones have. He said, 'Go away. Go away. Go away.'

"I walked across the lobby and curled up on the sofa, obeying my master. It was very late; he let me sleep. About two hours later I woke up, half sober. I remembered the corridor, talking to the clerk, but nothing before.

"I practiced pronouncing my name, shuffled over, asked for my key. The clerk was chipper and cheery, saying, 'Yes, indeed, sir! Here you are, sir! Have a pleasant day, sir!'

"I went upstairs and let myself into my empty room and, except for a fleeting mild surprise not to find myself in bed, knew I was sobering up. To this day, when faced with a wildly strange circumstance, I sometimes say, 'Go away. Go away. Go away.' I think of it as the Room Clerk's Spell."

Clerks come in various degrees of proficiency. Howard L. Dayton of Howard Dayton Enterprises remembers a night clerk he once hired at Casa Ybel Resort at Sanibel Island, Fla. The clerk and his wife were quartered in a unit right next to the lake.

The clerk had been working there an entire month when, one night, his wife rushed in screaming that her husband was drowning. He was fished out of the lake and taken to his room—which was full of empty Scotch bottles. Evidently he always turned right, toward the package store, but that night he made a wrong turn, and his wife was in a screaming rage at the management.

"We've been here a month," she shouted. "Why didn't somebody warn us there was a lake there?"

Any veteran clerk is bound to get blasé. He sees it all. People see the room notice which says "Check-out Time: 2 P.M." and call up to say they can't possibly stay that late without missing their train or plane. The number of would-be Lotharios who confuse the clerk with the resident pimp—and ask him the rates on local girls—is depressing. At the opposite extreme are straitlaced folk who have heard about all the sin in the big city and are ever ready to strike out at the first sign of evil. E. Bill

Green, managing director of the Bourbon Orleans, tells of the elderly, stern-visaged rural resident who was registering on his first visit to "sinful" New Orleans.

"How many in your party, sir?" asked the room clerk.

"Mind what you say, sonny! There ain't going to be no party!" The guest was indignant. "Just me and Mama!"

It's possible to get too blasé. In Kansas City an otherwise good hotel is cursed by its proximity to the railroad yards. One guest who checked in called down in less than an hour.

"Hey," he said. "Get somebody up to my room right now."

"Yes, sir," tiredly said the clerk, used to complaints about switch engine noise on the north side. "We'll move you to another room which you will find more satisfactory. It may take a few minutes to get someone up for your luggage."

There was a short, puzzled pause.

"Never mind, I'll carry my own luggage," the guest said. "This goddamn room's on fire!"

At the Sir Walter in Raleigh, N.C., a hippie checked in —with four lumpy duffle bags—and registered for a single rate. The bellman struggled to the room with what seemed like an uncommonly large amount of luggage for an antimaterialistic sort. He went after more luggage racks and was delayed. When he came back the bearded guest was gone—but now there were eleven duffle bags, four bedrolls, and two camp stoves.

The bellman told the clerk, who told the assistant manager, who went up and locked the room with the double-locking key. Later the outraged hippie stalked up to the clerk.

"Hey, Dad," he said. "You gimme the wrong key. This won't open my room."

Coldly, the clerk said, "Sir, did you wish to inquire about our commune rates?"

"Never mind, we'll blow," said the hippie, whose seven friends were hiding in the alley. "What you doing in this racket when you can read minds?"

At the Royal Orleans a man and his "wife" checked in. She was a knockout. After fifteen minutes an order came down for champagne. Ah, young love. After thirty minutes the husband came charging into the lobby.

"Where do I pay my bill?" he growled.

The clerk asked if something was wrong with the service or the room.

"None of your business," the guest snarled. "I just want outta here!"

"May I ask if your wife is checking out also?"

"If I ever catch that sonofabitch," the guest roared, "he'll check right out of the whole damn world!"

That hadn't been his wife. That hadn't even been a lady. That was a female impersonator . . .

Part of the clerk's job is to size up any and every registering guest. Suicides have been prevented by the perception of a room clerk who simply *feels* that this particular guy is something more than just another depressed loner —and checks up on him. He knows the rules of thumb about who's married and who isn't. (Married men tend to come through a revolving door before their wives— but the male *always* lets the illicit lady go first. Newlyweds always wear new shoes.) There's humor in the register signing sometimes. Only a rattled newlywed would sign "Mr. and Mrs. Sam Jones and wife." Between the first name and the last name there is sometimes a significant pause. A room clerk at the Mark Hopkins in San Francisco watched a swarthy mobster-type swiftly sign his first name, which, we'll say, was "Angelo."

Suddenly Angelo paused, knitted his thick dark brows in creative thought, then wrote his other name for the occasion: "Muligan."

Angelo Muligan obviously wasn't the kind of man you insulted by pointing out that Mulligan usually had two l's, but a house officer is always interested in these little things.

You don't need a lot of ESP to know that some people are simply screwballs. You just need to be able to see over the desk. At the Bon Air Hotel in Augusta, Ga., a well-dressed man was standing at the counter when the clerk looked up. The man wanted a single.

"Yes sir," said the clerk. Then he noticed a bellman standing behind the man, pointing down. This is a hotel signal meaning, usually, "No luggage."

"Would you care to pay the overnight rate now?" the clerk asked.

"Shertainly," said the man, reaching toward his hip pocket for his wallet and staggering back a couple of steps as he did so. Now the clerk had a fuller view. The man was well-dressed, all right, from the waist up. He was nude from the waist down, having forgotten not only his wallet but his pants. He got a single in the Augusta jail.

Being a room clerk calls for diplomacy in the face of adversity. Still remembered is the classic coolness of a clerk some years ago at the Chase Hotel in St. Louis.

In swept a matron of vast fortune and social clout with her pet Pomeranian and harried husband. She put the pooch up on the desk, complaining how *teddibly* poor

He hadn't forgotten just his wallet . . . he had
forgotten his pants.

little Pom-Pom had been treated at that *awful* hotel in New York. The clerk indicated that Pom-Pom's slightest wish would be his command.

"Hearum's nice mans?" she gushed to the surly little dog. "Pom-Pom's donna be *so* happy-happy here!"

Pom-Pom responded by languidly raising one leg and soaking the registration book. The long suffering husband closed his eyes in anguish. Even the woman was a bit taken aback. The clerk carried it off. He swept the book under the counter and in the same motion handed the woman the pen she had signed with.

"Accept this as a souvenir for Pom-Pom from the modern Chase Hotel," the clerk said, "where all the pens write under water."

They say the husband smiled for the first time that anybody could remember. We don't know where the clerk is now. We keep looking for his appointment as head of the Diplomatic Service.

Hotels make up a world with its own history and language. The word "hotel" itself is of ancient origin. (The medieval Latin *hospitale;* old French *osterie.*) There is, of course, Biblical mention of the inn. Chaucer's "Tabard" had all the essentials of a modern hotel: a sign, a host, a staff of servants, a table d'hôte meal . . . and a reckoning or bill.

In 1577 the Reverend William Harrison wrote in his *Descriptions of England* a passage which could still describe next year's fashion hotel, and not be too far off.

Those townes we call thorowfaires have great and sumptuous innes builded in them . . . verie well furnished with naperie . . . each commer is sure to lie in clean sheets, wherein no man hath beene lodged since they came from the laundresse . . . there is no greater securities anie where for travellers than in the greatest inns . . .

Old hotels often gave rooms names instead of numbers: the Rose Room, Crown Room, Star Room, and so on. And travel writers haven't changed much, either. A seventeenth century writer named Richard Brathwait went four times on horseback from Oxford to London between 1610 and 1630. And what did he write about? The beer and the hostesses, naturally, and the joys of such inns as The Bull, The Bell, The Rotherham, The Cock. He was known among innkeepers of the time as "Drunken Barnaby." We don't know why, unless he had reason to register under a phony name quite often. (It beats Angelo Muligan.)

The stagecoach, the train, even the bicycle, and certainly the motorcar brought their own innovations to the industry. In basic ways, however, it remains the same. It's an old game and hospitality is still the name of it. That each hotel grows its own personality is a fact; inexplicable, perhaps, but a fact. They become as different over the years as humans become different with years . . . and some seem born (built) with their own character. Two hotels built during the same period, completed the same month, and physically much similar, will *feel* different.

There are hotels in which nothing works right, nothing has ever worked right, and nothing will ever work right. Eventually, the most realistic manager comes to accept it —and regular guests come to love it. If things started working right they would leave. Who wants an old, loved, eccentric friend suddenly to turn efficient?

Ghosts? If so, leave them alone . . .

But take, let us say, New York's elderly and beautiful St. Regis. It is . . . patrician, genteel. Take also the venerable Algonquin. It is . . . knowing, a bit raffish.

Is this solely because writers and artists have traditionally stayed at the Algonquin while aristocrats of a more seemly sort have stayed at the St. Regis? Maybe. But it is more, too. The Algonquin is the kind of individual perfectly capable of giving the St. Regis a hotfoot . . .

At some point the impression given by a hotel defies all explanation and the total becomes more than the sum of the component ghosts. Some things *can* be explained, and one of the immediate impressions of a hotel is the doorman, embodiment of the palace guard syndrome. We are all latent royalty, and a good doorman brings it out.

There have been great characters among hotel doormen. One of the best known of them all, Mike of the Hotel Mayflower in Washington, D.C., amassed a small fortune partly through his seemingly uncanny ability to remember everybody's name. We all like to be remembered.

The fact is Mike could barely speak English at all when he came from Russia. He wouldn't say anybody's name. But he found he could make *any* noise as enthusiastic greeting, and everybody assumed it was that most beautiful of all sounds—a person's own name. (Maybe with a little Russian accent.)

Doormen earn their money. The entrance of any good-sized hotel would be a confused shambles without them. Only in Miami and Las Vegas are doormen actually big businessmen—but in these places no other term would describe them. A very few doormen, in fact, *pay* up to fifty thousand dollars a year for the door concession.

Even then it isn't simply a heaven-sent shower of gratuities and featherbedding. It's a businesslike contract between the hotel and the concession bidder to take over the entire responsibility of manning the hotel's front entrance.

In addition to tips, parking fees, commissions on auto rentals and sight-seeing trips, the resort doorman collects fees from nightclubs and restaurants for steering patronage to them.

During something like a Sinatra opening at the Fontainebleau, or a big convention anywhere, a hotel driveway would be like a cross between Dante's Inferno and the Keystone Cops without a master strategist running things.

Aside from Big Business doormen, however, the usual doorman makes his tips largely through some form of person-to-person service. His mental—and sometimes his physical—agility, his personality, and his ingenuity determine his profits.

Any auto can disgorge a screwball.

At the Ambassador in Los Angeles, a doorman was taking a suitcase out of a cab when the practical-joking arrival shouted, "Hey, be careful! That's got a bomb in it!"

The doorman sprinted to the nearest watertap with the suitcase, flicked the catches, yanked open the suitcase, and soaked the clothing and contents.

"Goddammit," moaned the suitcase owner. "There ain't no bomb. I was just trying to be funny."

"Well, sir," said the doorman, "You succeeded. Everybody's laughing."

Anthony M. Rey, general manager of Atlantic City's famous Chalfonte-Haddon Hall, has many special weekend events at the hotel (Caribbean Carnival, Winter Circus), and it's not uncommon for animal acts to be brought in. There have been llamas, dancing dogs, and a baby elephant waiting in corridors off the main hall to go on stage. Once a chimp on roller skates jumped off stage and headed for the lounge, doing figure eights among the potted palms.

"What's that big monkey doing in there on roller skates?" a startled passerby asked the doorman.

"It's tough to get a cab this time of night," was the deadpan reply.

Publicity men drive doormen crazy. Eventually every publicity man comes up with the idea of having an animal check into the hotel. Doormen have solemnly ushered in Elsie the Cow, Clarence the Cross-Eyed Lion, Sabu the Elephant Boy, plus elephant, Mr. Ed the Talking Horse, dancing bears, seals.

Animals are very poor tippers. Bing at the McAllister in Miami looked down once at the organ-grinder's monkey who was holding its tin cup out.

"Okay, but I shouldn't," he said, dropping a coin in the cup. "Not after all the times you guys have stiffed me."

Outside the Jefferson Hotel in St. Louis a visiting British lecturer on birds of prey strode up to the doorman, with an eagle perched on his shoulder.

"Could you keep an eye out for the people from the museum who are supposed to pick me up?" he asked worriedly.

"O.K.," said the doorman. "You hide around the corner and I'll give you the high sign when they're gone."

Big Kenny, doorman at the Columbus Hotel in Miami, has "Columbus" emblazoned across his cap and chest pocket. He stands under a marquee saying "Columbus" in huge neon letters. Brass plaques saying "Columbus" are behind him.

All day long, every day and night, people by the dozen ask him, "Say, is this the Columbus?"

Oh, yes, doormen earn their money . . .

They're not all paragons, of course. Former executives of New York City's defunct Hotel Astor still shudder at the memory of the big doorman who stood at the 44th Street side entrance, a picture of dignity. It was a false picture, the general manager found to his shocked surprise.

Just as the manager happened by one day the doorman, standing on the lowest step, leaned far back, snapped his head forward . . . and emitted a mighty spurt of tobacco juice. It barely cleared the heads of two startled women walking by. Taxi driver spectators cheered. The manager did not cheer. He fired the doorman on the spot . . . and then had to rehire him. Why?

Because the hotelworker's union is strong and it made a case that the doorman had never been told *not* to chew tobacco on duty, or *not* to spit over the heads of little old ladies. (Compose a sign about that.)

A rookie cop new on the beat is a doorman's nightmare. Any doorman has to be somewhat flexible about no-parking rules within his limited space, not only to take care of his good tippers but to handle arriving traffic efficiently.

Veteran cops know this. Rookies go by the book. You can tell the arrival of a young cop. There are so many yellow parking tickets around that the street looks like a meadow in daisy season. Do you argue with the rookie, who, after all, is trying to do his job?

"Nope," said a veteran doorman. "You do *exactly what he tells you to do*. Before long, you got a traffic jam that's a real dandy. I let the rookie's sergeant explain the facts of life. Police sergeants do that so well."

Many doormen's uniforms could be the envy of any admiral. Young servicemen often salute doormen—all of whom toss a snappy salute back.

The uniform has practical reasons. A uniform identifies the doorman, yes, but it does more. Any homegrown psychiatrist can tell you that most of us get bigger kicks having someone do our bidding who looks like a full field marshall than like a lackey in, say, bib overalls. Collectively, we may be so democratic that we snicker when the White House tries to gussy up *its* palace guards real hotshot. Individually, we like the regal system—if we get to play king.

Widespread use of uniforms or livery of any sort for hotel employees is relatively new. In his excellent book on the Statler operation (*A Bed for the Night*), Rufus Jarman writes that James Breslin (not the journalist), owner of the old Gilsey House in New York, put uniforms on his bellmen in 1877; shortly thereafter he also put doormen and elevator operators into uniform. Until then the only livery had been worn by porters—a round hard cap with a stiff visor and a brass plate. Use of uniforms spread swiftly in the competitive hotel business.

But it wasn't really new. European inns centuries ago sometimes had an early version of doormen, wearing uniforms. They protected arriving and departing guests from footpads and cutpurses, and the modern-day doorman isn't all that removed from this function. You're usually safe from purse snatchers outside a hotel largely because any good doorman can spot a thief—and it's the doorman more than anybody else who keeps the entrance clear of ladies of prey: the lasses with the come-hither look in their eyes and the chloral hydrate knockout drops in their purse.

The doorman, some historians say, came from the institution of the stagecoach footman, and served the same purpose. Protection.

The uniform still means authority today. Drunks respond more quickly to somebody with military brushes on his shoulders. The most independent of all creatures —New York cabdrivers—would be the first to sneer at the idea of their response to *any* authority figure. But, rest assured, if civilian garb moved traffic faster, every doorman in America would be wearing a very conservative Brooks Brothers suit.

A doorman—he'll tell you with a sigh—needs all the authority he can muster, fake, or borrow, for his job takes unexpected turns. It was Bing, at the McAllister, who watched two flashily dressed men pull up to the entrance in a rental car, hand him a couple of bucks, and say, "Keep the car right here—we'll be right back."

They went in. Promptly, following procedure, he took the keys from the car. He hung them on the board of key hooks all doormen have. About two minutes later the two men raced out, obviously panic-stricken; slammed into Bing, knocking him down. The keys scattered on the sidewalk. The men piled into the car. The driver squealed in fear:

"Keys! Where's the keys, you stupid bastard?"

The other man leaped out and was crawling around on the sidewalk with Bing, searching for the keys. Bing found them. The man grabbed them—and just then a large, red-faced furious man wearing a ten-gallon sombrero came charging out of the hotel. You could tell he wasn't happy.

Spotting the guy on all fours, the one with the keys, he screamed like a scalded panther and punted him six feet. Terrified, keening in a high-pitched moan of fear, the flashily-dressed puntee described a short arc, came up on the first bounce, and went through the window of the car screaming, "Get out of here!"

"I'll kill 'em," I'll kill 'em," the large cowboy sort was bellowing. The driver was trying to get the keys into the ignition, which is tough to do when somebody is reaching through the window pounding you on top of the head with a fist like a Tennessee ham.

But he got it started and the car roared off. A police car screeched up.

"What's the trouble here, Mister?" called one of the cops who piled out.

"Trouble? I'll tell you what the trouble is!" The red-faced man was snorting, frothing, shaking his fist. "Those two dirty . . . uh . . . "

Suddenly, he fell silent.

Meekly, then, as Bing, the cops, and the crowd watched, he said in a small voice, "No trouble, officers."

And he turned and walked swiftly back into the hotel. Bing and the cops looked blank. The police shrugged, left.

But Bing made it a point to find out.

The two flashy men were male prostitutes. They had gone into the hotel to pick up—by previous arrangement —a lonely, wealthy lady guest whose husband was away.

They had just called Her Ladyship on the lobby phone and were informing her that her lover boys awaited when, of all people, the husband, returning unexpectedly, happened to overhear them talking to his wife.

He went at the pay-boys with mayhem in his heart. It was two frightened male whores who ricocheted off Bing. It was a wronged husband, in full cry of righteous wrath, who was trying to get in a little justifiable homicide.

It was at this point of the plot that the police asked, "What's the trouble, Mister?"

And it then became apparent that his sudden meek silence was perfectly logical.

Think it over. What could any strong masculine type say?

Different doormen have different talents. One of the best known doormen in the country is Stewart, so well-known he goes by that name alone, at the Sir Walter Hotel in Raleigh, N.C. He's old school hospitality, overwhelms you with personality and, smile glistening and apple-cheeks aglow, out-politicians the politicos in that state capital . . . actually greeting them all happily by shouted name. A greeting from Stewart is a status symbol among the dignitaries.

Doormen have become mobile at many of the newer motor inns at airports where they drive courtesy buses to and from the terminal. At O'Hare airport in Chicago where one motor lodge uses little Volkswagen buses, the doorman sells the idea of "individual, personalized buses." (You get more tips that way than by describing them as cramped.)

The Hollenden in Cleveland has lettered across the

sterns of its courtesy buses: 25 SECONDS FROM OUR DOOR
TO THE MUNICIPAL AUDITORIUM. This was a gag slogan
invented by John Nolan when he was sales manager, and
in tiny print beneath is this qualification . . . *if you're
shot from a cannon.* Doormen capitalized on it—when
customers groused about the distance, doormen handed
them a blowup of the fine print. Laughs get tips.

Should you tip a doorman?

*Sure, if he performs a service and you can afford it and
feel you should.* That's all this book has to say about
tipping. Tipping is a personal matter and if you need
advice on it read Temple Fielding, who knows everything
there is to know about travel, and/or Amy Vanderbilt,
who also does.

Amy Vanderbilt told the authors of this book, "I've
sold millions of books and written about every aspect of
what to do when, and it all boils down to exactly two
things. Always under any circumstance do what simple
good manners tells you to do, and if you don't know
what constitutes good manners in a given circumstance
never be afraid to ask." We can't add anything to that.

One hotel doorman was baffled about a lot of grins on
the faces of arriving customers, plus several rather
pointed queries asking where the girls were. Finally he
walked around and looked at the sign painted on the back
of the bus from the airport. Instead of saying THIRTY-FIVE
SECONDS FROM RAMP TO ROOM, somebody had changed
it to THIRTY-FIVE SECONDS FROM RAMP TO RUMP.

You get con men doormen. At Chicago's O'Hare Inn
one of the sharp ones would whisper to arriving guests,
"Don't quote me, but this is a big, rambling layout. To
avoid getting a room with one of those long walks from
the desk, just tell the clerk you've got a heart condition

or a hernia and your doctor doesn't want you to do a lot of walking."

He really got astronomical tips. The room clerk, of course, had long since tumbled to the gag; he would merely give that room clerk smile and assign whatever room was available. He said he had seen more ailments than Marcus Welby, M.D.

If some doormen, particularly in the larger cities and most specifically in New York, act a bit high and mighty —the Admiral complex—it may be purposeful intimidation; there's a theory in many tip-oriented fields that it's good to more or less *scare* the customer into shelling out by being some sort of authority figure.

Sometimes it works, sometimes it doesn't. One doorman in New York City makes a lot more with the opposite approach. He is so drawling country-boy friendly and so quick to help and so absolutely downhome chummy that never a day goes by but what people say, "Gee, it's nice to see a friendly New Yorker for a change."

And he says, "Wal, suh, I reckon I jest ain't been in the big city long enough to larn no better."

The tips pour in. He's a native of the Bronx.

So, notice the doormen. They're interesting people. And—certainly—whether they seem to or not—they notice you.

The experienced doorman can read arriving guests like a carnival palmist. Just by looking at you he can almost surely tell: whether or not you have a reservation; whether you're coming to dine or stay as a guest (and before he knows if you have luggage); whether you're a good tipper (before you reach in your pocket); whether the girl you're with is your wife, your secretary, or a pickup; if you're honeymooners; whether you're there for

business or a good time . . . and an awful lot about
whether you're some kind of booster, deadbeat, or skipper.

And he never seems to notice you at all.

In many ways, the entire hotel business is like that . . .

And, like the hotel business, doormen prize the gift of
discretion.

The talented author Gay Talese, writing in *Esquire,* had
this observation on doormen:

> Knowing that it is possible to see too much, most door-
> men in New York have developed an extraordinary sense
> of selective vision: they know what to see and what to
> ignore, when to be curious and when to be indolent—they
> are most often standing indoors, unaware, when there are
> accidents or arguments in front of their buildings, and they
> are usually in the street seeking taxicabs when burglars are
> escaping through the lobby. Although a doorman may dis-
> approve of bribery and adultery, his back is invariably
> turned when the superintendent is handing money to the
> fire inspector or when a tenant whose wife is away escorts
> a young woman into the elevator—which is not to accuse
> the doorman of hypocrisy or cowardice but merely to sug-
> gest that doormen have perhaps learned through experience
> that nothing is to be gained by serving as a material witness
> to life's unseemly sights or to the madness of the city.

One doorman says this trait Talese defines as selective
vision is the ability to *appear* never to be looking at anything. "You learn it," he said, "by seeming never to look
as girls in miniskirts get out of cars."

By tradition no good hotelman is overtly nosey and
certainly not given to gossip.

Guests do not get gossiped about. Your privacy is certainly safe.

Scandal is bad for business, in the first place. That's part of the reason for the hotelman's look: the middle-distance stare.

The good doorman has it, the good clerk has it—it's as standard as the lobby furnishings.

Just wait until you get upstairs.

3

Give It Back to the Indians

A five thousand dollar government grant to finance a study to determine whether it would be feasible to build a motel on the Micosukee Indian Reservation in Dade County was announced in Washington. The tribe proposes to build a motel adjacent to an existing service station and restaurant . . .

(*Associated Press*)

The Hiawatha Arms

Far from shores of Gitchee Gumee
By the subsidized great highway
Stood Running Irving's wigwam
Making wampum like a madman

Dark behind it rose the forest
And the Cocktail Lounge and Gift Shoppe

Rose the pines with cones upon them;
And the Tamiami Trail before it
Brought the tourists by the dozen;
Brought the shining Yankee dollar.

At the door on summer evening
Sat the little Running Irving;
Heard the rustling of the bank notes,
Heard the lapping of the tourists,
Sounds of music, words of wonder.

"Minne-wawa!" said the pine trees,
Tourists calling "Ice'n'soda!"
Saw the neon, No-Vacan-see,
Flitting in the dark of evening,
Ere in sleep he closed his eyelids,
Ere he dreamed in soft white moonlight,
Of Great Check-Out Time in Sky.

Mighty hunter, Running Irving,
Learning every tourist language,
Learned their names and all their secrets
How they bought the five-buck conch shell,
Funny co-co-nut; stuffed al-li-gator—

Talked with them where'ere he met them,
Called them, "Running Irving's Pigeons,"
Chuckled, "Whose tongue forked now?"
Bulldozed out ten more acres,
For additional units to the south.

Then, Little Running Irving,
Big brother to the beaver,
Brave foe of bear and panther,
Whose heritage was the forest,
Hired a resident manager, Ar-Thur,

Moved to the Fon-Taine-Bleau.

And he sings the song of landlords,
In the chant the realtors taught him;
"Hotcha-cha, the Noble White Man,
Swarms in and fills my wigwam,
And, in truth, no more of that Lo,
The Poor Indian Jazz for me."

John Keasler

4

Who's That Knocking at Our Door?
(Cried the fair young maiden)

LOOK OUT FOR YOUR SAFETY! YOU MAY BE ENTICED AWAY BY SOMEONE AT STREET WHO MAKE FOR YOU TO CARE OF YOUR COMPANY IN THE EVENING. THESE MEN OR WOMEN ARE MADE A CAT'S PAWS OF GANGSTERS IN CONNECTION WITH SOME GROUPS OF PROSTITUTION. THEY ARE GETTING UP TO SHOVE YOU AROUND!!! OR MAKE AN ASSAULT YOU. WE CALL YOUR ATTENTION TO OUTRAGEOUS FELLOWS.

(Sign in a hotel in Kyoto, Japan)

She was a pretty young thing. She was demure. She had downcast eyes. She was a hooker.

The house detective knew she was hustling in the Taft Hotel in New York and had been trying for months to catch her at it, but he hadn't been able to—had failed to catch her in, or entering, a guest's room. It had become a cause with him.

This was back during World War II. The Taft was a busy, booming place, directed by a great manager and promoter named Alfred Lewis. This particular house detective, like all good house officers, had a memory like a computer. This fresh-faced innocent showed up entirely too often, with her cute little wiggle, trolling around the crowded lobby, keeping the bait in motion.

The house detective knew blasted well she was always either leaving after a trick or working up new business but she was swift, elusive, and he hadn't been able to nab her. After a few months of this cat-and-mouse game he didn't know who was the mouse. Then one evening, by luck, he knew he had her! He spotted her far down a corridor entering a room with a handsome young Army captain who had been staying there, alone, for a week.

The house detective leaned against the wall and waited. After a while he snuffed out his cigarette and took out his house key. Silently he slipped the key into the lock, turned it—and burst in.

"O.K., Sister," he growled, as the startled couple in bed grabbed for cover and looked up at him bug-eyed. "C'mon, and give me no trouble. I been watching you for months."

"You bastard!" shouted the captain, leaping out of bed. "I'll brain you! You can't talk to my wife like that!"

And the captain grabbed a paper from the dresser and shoved it under the house officer's nose. It was a marriage license . . . dated earlier the same day.

"Oh, boo hoo hoo," caterwauled the outraged maiden, trying to keep from laughing.

The captain beat the house officer downstairs, still buttoning up and raging. The legal department reportedly settled.

The job of a hotel house detective always has these demolition-squad overtones. You never know what's going to blow up in your face.

Nothing is more inaccurate than the Grade-Z movie depiction of a house detective as a bumbling oaf. Pure hokum. He's a smart cop and a skilled specialist or he doesn't last. Many are retired policemen—and good ones. Increasingly, hotel security itself is a profession men grow up in. If a house detective is good—and if you're fairly good—you'll never know he exists. Most guests think they've never laid eyes on a house detective. But he's there. There may be many in huge hotels, which as much as a good-sized town need their own police departments. Smaller hotels may get along with one. One or many, the house law is indispensable if a hotel is to survive and prosper.

He's different from other policemen in one outstanding way. He must simultaneously manage to impose order without overtly cramping the general happy, freestyle atmosphere. But he's the one you need when the freestyle gets a bit too free. Take the case of group nude-tag in 1620-22.

Jack Egan, who came up through the ranks to become the general manager of the Commodore Hotel in New York, was a harried assistant manager when he got a call one night: orgy on the sixteenth floor.

He checked the folios—nothing particularly revealing there. He called the house officer and headed upstairs. They listened outside 1620-22. (You hear best with your ear at the crack on the hinge side.) Obviously it wasn't a prayer meeting—high-pitched female giggles, male laughter, and suddenly, the galumph-galumphing of what sounded like hippos at play. The noise rose to such crescendo that nobody answered Egan's knock. He and the house detective hurried down corridors and into an unoccupied room across the court. They looked across toward the scene of the action. Some scene.

Six men and six girls, all completely nude, were racing around the room. The drapes weren't even drawn. They were clambering and squealing around, scrambling across chairs, beds, tables, and even up on the dresser.

It seemed to be either an unusually demented form of tag, or catch-as-catch-can follow-the-leader. (The naked redhead up on the dresser seemed to be the leader—at least lots of the men were following her intently.) Egan and the house detective didn't stay watching long enough to learn all the ground rules—they rushed back around and, opening the door with the pass key, went in.

"We're getting complaints," Egan said sternly, and—"

"Complaints?" innocently asked a portly man, attired only in a cigar. "About what?"

"Do you really want an official list?" asked the house officer.

Muttering, the tycoon type started pulling on his pants. It's a bit difficult to maintain an air of command when you're nude, with eleven other nudists in your rooms including a naked redhead on the dresser.

Swiftly, the males began dressing—the girls went into the other room to dress modestly away from prying eyes. Once an orgy loses its spirit everybody might as well go home.

Only then did Egan notice a seventh man, sitting in a far corner on the edge of his chair, completely dressed— he even had his hat on—and with his briefcase primly in

his lap. He looked like a Prudential salesman in Gomor-
rah.

Egan said, "What's your story, friend?"

Wistfully, the so-proper gent looked up through his
rimless glasses and, rather sadly, replied, "My girl was
late."

Complaints about what? It wasn't a bad response to
an embarrassing situation. One of the best comebacks of
all time, for pure gall, however, was recalled by a house
officer in the Bahamas at a resort hotel in Freeport. Down
a corridor he saw a nude girl dash into the hall, screaming
with laughter, then dash back in. He walked down, looked
in—she had left the door ajar—and a certain indus-
trialist was wrestling and laughing in bed with three girls,
all as nude as he was.

"I'm the house officer!" he began.

The man looked up and said angrily, "Yeah? Well,
just what the hell kind of a place do you think you're
running here?"

Experienced house officers sometimes have to steer
younger house dicks through the quicksand bog called
human nature.

"I know that old bat's stolen something," a young officer
said to a veteran at one of the higher-priced Miami Beach
spots.

"Which one?" said the old-timer.

"The crummy-looking old gal in the torn sneakers.
She just stuck a paper bag down behind the sofa pillow."
He jerked his head toward a furtive-looking woman on a
sofa in the lobby. "Should I grab her?"

"I wouldn't advise it," said the old-timer. "She's got
enough money to buy the joint and fire you—she's got

rolls in that bag. She steals enough every day at breakfast for her lunch."

As a longtime seasonal guest, she paid the sixty dollar a day rate for weeks at the top of the season without a whimper . . . but tried to take it out in trade—in rolls.

You don't judge people by what they look like—and the bigger the hotel the wider variety of oddballs you get. In Miami Beach, house officers keep an eye open for regular freeloaders—usually aging women dressed fit to kill—who somehow get their hands on a house key, for identification. They attend every function for guests of a big, expensive hotel . . . but live in a hole-in-the-wall seventh rate hotel down the street.

"Sometimes they actually come in and complain about our movies," one house officer groused to another.

"Yeah," said the second house officer. "One was giving me hell the other night because she didn't like our bingo prizes as much as the prizes at the Americana."

Admittedly, Miami Beach is the well-known something else . . .

MIAMI BEACH

Glittery Oz, out there on a bagel and banknote: Atlantis risen from an ocean of if-come bets. Air plant of cities, growing on climate and nerve; diamond-studded mirage with palms made of the best plastic money can buy.

Each hotel tries to outglisten and outglitter the others. The array of chromium, glass, and neon palaces seems unending. Any one of these edifices would be the out-

standing hotel in any other city; the Taj Mahal would
go broke in competition in one season; there was nothing
like Miami Beach in the Arabian, you should pardon the
expression, Nights.

Here the hotels stretch in rows and the lobbies could
house a sultan's palace. Lobbies are so appointed and
designed that when Mama takes her seat in regal ermine,
or sable, with her sequined gown and the rhinestones on
her heels, and the two hundred bucks worth of hairdo,
she is spotlighted; a baby spot is aimed from the ceiling
to highlight each and every chair. Every queen's throne
is in a baby spot . . . oh, *gawjis,* simply *gawjis!*

In the daytime a thousand glistening hides lie poolside
on rows of wooden pallets. Row upon row, shelves of
gleaming, greased, smoldering meat baking in the sun.
From an upstairs window it looks like a packing house.

It's the thing to do.

Cabana-boys in pseudo-sailor outfits stay on a dead and
fevered run to service the supreme beings who *have their
own cabana.* (That's *the* thing to do.) They hasten with
food, with cigars, with cards for a little gin, with suntan
oil, and an occasional, but only occasional, drink. Book-
makers furtively (but not very) patrol the cabana area.
What opulence! What . . . fun?

You may find a strange apathy. Are the guests happy?
Probably, but to show it would be unsophisticated and
not the thing to do. Certainly they want to be seen; oh,
yes, be seen. They want to spend. They want to spend
and spend and spend—they brag about how much they
got soaked, and nightclub shows are often judged by the
size of the tab, and the price of a room is a status symbol. Miami Beach hotel owners, who are the smartest
and craftiest hotelmen in the world, bar none, are not

unaware of this. If getting soaked is a status symbol, who is to say the status seeker nay? Soak it to 'em; that's the thing to do.

And the service staff is magnificent too: they wear handsomely-fitted jackets and wing collars and white gloves. And the lobbies have marble floors and oriental rugs and crystal chandeliers and . . . tsk tsk . . . scores of rubberneckers.

Miami Beach is a place where tourists throng to look at richer tourists. Trying to stop sightseers from jamming his lobby at the Fontainebleau, Ben Novack, owner of that sumptuous hotel, turned the hotel into a "private club for members only." It was supposed to keep the sightseers out of the lobby. It didn't work, of course. The middle class flocks in to see the upper class, and the upper class lolls languidly, electrified only by the sight of America's royalty . . . a *celebrity!*

All the moneyed princes hope to see this month's In celebrity; they knock over their suntan oil when a celebrity goes by; the comedian who last year was playing the Bronx deigns to give an autograph. Even the court jesters in Miami Beach have court jesters; they sweep by with a retinue.

Jokes about Miami Beach are part of the tapestry of the place. About ostentatious guests:

"Should I wear my ermine or my sable?" she asks hubby, dressing in her room.

"I dunno. The sable."

"My silk gown or the sequined?"

"The silk, I guess. C'mon, hurry up!"

"My emerald headband or the diamond tiara?"

"Wear anything!" he shouts. "Just hurry—we're going to be late for breakfast!"

About hotelmen themselves:

"I'm worried," says one hotel owner to another. "I'm down seven percent for April. April is awful!"

"You're worried?" says the other. "My son is kicked out of college, my daughter is becoming a hippie, my wife nags me all the time, and my arthritis is killing me. What could be worse than that?"

"May."

But the jokes never quite catch up to the reality. In *My-yam-mee Beach* nothing, in fact, intrudes on reality . . . because it's the world's capital of true unreal. That's its charm.

And off in the wings of unreality are the everpresent sharp-eyed keepers of the naive—hotel house officers.

The opulent get what they want, or think they want, at the snap of a credit card.

What they don't get, except amazingly infrequently, is mugged, rolled, blackmailed, and hustled. The reason, largely, is the security force in hotels, cooperating with local police. In resort hotels where compulsive overtipping is rampant, the house detective is the one employee nobody would ever think of tipping.

They might think of bribing him.

Success is unlikely.

"If a house officer goes on the take," said one owner, "the whole operation goes down the drain."

Rental love, unchecked, can ruin a hotel—keeping prostitution operations at a minimum is one of the house officer's chief duties. Why? Morals? No. Your morals are your business. The hotel is the house detective's business. And whores are bad for business.

The complete elimination of prostitution from a hotel or motel is an impossible task. Commercial sex has a

longer history than house detectives. But a successful
first-rate hotel or motor inn cannot tolerate obvious sex
traffic.

*The hotel manager can't protect the morals of his guest
but he sure better protect the reputation of his hotel.*

If word gets out about a hotel being run wide open it
loses local class trade and, eventually, even visiting firemen are going to be told by their wives to stay out of
there. If pros are allowed free reign, business may boom
—but only temporarily. After a year or so, business will
sag mysteriously, uncontrollably.

Shabby morals in a hotel operation will drive good
business away just as surely as physical deterioration will
chase away trade.

As soon as a house officer takes payoffs, the house has
had it.

Obvious sex traffic—that's a subtle but important point.
It's a fact of life, known and tacitly accepted, that in
some of the nation's snazziest hotels guests sometimes put
the services of call girls on their credit card accounts.
"Stenographic service" or "research"—and it's deductible.
But who's to know . . . or for that matter care . . . if
the prim, chic, shapely stranger in B. J. Bigcash's suite
—suite not room—is really an excellent typist?

It's the foyer full of floozies that gives a place a bad
name. In a North Carolina hotel the place was suddenly
overrun with prostitutes. The management decided to
bring in a specialist, a house officer in another city known
far and wide in hotel circles as The Avenger.

Dick Arey, general manager of the Washington Duke
in Durham, N.C., tells the story—a classic in the hotel
business.

The Avenger wasn't exactly admired by his colleagues.

He was a bit too dedicated to breaking in on couples in illicit beds. But he had a sixth sense for it. In one evening he had been known to break in on as many as seven couples and get a caught-in-the-very-act seven-for-seven. A psychologist could have written a book on him.

But the manager in the distant city needed a stranger to set the trap and nobody knew more ropes than the sin-stomping Avenger. He went to the particular city and checked in; began to make the typical queries about how-does-a-guy-find-a-girl. He found the bellhop pimp very shortly.

"Now, leave your door unlatched so she can come straight in," the bellhop said. "Just leave the door open a crack and wait."

He cracked his room door, turned off the lights and, fully clothed, went into the bathroom, turned off that light, eased the door almost shut and waited. He knew his business.

Before long he heard the room door creak open, then close softly. He heard a tentative, female whisper: "Hello?"

In a stage whisper, he answered through the slightly opened bathroom door, "Hop into bed—I'll be right there."

He heard the wispy undressing sounds, the mattress creak as she lay back. He charged in, snapped on the glaring light and, triumphantly, wheeled around from the light switch to arrest the naked woman.

It was his own wife.

She hadn't been visiting her aunt all those times after all. He turned, walked out. Nobody in the business has seen The Avenger since.

The house dick's job is anti-sin, yes, but it's the screwball episodes that keep him the busiest.

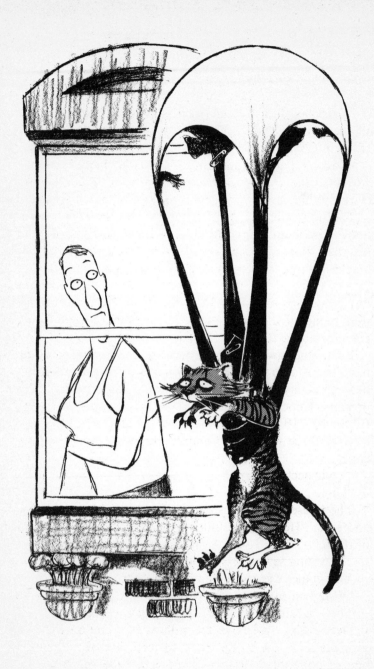

"Cats are parachuting out of a sixth floor window!"

"Cats are parachuting out of a sixth floor window," shouted an excited passerby, running into the Barringer Hotel in Charlotte, N.C.

"Katz *is* parachuting out of a sixth floor window," corrected the weary room clerk. You can't shake a room clerk. "When he lands tell him to come in and check out."

The house detective went out for the para-cat. Somebody had made a parachute for it of pillowcases and neckties. It landed unharmed. Somewhere in the upper reaches, a guest or guests needed the policy explained. (NO CATS TO PARACHUTE FROM WINDOWS.) What do you do? Knock on doors on the sixth floor asking people if they parachuted a cat out of the window? You will not get informative replies or make new friends this way.

First, you narrow down possible rooms which could have been jump sites. The neckties are GI. The house—near an Army post—is full of soldiers. Check folios. Go upstairs. Knock on 610-612-614. "Is this your cat?" No. Eliminate 710-712-714.

At 510 the sergeant who answers says, "No sir. Not my cat."

"Your neckties?"

"Uh . . ."

The house officer looks at the bed, at the bare pillows, and says, "Here's your pillowcases, Sergeant. What's left of them."

The young sergeant is flustered.

You glance toward the bathroom door.

"Will your visitors be leaving soon?"

The sergeant blurts "Yes *sir*. Very damn soon."

Downstairs, you have the pillowcases put on his bill, give the stray cat to the cook to feed, and are having a cup of coffee and don't look up when the sergeant, another noncom, and two college girl guests walk swiftly out.

They think you're a mind reader. You're glad you saw the four glasses, two with lipstick smudges, stuck back under the bedside table. Even nice kids like that can get in trouble in a hotel room . . .

"Hey," says the assistant manager, just as you are preparing, finally, to finish one cup of coffee without interruption. "You wanna come up to 430 with me? Some drunk has got his foot caught in the commode."

5

Tips from the Unrepentant Roué

PLEASE DO NOT TAKE LADIES TO YOUR ROOM
UP THE BACK STAIRS. THEY HAVE JUST BEEN
PAINTED.

(Sign in a hotel in Topeka, Kan.)

"Son," said the old roué to a younger man in whom he
detected a certain potential. "Son, as you travel through
Life you will notice that shapely temptation is jiggling and
bouncing along every byway and often on the sidewalks.
I trust you will withstand that temptation, Son, particularly
when temptation wears a tight jersey blouse. I urge you to
steel yourself."

And the old roué looked enigmatically into the flickering
flames of memory and then he spake thus, "On the other
hand, my boy, if temptation wins, remember only this.
Never get a bedroom—always take the suite."

"But I do not understand, Wise Old Roué," said the

younger man. "Does not the suite come at a more costly rate?"

"My boy," said the old roué, "there are things we may not understand but would do well to accept. One of them is this. Hotels have a strange policy. It is that it is wrong to entertain a young lady in your bedroom, but it is perfectly all right to entertain a lady in your suite. Believe me, my boy, and mark it well—in the long run the suite is a hell of a lot cheaper."

The old roué is right. A suite is usually rented at a flat rate. The hotel loses nothing if you bring in a friend. As to why it's accepted policy to have a woman visitor in your suite but not in your room, nobody seems certain.

House officers must keep down obvious sex traffic. There are only two ways for the male guest to get an illicit love into his room. He brazenly registers or he sneaks her in. There are plenty of ways to get into trouble by either method, but some procedures are less obvious than others.

If you and your girl plan to arrive and register together, have at least two pieces of baggage. Make sure she has a wedding ring on, or a glove. You have your choice of dangers: your own name or a phony. The imagination in choosing false names is surprisingly often offset by a guest later trying to use a credit card with his own name. Or forgetting entirely who he is supposed to be.

The sneak-in approach requires that you go in and register and get word to your little chum about your room number. Nervousness accompanies most illicit affairs—a man somewhere right now is sitting in 1210 chain-smoking while some guy in 1012, the number mistakenly given, has had his faith renewed in Santa Claus.

The lady should never stop and call your room on the house phone. Obviously—one would think, but it happens —she shouldn't try to sneak in *with* luggage. The best time to sneak in is between five and seven P.M. when hotel traffic is fairly heavy and many people are coming and going. Also, the maids are off. During those hours, one more unescorted woman riding the elevators is less likely to attract attention.

Any unescorted woman going up later is bound to attract attention. If she's not registered, who is she? The clerk knows she's not the Avon Lady and Salvation Army lassies have tambourines. Use the rush hour.

Tell her to go straight up. The overly bold front in the lobby of buying a paper, asking the clerk or bell captain for the time, and all the things to avoid looking guilty—look guilty. *Go straight up.* Have her memorize it. Tell her which way to turn upon leaving the elevator.

She's there! Sigh . . .

Isn't the phone shockingly loud?

The somewhat robot-sounding voice wants to know if you have a visitor in your room.

Always say yes.

He wouldn't call to ask if he didn't know the answer. Don't panic. Just say yes, you have a visitor and she's just leaving. That's all you need to do, if you're caught . . . except make sure she leaves.

(Sometimes the hotel employee doing the calling is in a vacant room within sight of your door to make *sure*.)

You can say it's your wife. He'll ask her to come down and register.

You can say it's a childhood friend who drove all the way across town to see you. He'll be happy for you, and offer you every bit of hospitality the lobby can afford—

She's there! Sigh . . .
Isn't the phone shockingly loud?

because unregistered visitors of the opposite gender in the room are against policy.

(That general policy may at first glance seem strangely old-fashioned in today's Swinging Seventies, but general policy it *is*. Whatever the so-called Sexual Revolution means to others, it could mean a sea of red ink to hotelmen—who, whatever else, are unlikely ever to get very permissive about the key word . . . *unregistered*. However the battle for sexual freedom goes, the warriors damn well better register before going upstairs to join the fray.)

Now, when the desk calls your room on this lady-guest matter you can reply by saying it's all business, business, business, and that your female visitor is, oh, an important buyer. The hotelman will reply by offering you all the conveniences of the lobby, or perhaps a conference room.

You can say it's a secretary or your researcher. You may then feel a bit silly feeding quarters into a pay typewriter in a conference room for a sulky redhead whose fingernails are far too long for typing.

Or, if he calls, you can say it's your mother.

It's O.K. if it's your mother . . .

. . . *If* it's your mother.

Of course, if it was your mother he probably wouldn't have called.

The facts are these. A hotel is a civilization of its own, and highly civilized at that. When you walk in, no matter how crowded it looks to you, you're walking onto somebody else's turf. Individually, you're a stranger—but not so anonymous as you think. There are types and ways to recognize them.

Your morals are important only to the extent they reflect on the house. Your manner of registration, if we must be blunt, boils down to economic pay dirt: single occupancy registration doesn't mean a second party comes in free.

Yes, you have a right to your individual outlook. The hotel has a right to its policy. And there is nothing more.

Franklin Moore, widely known former head of the Penn-Harris Hotel in Harrisburg, has a great fund of humor and philosophy about hotels. There is a story about the downfall of a practiced sinner we'll call Bill Filander.

"Now, old Bill was a fine politician but he suffered a fatal weakness," said Moore. "He got absent-minded— dangerous for any politician, dangerous for any philanderer . . . potentially disastrous for a woman-chasing politician like old Bill Filander.

"Well, one day he was with his real wife, politicking at a woman's club meeting. The hostess pushed the big guest book across the speaker's table for Bill Filander to sign. He was so busy talking and handshaking that he registered as Mr. and Mrs. Joe Jones."

"Once upon a time," mused the old roué, "I knew a fellow hobbyist who truly believed in being prepared. He carried a woman's white glove in his pocket at all times, in the event he unexpectedly managed to fall prey to the Temptation besetting us all. He carried the left glove only. A man of sentiment, he was. So many times, before entering a lobby to register, he would take the left hand of his new lady-love tenderly, and slip on the glove, saying softly, 'With this glove, I thee wed.'

"But once he forgot his registered name in Cleveland and signed for champagne with his St. Louis monicker. I find sentiment far less nerve-racking in a suite, where I care not who knocks upon my door."

FOOTNOTE ON MORALITY

Hotels, indeed, are individuals. To generalize about individuals is, at best, pointless. Some individuals are more individual than others. To understand hotels, however, one basic rule applies: the first duty is economic survival or everything else fast becomes idle theory.

Sex is part of the rental-bed business. It always will be. Let two actual case histories show two ways this reality can be handled.

A certain hotel in Washington State was one which chose to encourage affaires d'amour. It flourished on the s.s. trade (short stay, in hotel language.) It even had code names for its better known playboys. The general manager himself dubbed them: Cisco Kid, Wyatt Earp, Doc Holliday, Jesse James, Billy the Kid, the Lone Ranger. Prominent men, some of the fastest cads in the West.

A regular would call the general manager, who would give him a room number over the phone. A bellboy would leave the room door open, the key lying on the bed. Say it was Billy the Kid who had called.

All Billy had to do—the sly old goat—was to slip in a side door unseen. He could go directly to his room without going near the front desk and have his companion join him there. Later, he could slip out as unobtrusively. He would receive and pay his bill by mail. To borrow a banking phrase, it was indeed a full-service hotel.

The manager could not have been more helpful. One

time Billy the Kid was on the sixteenth floor with a woman in his safely secret room. The Cisco Kid arrived and headed toward his own hideout on the sixteenth floor. But who was with the Cisco Kid this trip? Billy the Kid's wife.

Suppose they ran into each other?

Both were prominent men—any confrontation would surely make the papers. The manager first tried to explain to the operators of the three elevators a complicated set of directions about not stopping at various points simultaneously, so the two couples wouldn't meet. This gave him nothing but three confused operators and a headache.

Being a dedicated manager, he did what any experienced manager would do. He put the assistant manager on the case—to operate a single elevator and keep an eye open in case either couple got on—then make a fast express out of it.

He put "Out of Order" signs on the other two elevators until the gunfighters were out of the old corral.

It worked.

Why did such a—well—*thoughtful* hotel go on the skids? Romantics might attribute its doom to automatic elevators: they might say that automatic elevators installed later had no passion or understanding. Romantics might sadly say, holding sombreros over their breasts, that it was part of the passing of the Rugged West. But they would be unrealistic.

The truth?

A hotel can't hide its reputation, and when the reputation gets a bit murky it's not just the good trade that leaves—the playboy regulars are among the first to go.

"Commit these things to memory, Son, for they will stand you in good stead." And the old roué poured his shot glass full and looked into the amber sour mash. "Carry a grip with buckle straps; they never fall open when you're running. Always treat a lady a bit like a scarlet woman; treat a roundheel as you would virtue on a pedestal. Above all, my boy, always stay at a respectable hotel . . . all women immediately know class."

The second case history concerns a hotel that hit the skids. It swarmed with prostitutes and homosexuals. Absentee owners had made the bad mistake of putting a man with no hotel experience in charge.

He had no idea how to cope with commercial sex. The hotel, in a respectable community, began to lose big money fast. The owners sold to professional hotel people.

"The very day we closed the deal," a member of the purchasing firm told the authors of this book, "a broad phoned me in my room, pretending she knew me from another city. Obviously, an employee had tipped her off —how would she get my room number? Or know my wife wasn't with me? I brushed her off—she cursed me with every four-letter word in the book.

"I went downstairs to talk to the new manager. The phone on the bell captain's desk rang. The bell captain was gone and the manager answered. 'Send two broads up right away,' said the male voice. 'Make sure one is Maybelle.'

"Our new food and beverage manager checked in later that day. His room phone rang. A female voice said, 'Hi, honey. You looked so lonely in the lobby I thought you might want a little company.'

"Within one day," the hotelman said, "My manager,

my food manager, and I had been propositioned. We got rid of the whores and the property is profitable again."

In the hotel business Morals and Money are filed under M. They're that close!

6

I'm Your Assistant—Please, Lady!—Manager

YOU NOT SEEING
YOU DESIRING
SO REQUESTING!
ASKING TO THE
ASS,T. MAN.

(Front desk sign in a Singapore hotel)

George Thomas Cullen, who ran the Sheraton Biltmore in Providence, R.I., did what any experienced general manager would do when informed that Lady Godiva, not even wearing her horse, was trying to get off an elevator and parade through the lobby. He called his assistant manager.

There's irony in the very title of a hotel assistant manager. If there's one man in the world of hotels, where

69

rules never catch up with transgressions, who *needs* assistance, it's the harried assistant manager.

This one came running.

Indeed, the assistant manager noted, there was, forsooth, a nude woman in the elevator. She was quite happily stoned, and had decided to go for a ride on the Otis.

Now she was thinking in terms of a stroll around the premises.

"Ah, yes," said the assistant manager, snatching the blanket a bellhop handed him and draping it around her. "But we mustn't get chilled. Now, madam, before you take your little walk I think I should warn you that . . . "

And the elevator door closed. After several minutes, having talked her back down the corridor and into her room, and making sure a house officer was keeping an eye on the door, the assistant manager reappeared, perspiring.

"What did you tell her to get her upstairs?" the bell captain asked.

"I told her the lobby was full of reporters and photographers," he said. "She said she *detested* cheap publicity. I told her I knew she was a lady the second I laid eyes on her."

An important phase in the development of a topflight manager is the period he must undergo in learning to deal directly with the public. The spot where a budding executive best gets his public relations lumps is as assistant manager: a spot to try men's souls.

He's a buffer between top management and a wildly varied public, and he's buffeted by both. He's the one, figuratively and literally, who is forever trying to define exactly what unnecessary loud screaming is. He's on a tightwire of tact over a canyon of potential disaster. And assistant managers never get to work with a net.

You adapt to conditions. Adaptability has to be as wild as the conditions. Edward Buckley, ex-general manager of Chicago's Edgewater Beach Hotel, remembers an assistant manager who adapted himself smoothly right out of a life potentially fraught with contusions and abrasions. Bouncers kept quitting the hotel's brawl-ridden bar. In fact, the bouncers were getting bounced.

The hotel, managed by a friend of Buckley's, was in an industrial city and the clientele of the bar was rough. Police were indifferent and bouncers kept leaving for calmer climes. The assistant manager was told by the manager, between bouncers, to try to keep things down in the bar—personally—or else find a bouncer who could.

The assistant manager hired a bouncer, you can bet, that very day—the bouncer stayed and merely by walking between combatants turned every fight thereafter into laughter.

The assistant manager had hired a midget as bouncer. Now, *that's* adapting.

An assistant manager is in the position of a first sergeant—with one decided disadvantage. He has to do what the CO (manager) orders, but he has to make his troops (guests) happy too. Arthur Miller's classic definition of a salesman is somebody "out there on a smile and a shoeshine." An assistant manager is in there with a bland smile and nervous indigestion. Charles Laughton, the great English actor, pegged the manager/assistant manager relationship pretty well, having himself grown up in a family of northern England hotel-keepers.

Laughton frequently stopped at the Pontchartrain in

New Orleans. Owner Lysle Aschaffenburg and Laughton became friends. Eventually, Lysle asked Laughton what, specifically, attracted him to the Pontchartrain as a regular, repeat visitor.

"On my first visit, I noticed it was a family-operated hotel," said Laughton. "And it made me nostalgic for my own younger days."

Lysle asked, "How did you know it was family-run, on your first visit?"

"When I first checked in," said Laughton, "your assistant manager was standing up to you in an argument. When he wasn't fired on the spot I knew that, naturally, he had to be your son."

Sympathy, then, is not always forthcoming from top management. Kind behavior is not to be expected unvaryingly from the guests. At the Mayflower Hotel in Washington, the house was packed with women attending a convention of a national group. The assistant manager received an "emergency" call and raced upstairs, knocked, and the door opened.

A dozen women grabbed him, jerked him into the room, threw him on the bed, ripped off his pants, threw them out the window, shoved him back out in the corridor, and slammed the door. Conventions can bring out the hell-raising syndrome in women, too, is the moral to draw from that.

At the 1000-room Sheraton Cleveland, run by Allen James Lowe, it was an assistant manager who looked up to see an irate woman demanding he cash her three hundred dollar personal check. She wasn't even a guest. The hotel gets a tremendous amount of foreign foot traffic from the railroad station and Terminal Tower office building.

. . . so, still standing there . . .

"I'm sorry, madam," said the assistant manager. "It is against hotel policy."

She was furious. (A great many people, everywhere, somehow feel it is part of a hotel's function to cash checks. Nobody has ever explained this.)

"Is that your last word?" she demanded, drawing herself up haughtily.

"I'm afraid so, madam."

Still standing, glaring at him, the picture of outrage, she vengefully urinated on his beautiful white carpet, turned, and strode out.

Some days are enough to break the usually cool composure of the most imperturbable assistant manager. At the John Marshall in Richmond, Assistant Manager L. G. Maxey had already put up with a half-dozen overbooked and highly abusive arrivals who took out the reservation office's mistake on—of course—the assistant manager.

He had been held personally responsible for Richmond's sewage system because a fifth floor john was stopped up. He had diagnosed a case of measles on the seventh floor and been told by the child's parents not to be so nosey. He had just learned that a one hundred dollar check he had personally okayed was back from the bank like a handball off a wall.

Such was his state of mind when a woman walked up to him, breathed gin in his face, and cried that if he did not immediately and forthwith get her a room, her plan was to kill herself.

"If you do, madam, go somewhere else to bleed," said Mr. Maxey. "I've had enough troubles for one day."

He turned and walked away. It took a while for his

reply to sink in—then the woman went wild with rage and did several interesting things. First, after gasping in sufficient air, she screamed like an outraged hyena. She then raced around the lobby, ripping the newspapers out of the grasp of several lobby lizards, scaring them no end. She ripped these into shreds, scattering confetti as she raced in figure eights around the lobby, seeking Mr. Maxey. She dashed into his office, and even crawled under his desk, looking for him.

Racing back, looking about wildly, failing still to find him, she ran over and belted the bell captain full in the mouth. She then dashed out of the hotel and was never seen again. Mr. Maxey, who had been resting up in booth three of the gentlemen's room, waited a considerable interval, then emerged.

"Jeeth Chrith," the bell captain spluttered, tentatively moving a loose tooth with his tongue. "What did you *say* to that maniac?"

"Hm?" said Mr. Maxey, blandly, as the manager walked into hearing. "Why, merely that we were full. She seemed depressed."

When the boss is away, the assistant is responsible. Suicides are a dread of hotelmen. The assistant in a Dallas hotel got the word one afternoon—jumper on the ledge!

A crowd gathered, with the usual ghouls shouting "Jump, jump!" Police and fire equipment arrived. Nobody could get close to the man on the ledge—each time somebody tried to he threatened to leap. Seven floors.

The assistant manager had checked the folio. The man had been there four days. He had been ordering bourbon by the pint or half pint. This is one sure sign of an alcoholic: only journeymen drunks consistently buy pints or half pints. The assistant manager promptly sent out for a half pint of bourbon.

"Hey," he shouted out the room window to the man on the ledge, and he waved the bourbon bottle. "Why don't you come in and have a drink and let's talk this over?"

"P'pass it out," the man chattered.

"No, come in and have a drink. You can make it."

Inch by inch, the man, one eye on the bottle, made it back along the ledge. He tumbled into the room with a half-dozen pair of hands helping him.

"Gimme that!" he blurted, twisting the cap off, and draining most of the half pint in three long pulls. He shuddered, sat on the edge of the bed and managed to keep the booze down. Thus bolstered, he looked up at the assembly and, rather conversationally, said, "Wow. That's the last time I ever try suicide as long as I live. I like to of fell off that goddamn ledge!"

Hotels don't like to talk about suicides. Suicides attract suicides—at least so hotelmen insist. Too many times they've known of suicides, jumpers, who left in the room a newspaper folded to the story of a recent jumper . . . from the same hotel.

Jumpers lead in the hotel suicide rate, hangings are next, then sleeping pills, and finally guns. Suicides often follow strangely constant rules. They usually leave their rooms neat. Males are usually shaven and neatly dressed and women have their hair done. Wrist slashers are careful to bleed in wash basins; throat cutters often sit in the bathtub. Many leave notes apologizing for the trouble they've caused. Young hotelmen coming along are no more exempt from occasional violence and horror than cops or newspapermen.

In the newspaper business a famous lead on the suicide of a notorious gangster in Chicago, written by Ben Hecht, was simply: "He was neat. He hanged himself in the closet."

In fact, self-hangings in closets are far from rare. Michael T. McGarry, general manager of the Claridge Hotel, Atlantic City, has, like most experienced big league hotelmen, seen his share of suicides. When McGarry was at the Ben Franklin in Philadelphia some years ago, the house officer, an ex-police captain, matter-of-factly cut down a dead man who had hung himself in the closet with his necktie.

Trapped air left the body in a loud "whoof!" The wide-eyed maid who had discovered the body, and was already standing there terrified, turned and ran downstairs. Her reaction is better gauged by the fact she started running downstairs from the fourteenth floor and hadn't slowed at street level.

That house officer was old-breed. An assistant manager was young and impressionable. Together they answered another suicide report. A male guest was seated in the tub, nude, his head back moaning pitiably, and his wrists bleeding. The assistant manager was, as they say, distraught. The ex-police captain knew an attention-grabbing phony when he saw one. He turned on the cold shower, whereupon the "dying" guest jumped up.

"Get dressed and get the hell out of here," the house officer growled. "We ain't nursemaids to some jerk whose girl has dumped 'im."

The guest dressed and checked out hastily. Things like that tend to educate an assistant manager.

McGarry himself, however, was impressed with the firm grasp on reality that particular house detective had.

At the Ben Franklin, a bellman had reported to Manager McGarry that a young, well-dressed man who had just checked into a room on the seventh floor was acting strangely.

(The guest had, upon first entering the room, immediately walked to the window, thrown it open, stared out. Most times this would mean nothing. To this bellman, this was not one of those times.)

McGarry went up, knocked, got no answer, and opened the door with the passkey.

The guest had one foot on the sill, ready to go. McGarry grabbed him, wrestled with him—slammed him a hard left, then a right. It didn't faze the jumper. He wanted death. He wrestled his way back to the window and this time tried to pull McGarry with him, and almost succeeded. McGarry barely managed to get loose before the jumper plummeted to his death.

The house officer went down with McGarry to the corpse in the courtyard. When the detective heard the part about the man trying to pull McGarry with him, he frowned, leaned over, took the dead man's wallet and carefully extracted the price of the room, sending a bell-hop to pay the bill.

"If we charged for jumping like we do for sleeping we could put a stop to some of this damn foolishness," the detective snarled.

A budding young and eager hotel executive, then, does not lead a cloistered life. Neal Lang, a top pro respected by top pros, came up the long hard route; learned to think on his feet as a subexecutive and was passing it along to subordinates when he invented the damper on sin. It's still one of those classics of simplicity that can only be termed genius.

Neal was manager of the Sheraton-Cadillac in Detroit when sex started rearing its blondined head—up and down every corridor, it sometimes seemed. Prostitution was suddenly a highly organized industry. Pimps were waiting at the police station, bailing out whores who seemed to be back almost as fast as the hotel could get them arrested. What to do? Neal Lang thought about it —and adapted.

What is a hustler's greatest asset? Yes, of course . . . but before that? Her appearance. The girls, to meet competition, must be dressed well, coiffed, jewelled, perfumed, the works. O.K., thought Lang.

"When you catch a hustler," he told his assistant and the house detectives, "don't turn her over to the cops. Take her through that door."

As each carefully costumed prostitute was led through the door, she was smirking smugly—until the tub of water hit her.

There was no paddy wagon outside in the alley. Only two maintenance men with a washtub full of water for each scarlet lady as she emerged.

Slosh! Soaked . . . head to tail.

What's a girl to do? Except curse in rage, go drippingly home and change, fume over a ruined hairdo, and vow never to go back to *that* crazy hotel. Who propositions a drowned mouse?

Two episodes exemplify the you-can't-win position of the assistant manager, caught as he is between the masses and the management; often damned by both.

Joe Crocy went on to become one of the South's best-known hotel managers, and it may be that an experience like this molded him in that direction . . .

Years ago when he was assistant manager of the Dink-ler Ansley Hotel in Atlanta, he got a call one night that an enterprising hustler was operating in a room on the ninth floor, with a very rapid rate of turnover, so to speak.

He pulled out her bill, went upstairs and hammered on her door. The tinsel-haired blonde swept open the door with a smile that would warm the heart of an Eskimo elder. "O.K., Sister, on your way," Joe snapped, flashing her bill.

After the usual phony, deeply offended protests she said, "O.K., honey, I'll check out in about an hour."

"In a pig's foot," said Joe, or words to that effect. "You'll check out right now. I'll carry your baggage."

He grabbed her limited luggage and down the corridor they went and into an elevator. There was a banquet that night at the Paradise Rooftop Ballroom and just about every prominent businessman in Atlanta was there. The down elevator was crowded when they got on.

All the men knew Joe and greeted him, giving the knowing eye to the obvious floozy in his company (whose bag he was carrying). More men got on at each stop and, of course, sized up the situation immediately. (Wrongly, but immediately.) Joe turned red at all the elbow-nudging, but maintained a dignified silence.

Reaching the lobby, all the men stepped aside to let the woman parade out, followed by red-necked, sweating Joe Crocy.

With a fine sense of timing, the girl stopped right outside the elevator, turned, and in front of about twenty grinning males, threw her arms around Joe, kissed him full on the mouth, and said loudly, "Joe, Baby, thank you for a simply *scrumptious* weekend, Lover. Call me anytime."

She took her bag and flounced away at full jiggle.

The other example of the assistant manager's Dilemma of Life follows. The Ambassador Hotel on Park Avenue (later the Sheraton East and now gone and mourned in the name of Progress) was always very elegant—not so vulnerable to theft as many other hotels, because its high-class clientele didn't usually do a lot of stealing, comparatively.

However, it bought the best and when two expensive blankets, brand-new and fluffy, were placed in the room of a departing guest and were missing after she checked out an hour later, it became the job of the assistant manager to write her his most diplomatic perhaps-packed-by-mistake note. He did.

A few days later the assistant manager got the following letter in reply:

> Sir!
>
> How dare you accuse me of being a common thief? My father was a brigadier general. My uncle was a federal judge.
>
> The audacity of you commercial people is nothing short of amazing. If my father were alive he would certainly put you in your place.
>
> If this is an exemplification of your hospitality, I shall never stay in your terrible hotel again. Also, my father is a friend of the owners and they shall hear of your presumption. Your goddamn blankets are being shipped under separate cover.

The job of assistant manager is front-line training for a life with an aura of the unexpected, which aura often comes on like this:

Hugh J. Connor, general manager of the Barbizon in New York City, came to his office to start the day. What was new?

"Somebody seems to have stolen the kitchen exhaust fan," said the room clerk.

"Did you see anybody suspicious?" asked Connor.

"Well," said a bellman. "There was this fellow I saw in a bathing suit going out the service entrance."

As the Barbizon is in mid-Manhattan and nowhere near a beach, this seemed fairly suspicious.

"He looked very suspicious," added the bellman. "He had a monkey on his shoulder."

"I see," said Mr. Connor, and called for the assistant manager, who explained. That was the exhaust vent cleaner, and he always changed into bathing trunks because it was a dirty job—and he used a monkey as his chimney sweep.

"I see," said Mr. Connor. "Do you mind telling me why he took our exhaust fan?"

"Sir, I hesitate to tell you this," said the assistant manager, "but he says he's keeping our exhaust fan unless we also pay his monkey union rates . . . "

And the day hadn't even started.

A card on every table in the Statler-Hilton in Dallas says, enigmatically and in its entirety: *For* ENTERTAIN-MENT *in the hotel, see the assistant manager.*

A tall and thought-provoking order. But rest assured the assistant manager is doing his damndest. Someday he may be a manager, and the reason they're hard to fool is that all of them have been there.

Learn Hotel Assistant Management!!!
An Aptitude Quiz

(Are you the ideal assistant manager? No, *nobody* is the ideal assistant manager, or both Tums and Bayer would go out of business. However, just for fun, see what you would have done as assistant manager in these three situations, all factual. And—who knows—you may be in the wrong business. Assistant managers say they're in the wrong business, too, but, somehow, they stay there . . .)

1. Dick Keeley gives us this one from his days at the John Marshall in Richmond. Big hassle on the eighth floor! He rushes up. A nude man and woman in bed— two fully clothed, and furious, women at the foot of the bed. The man is a prominent politician, the bedmate his "secretary." The two women are the politician's wife and . . . some men are born losers . . . his mother-in-law.

Somehow the wife and mother-in-law aren't buying this statesman's story that the poor girl had a heart attack down in the restaurant and he brought her up for first aid. (Aren't politicians great?)

The problem: The two women are raising teetotal hell and have told Keeley that if he doesn't immediately call the police, they will. The publicity, Keeley knows, is going to be big—it's a big politician—and bad. The problem: What do you say to avoid the publicity?

2. You're assistant manager of the Plaza in New York. A famous Hollywood producer is checked in for what looks like an extended binge and orgy. So many hustlers are in and out of his suite that complaints are

Somehow the wife and mother-in-law aren't buying this statesman's story that the poor girl had a heart attack down in the restaurant and he brought her up for first aid. (Aren't politicians great?)

coming in from other guests. The guest has been asked by the manager to check out and, good naturedly but flatly, has told the manager to soak his head—he likes it just where he is.

If the manager physically throws this VIP out, it will be a mess in the papers—the VIP in this case doesn't really give a damn and knows he's got management over a barrel. It's a Mexican standoff. Again, the manager does what any alert manager does. He calls the assistant manager and says, "Make that bastard so uncomfortable he'll check out on his own accord."

Your problem: At least four ways to make a guest uncomfortable.

3. Now you're assistant manager at the elegant Century Plaza in Los Angeles, one of the best-run hotels in the world. (See how you travel and meet interesting people in the hotel business? You've only been an assistant manager ten minutes and already you've taken your migraine coast to coast.)

A bellman smells smoke on the eighteenth floor! You follow procedure. You call the engine room, give the reported room number from which the smoke is coming to hotel fire fighters, and you rush upstairs. (You did yank the folios, didn't you? Of course you did.) On the elevator you glance at the records; nothing unusual; a young couple.

No answer to your knock. You've got the passkey. (Or you're fired and can read no further.) You open the door . . . charge in. Smoke is pouring from a mattress which in one spot is beginning to smolder dangerously red.

Nobody is *in* the room, but . . .

. . . on the balcony which overlooks Santa Monica, and clearly silhouetted against the city lights through the very sheer drapes, beneath a full moon which may have contributed to their decision, completely nude and ob-livious to any other fire in the world, is a couple appar-ently reaching the crescendo of la grande amour.

Got the picture? O.K. Do you:

A. *Bang on the glass doors on the theory it's better for you to embarrass them than wait for firemen to do so?*

B. *Stand in the corridor with the door closed be-hind you and delay the firemen a few minutes?*

C. *Run next door to the room you know is vacant, go out on that balcony, and shout as though to somebody back in your room: "Hey, Matilda, I think the room next door is on fire!"*

D. *Try to assess a quick time-motion study between which will break into flame first: the smoldering mattress or the couple spontaneously combusting.*

E. *Run back downstairs and see if your house policy has a rule on this.*

F. *Other.*

While you're thinking about these hotel problems, one quick story about how hotelmen *always* think about hotel problems.

The lovely Zsa Zsa Gabor—who once sent one of your authors to take her poodle for a walk in the Fontainebleau and was so overcome by his charm that she later allowed him to kiss her poodle—tells of a honeymoon night with Conrad Hilton.

Their suite was filled with flowers, with buckets of champagne, with the fragrance and presence of Zsa Zsa. Soft music, dim lights. Zsa Zsa, perfumed, drifted from her bath in a filmy undressing gown. She floated over to Conrad who was seated in a chair, observing his lovely love.

In her softest, sexiest, Hungarian tones, she purred into his ear, "Vot are you theenking, my beeg handsome dollink luffer?"

"I am dreaming . . . " said Conrad Hilton, softly, his own eyes aglow in anticipation, "of how I'm going to grab the Blackstone away from that Ernie Henderson."

Your Aptitude Answers (*Forget* Zsa Zsa . . .)

1. You *don't* mention hotel publicity. You *do* say to the wife and mother-in-law, "Of course I'll call the police! I'm sorry the publicity will cause your husband to lose his job . . . and with it, your income."

You never saw such a quick pair of publicity-haters, Keeley recalled. They left, still mad but too practical to let revenge stop hubby's paycheck. (The incident had a great switch. "They'll get over it," sighed the relieved politician. The hitherto silent girl in bed sat bolt upright and snarled, "Your wife may, but I won't. You said you were through with her, you two-timing son of a bitch!" And with that, she belted the statesman right in the mouth.)

2. Each telephone call the VIP, or anybody in his room, made was disconnected in midconversation. Operators called back repeatedly to ask if he had been disconnected. Each day the maids made his bed with ripped sheets. They removed toilet tissue. Each call for tissue was answered two hours later, but answered by at least three maids at intervals. There were repeated knocks on his door to bring Kleenex, extra towels, "Do Not Disturb" signs. Each room service order took a minimum of two hours to deliver. Each order had the most important item

missing. Each such item was then delivered at least twice after complaint. Light bulbs were replaced with burned-out bulbs. Window shades on the sun side were removed for cleaning. Time calls were made by mistake at dawn each day. On the fourth day the VIP checked out.

He stopped by the office and handed the assistant manager an expensive, gift-wrapped decanter of marvelous Scotch. "My compliments, sir," he said, shaking the assistant manager's hand. "I always admire a pro."

3. You bang on that balcony door and get them and the mattress fire out immediately! You want the joint to burn down, you softhearted romantic?

7

Bitch, Bitch, Bitch!

GUESTS ARE EXPECTED TO COMPLAIN TO THE
MANAGEMENT FROM NINE TO ELEVEN EACH
MORNING

(*Sign over desk of an Athens hotel*)

In a large building filled with strangers, and with employees who sometimes seem the strangest of all, no hotel
can ever be complaint-free.

And, surely, complaints aren't confined to any nine-
to-eleven period, except in some hotelman's Utopia; not
in this particular vale of tears and laughter.

Complaints have no real relationship to quality of
service. Which is to say, you can't satisfy everybody.

And hotel complaints usually seem to have that added
dimension of mind-bending involution peculiar to the
hotel world.

"There's a rat in here!" screamed a woman in the cocktail lounge of the Pocono Manor up in Pennsylvania resort country. The then assistant manager, Karl Fischer, led the clattering, squalling rat hunt. Fischer knew exactly the right tool for a rat (he attributes this to having been trained at Cornell University's School of Hotel Administration), so he got a broom and held the animal firmly in a corner of the dimly lit lounge, as screeching women stood on chairs and the headwaiter rushed up with a metal can to clap over it.

Fortunately, the "rat" gave him one of the classiest lines ever attributed to a hotelman.

"This is no rat," Fischer announced. "It's a mink."

It had strayed away from a mink farm in the area. Pure class.

Occasionally complaints cancel each other out.

"A French poodle just came in through my window and got in bed with me!" complained a badly shaken General Motors executive at the Sheraton-Cadillac one morning. His room was on the twenty-eighth floor, as the clerk pointed out.

"Goddamn it!" shouted the guest. "If my room was on the first floor I wouldn't be shaking like this!"

As the clerk mulled this over, another call came from a distraught lady guest. Her doggie, boo hoo, had just gone out the window. It didn't even leave a note.

Yes. Cherie the Poodle had gotten out of her mistress' bed early and, being a lady, gone outside to the bathroom—twenty-eight stories above Detroit—then after a morning constitutional on the three-foot wide ledge had gotten into the wrong room. Accidentally, so it appeared. (But you know those French females.)

At the Claridge in Atlantic City, guests were complaining that somebody came in their room and ate their room-service delivered breakfast while they were shaving, or whatever.

"They sounded like Papa Bear growling that somebody had eaten his porridge," the clerk said, and there was some concern about a possible Mad Breakfast-Snatcher on the loose—until a seagull was caught taking home the bacon. The screens had been taken out until the summer season, much to the seagulls' delight. It also explained the complaint of a drunk who insisted a raven kept perching on his dresser—which would make anybody nervous.

Things like this engender a certain calm in hotel managers, basically, for they know complaints are bound to happen; the house odds are against them.

The ability to handle whatever strange complaint arises becomes finely honed.

The straight non sequitur is sometimes quite effective with written complaints.

Here's an example. It's a complaint to a Washington hotel we won't name because it doesn't deserve the following blast, but got it anyhow.

> . . . and furthermore, your staff was rude, the food was awful, the room drafty, and the wash basin was a trickle.
>
> I hope to hell you and your idiot staff had a most happy holiday season because thanks to your stupid crew and your overpriced bar, me and mine had a perfectly rotten holiday season . . .

After pondering this, the manager gave up trying to isolate each—unfounded—gripe and simply dictated:

> Thank you for your warm and friendly holiday greeting. It was most gracious of you to write. We will look

forward to your return to our hospitable inn, soon and often. May your every New Year's wish be granted.

The nicest part about that bit of public relations is that it is well-calculated to drive the recipient right up the wall, but leave him without a comeback.

The former manager of the Plaza in New York uses one of the most effective gambits in answering written complaint letters.

Immediately, he calls the complainer person-to-person, long distance, wherever he is in the country.

"I just this very minute got your letter, sir," he says, "and I want you to know that I'm awful sorry to learn your TV flickered all through John Wayne . . . it won't happen again, and if there's anything I can do, anything at all, to make it up to you . . . "

And the guy who gets a call like that is a friend for life.

"Uh, gee, you shouldn't have gone to all this bother," babbles the complainer, flattered half out of his wits. "I, uh, just wanted to call it to your attention. Gee, it's nice of you to . . . "

"It's nice of *you,* sir, to let us know."

The guest is return business forever. The couple of bucks for the call is actually less than the time cost of dictating a letter. Most important is the underlying truth. The hotel would have fixed the TV cheerfully, and before John Wayne disposed of the next Indian . . . if management had known about it. A big if indeed. It's the great blank area between anticipating complaints and satisfying complaints which leaves management forever frustrated. Here's the eternal conflict between the hopes of public-relations minded management and the attitude of some employees. Jack Kofoed, who writes a widely read column in the Miami *Herald,* sums it up.

Kofoed was having dinner at a swank Palm Beach hotel. At a table near him sat a striking pair: a gentleman in a handsome shantung silk dinner jacket and a lady in a beautiful dinner dress.

The waiter spilled a tureen of soup all over the gentleman's white jacket. He was naturally furious. The waiter couldn't have cared less and went about his business.

But the manager of the hotel happened to be in the room at the time. He rushed over to apologize.

"Sir, give me that coat," said the manager. "I'll have our valet clean it immediately and return it before you finish your dinner, and you are my personal guests for dinner. We are so sorry, sir."

The manager trotted off with the coat. A couple of minutes later the waiter stalked back into the room and saw the guest in his shirt sleeves.

"Hey," he snarled, poking the guest on the shoulder. "Youse can't eat in here widdout you got a coat on."

Among men who know hotels best, common courtesy is money in the bank and what one rude jerk of an employee can do to the house image is horrendous to contemplate.

It's probably never been summed up better than by the publicity genius named Hank Meyer. Hank is Florida's outstanding public relations man, his firm handles many giant accounts and while he, himself, is not a hotelman, a lot of hotelmen could profit from his experience. He's handled all of the City of Miami Beach's publicity, has been advisor to many large hotels and motel chains, and coordinates facilities of all Gold Coast hotels for the nearly inconceivably complicated shindigs called national political conventions.

Hank Meyer himself exemplifies the courteous soft sell; always seems to have time for the most intrusive time-waster, partly because he never knows where he'll find a space-grabbing idea, and primarily because he's naturally courteous himself.

He has brought many high-powered celebrities, from Arthur Godfrey to Jackie Gleason, to Miami Beach, hence enhancing its image.

Meyer one day read in a newspaper that Jackie Gleason, snowbound in New York, wished he could play golf every day. "You mean that, Jackie?" said Hank, getting right on the phone. "You know it, pal!" said the Great One. "I'll see that you play golf every day if you want to," said Hank, in his soft-spoken way. The result was Gleason moving his entire show to Miami Beach, telecasting from the convention hall, and Miami Beach reaping millions in publicity. (One courteous phone call—and a lot of moxie in the follow-up—is Meyer's formula.)

Whether you're in the hotel business or not, what Meyer has to say about courtesy—which sometimes seems to be a vanishing trait—may apply.

"The personnel of America's service industries," said Hank, "seems about equally divided between those who serve the public because they enjoy meeting people and those whose natural inclination seems more and more to be that of guard-dogs whose role in life is to take bites out of passersby."

Hank leaned back in his swivel chair in his penthouse suite on the Lincoln Road Mall and smiled his deceptively gentle little smile. "By that I mean, in case I am being too subtle, that too damn many people are just rotten mean."

"Now it's not too subtle," his interviewer said.

"Good," said Hank. "Because a rude employee often doesn't realize he's being rotten mean—maybe he's really a swell guy—and *acts* rotten mean out of a zeal to protect and defend the establishment he works for. He thinks he is keeping the place alive by what he considers firmness. He's not keeping it alive. He's the angel of death."

Hank is an institution now, but he's never forgotten what it means to be unknown in a place where even a stranger's smile means a lot.

"Any mammal leaving its den becomes wary," he said, "and ready to fight or flee. The human animal is no exception. When traveling, he craves comfort and reassurance and a familiarity he may not even need at home. Strangers in a strange town, even the jubilant enjoying a pleasure trip, are often just one icy remark away from a burst of anger or a case of the jitters.

"In any resortdom, the employee at any level whose normal emotional range runs from courteous to compassionate is worth his weight in travelers' checks. A warming voice and a friendly look are great assets.

"But, when the traveler hears his car whipped toward the garage with great screeching at the corners, the grandest hotel begins to look and sound like a loser. If bags are mislaid a rude put-off just may take a guest ten percent of the way to a nervous breakdown and certainly to an immediate checkout. Furthermore, he didn't bring a red flag with him to signal waiters or the coffee shop waitress and he expects consideration without having to send a telegram that his coffee is cold.

"Money transactions particularly," said Hank Meyer,

"make any stranger feel vulnerable, even when he could buy and sell everybody for a block around; when he feels or hears himself sized up as a potential forger the phrase 'Never come back here' starts ringing in his ears.

"And whether he's a manager with battalions serving under him or a car jockey who bosses nothing but a gearshift, he has the same problem—to bring out the best in a guest by exhibiting the best in himself.

"Discourtesy is a particularly wounding form of hari-kari because it eventually will cost the discourteous more than it costs his victims . . . and there are consequences to his employer, the street he's on, and the city he lives in.

"Courtesy means many happy returns and rudeness is what causes ghost towns and ghost hotels."

"Hank, we thank you," said *Keyhole*. "But you know what strikes us as a bit peculiar? If you're so good at publicity, why didn't you mention the name of a single client of yours in the lodging business?"

"Oh, I don't need to," said Mr. Meyer. "Everybody already knows about courtesy at all Quality Courts motels."

And, of course, hotelmen sometimes themselves inadvertently wrongly accuse or accidentally annoy a guest into what can only be construed as a legitimate complaint.

Norman Eldredge, for instance, well-known throughout the trade as the boss for years of the New York office of Thomas Cook & Son, worked as a night manager at the Bradford Hotel in Boston.

One night on a routine patrol of the upper floors he overheard a conversation behind a guest's door—the impassioned plea of a charged-up young swain convincing his lady love that she should *couchez avec* him, post-haste.

The man announced in no uncertain terms how this would relieve his eager desire and also transport her to a stage of undreamed of bliss. It was one hell of a sales pitch.

Norm, his admiration overcome by his sense of duty, took his passkey and entered the room across the hall. He called the room of the would-be lover and recited the usual, "Sir, do you have a lady in your room?"

(When they ask they always know.)

"No," came the answer.

"Well, sir, I beg to differ but—"

"There is no woman in my room!"

As the guest got angrier, Norm finally said flatly, "Well, I couldn't help overhearing you asking her to . . . ah, conversing with her."

"Come over and see for yourself!" the man said.

Norm did.

No girl.

The guest complained about the treatment.

Norman apologized.

The guest relented.

"That's O.K.," said the guest sheepishly. "I was just rehearsing my proposition in case I could *get* a girl to come to my room."

Indeed, the extra fey dimension. Although hotels have changed a lot physically since the old non–air-conditioned days when the seal story happened, human nature hasn't. The seal story happens, in some variation, everywhere all the time.

"The guy in the next room keeps his seals in our adjoining bathroom and my room smells like fish!" complained the guest in a New York show-biz hotel.

"Well, open the window," said the weary night clerk.

"What?! And let my pigeons out?"

John Monahan, who runs the Marco Polo in Miami Beach, is a vastly imaginative Irisher. The way he handled a chronic complainer worked wonders. This was a guy in a position to book in convention trade, but the more he was handled with kid gloves the nastier he got, throwing his weight around. Monahan finally got enough of it.

He got hold of a fairly frowzy, used, black silk negligee. He had it wrapped. He mailed it to Big-Shot's wife with a note purportedly from the hotel housekeeper.

"It was so nice to have you and your husband stay with us last Saturday," said the note. "We look forward to your return. We are sending a garment you forgot."

The wife had been at home all along.

Presumably the homecoming of Large Mouth was not a study in domestic bliss. He telephoned John, a beaten man, and said, "Okay, John. You win. I'll be nice."

He has been, too.

Many complaints can't be classified at all. They are things that happen once. They happen only in hotels. But no school teaches about them and they have only this in common: they have no precedent. As the spinster said after the burglar assaulted her, "By the time I figured out what was happening I didn't need the information anymore." At the Theresa Hotel in Harlem, where Fidel Castro and his lieutenants stayed during a UN session, and actually slaughtered and cooked chickens in their room, the manager was educated to anticipate future

complaints that some Cuban Communists were killing
and frying chickens in their suite. But just how often will
he get to use the knowledge in one lifetime?

Many years ago a Shah of Persia had a sheep be-
headed in his quarters. It's not a thing you would ordinarily be on the alert for.

In Evian, France, an Oriental potentate urinated in a
hotel elevator. This caused complaints from the prissy.
The manager, in turn, complained to the potentate. The
potentate bought the hotel and ordered everybody out,
including the management. The manager didn't even
have time to think up a sign for the elevator. It seems a
shame.

Hotelmen—the veterans—are, well, different. It may
not be apparent to the casual glance; won't be, in fact.
A lot of deception has rubbed off on them, and without
making them deceitful, has made them . . . aware.
Fully aware that today will more than likely bring them
some situation for which all their yesterdays failed to
prepare them. Their eyes are not so resigned as ready.
They are not so much incapable of being surprised, as
they are certain they will be surprised. Two things are
sudden death: being cynical and being naive. It is a veiled
look, there above the most decorous carnation, which
says: *never try to con an old conster, never snow an old
trooper.* But—no!—it is not world-weary wisdom that
says, solely, I have seen it all.

Rather it is a unique outlook which says: I've got to
figure out what's happening now before the game is over.
The successful survivors learn fast, or the game for them
is over. It's kibitzing the unknown. One incident, which
happened in the Variety Club in the Willard Hotel in
Washington, D.C., seems to sum up the outlook. It is, in

fact, a story about a kibitzer. He was always looking over the shoulders of the regular card players and was maddeningly free with his advice. The players, before he arrived one day, framed up a mythical game instead of the usual stud and draw.

The onlooking expert arrived. Immediately, the dealer shuffled, took four cards off the top of the deck, put them in his pocket. He gave six cards to the next player, who folded them and put them under the ash tray.

The next player got twenty cards. The next, one card, which he put in his pocket and said, "I've got a scrinch so I'll bet a buck."

The next player said, "Gung-ho your ring-a-ding. I filled my blamp."

"Looks like a busted wallaby," said the next player, "but I've got a blimp."

"I raise again!" said the dealer triumphantly. "I've got a flooney and I raise the limit!"

"Goddamn, man!" shouted the kibitzer. "How do you expect to beat a scrinch, a blimp, and a blamp with a lousy flooney?"

Hotelmen have to learn fast, with an added disadvantage: no matter who the kibitzing complainer is, you're expected to do something. Whatever the strange game is.

"Do something!" shouted a drunk who had telephoned the manager from his room. "When I look at my TV it looks back at me!"

Jack Lanahan, now president of Flagler System Hotels, tells the bemusing facts. He was sales manager for Dumont Television when it happened. The drunk kept calling the manager, who finally went to check, and looked into the Dumont "magic eye." A very real eye looked back. It was a mouse.

"Do something!" shouted the drunk. "When I look at my TV it looks back at me!"

The manager removed the mouse, calmed the drunk, went to his office and wrote a thoughtful letter to Lanahan, going to the heart of the matter as only a hotel manager could, concluding:

> So you, Lanahan, because your sets aren't mouse-proof, have left me a miserable man. Now the rest of my life I will have to give credence to every single drunk call . . . no longer can I brush off a single drunk!
>
> No matter what a drunk says, I will check it out! I average three drunk calls a week, 156 a year . . . this will take weeks out of my working life, and all because of you and your goddamn magic eye!

If you complain about your hotel TV and a man comes up to see if there's a mouse in it, you'll know why.

Possibly the record for complaints in quantity, a veritable Tower of Babel of multilingual complaining, has, until challenged successfully, gone to the quite awesome Barefooted One-World episode at the Mayflower. It was downright magnificent in scope.

Corneal J. Mack, who has been president of both the American and International Hotel Associations, was general manager. He has been host to ambassadors, presidents, and kings. The International Parliamentary Union was holding its biennial conference at the Mayflower.

Mack kept his men's room attendants on overtime to pick up and shine shoes he knew would be left outside doors overnight as per European custom.

It was a big convention. The attendants picked up more than 400 pairs of shoes that night and shined them nicely. It was all in the best European tradition except for one slight detail.

The attendants neglected to chalk corresponding room numbers on each pair of shoes. It's those little things that get you—and the next morning some 400 sock-clad diplomats were in the ballroom pawing through shoes, looking for their own. Dignitaries evidently travel with only one pair, even as you and I.

The Secretary of State himself called Mack on the carpet, but it was futile. The Secretary of State, try though he might, couldn't stay stern and broke up laughing . . .

The description of striped-pants diplomats squabbling over shoes, with an occasional bare big toe poked out of an internationally traveled sock, was too much. (Could you immediately spot your shoes in 400 pairs? Or, if you could, could the other 399 guys spot theirs?)

The fact they had to quarrel in different languages, with no translators, lends the added touch of class for the Complaint Championship.

(No fair counting UN sessions.)

So, the hotelman not only kibitzes, he must cope, and cope fast. There are very few iron-clad rules in handling complaints. What guidelines do exist are important to know and follow, however. One of hoteldom's firmest laws is this: never touch a guest in any way but a handshake, for legal and other reasons, including simple self-preservation.

Jim Crothers, who owns the Nassau Beach, mentioned the wisdom of this rule, telling of a resident manager he had—an impressive Britisher, suave, polished, poised, seemingly capable of handling anything.

The lordly Britisher always wore a fresh carnation, was marvelously tailored, and coped by sheer imperiousness of manner. He never quite regained command after breaking the no-touch rule, however. Overconfidence got him. (With British hotel managers, the imperiousness is the first to go.)

A loud drunk did it. Just one garden-variety drunk, no different, seemingly, than a thousand other lobby loud-mouths with the funny hats and the fanny-patting syndrome.

"Now see heah, m'good fellah," said the manager to the drunk—and, with condescending friendliness, *put his hand on the loudmouth's shoulder.*

Crothers sums up the result with a sentence Shakespeare might admire for beauty and cadence.

"In the twinkling of an eye he was flat on his ass, carnation, *broad-A,* and all."

That hosts manage to stay as genial as they do has been known to bring on fits of poesy, as follows.

Whatever Became of Mine Genial Host?

The late Al Koehl was president of Koehl, Landis and Landan, Inc., an ad agency in New York which specializes in hotel advertising, when he wrote this verse.

In the good old days the hotelman
Lived on a gracious Lucullan plan,
Smiling while guests so distingué
Partook of his table and cellar, for pay;
Schooled in the art of fine conversation,
Passing his days in endless vacation,
Chatting and supping and quaffing his fill,
While the cream of society fattened his till.
Whatever became of Mine Genial Host?

What dastardly doings have altered his post?
Where are the helpers he had in the past?
They're out on a strike, or off on a blast . . .

Now he's a plumber, an Einstein and foreman . . .
A housekeeper, chef, art critic and doorman;
And there on his desk, that great volume you saw,
Is an up-to-date treatise on labor and law!
He rarely sits down with his fashionable clients.
His career has become mathematical science.
Bookings and vacancies, profits and losses.
Income tax lawyers now serve as his bosses.

Vendors and spenders all add to his work,
And the help in the kitchen is going berserk!
Complaints and decisions, he pacifies all
From the Board of Directors to maids down the hall.
He can't leave his office, for out in the foyer
Lurks a chap who's reported to be Zsa Zsa's lawyer.
And if these aren't enough, alack and egad, man,
His office girl buzzes announcing the ad man.

Can he hide in the bath? No, he's never alone,
For now every john is equipped with a phone.
The heliport's calling to bring him a glowing
Report that the new rooftop pool's overflowing
So he'll run up the stairs, though his old heart implores
Because the new elevator is stuck between floors.
O! What will the eventual end of him be?
Next week's convention, or ceiling TV?
Bunions, lumbago, the new competition?
Hyperacidity . . . or malnutrition?
Cheer up; all too soon he'll go on vacation—
Doomed, damned and displaced by complete automation!

                                                    Al Koehl

At the risk of conflict with a fellow poet, and you know how sensitive we poets are, we admire Koehl's poesy more than his conclusion.

Perhaps the prophecies will come true of computerized, machine-managed hostelries. (If so, we can hardly wait to see how the maids are programmed.) But our own outlook differs. Thusly:

Send Up Mine Genial Host, This Damn
Robot's Blown a Fuse!

And the "automated" hotel,
Will have the same old quirk;
Hotelmen will catch the hell
When computers fail to work.

8

The Fontainebleau Papers

. . . But there is neither East nor West,
border, nor breed, nor birth/ When two strong
men stand face to face, though they come from
the ends of the earth!

> (*Kipling, "The Ballad of East and West")*

This complaint has gone down as a classic.

San Francisco, March 18, 1971

Hotel Fontainebleau
On the Ocean at 44th Street
Miami Beach, Florida

Attention: Resident Manager

Dear Sir:
Enclosed find remittance in the amount of $125.45
for my brief stay at, as my people say, the "Fon-tan-
bloo."

What a delightful experience! ! ! The opportunity for two full days to be surrounded by beehive hairdos, glittering bejeweled fingers and toes, and tons of sunburned adipose tissue. And all for $58.30 per day plus tax.

Each morning brought a new anticipatory thrill as I rushed down to the poolside to stroll among the bodies of the ultimate in Semitic womanhood. How my heart pounded as I observed them all browning their vulgar behinds in the Florida sunshine. What pride I felt; I'm sure Moses himself would have felt the same pride at the display of Jewish men at their leisure. Great oily, corpulent bodies steaming in the heat; mouths agape to show the pearly-white Manhattan Island tooth cappings. My viscera quivered with chauvinistic pleasure at the sight of them.

As I write this note my eyes dim with tears of nostalgia. I think of my bed with the plastic headboard and the sparkle ceiling. I think of the mattress stained with unidentified droppings and filled with the aroma of a whaling ship. Even now I feel it rocking and creaking underneath me. I think of the soggy sandwiches at lunch. I think of the algae at the swimming pool edge. I think most of all of the great, golden-haired big city Jewess; her huge rump thrust through an unfortunate inner tube; fiighting like a sweating, steaming hippo in the pool. Memories like this are priceless. At $58.30 per day plus tax, I considered this a bargain.

Very truly yours,
Signed: _____

P.S. Perhaps a portion of this remittance might be used to clean and fumigate the room in which I stayed. The third generation cockroaches that I encountered there were annoying to say the least.

(*Author's note:* Now *that* is a complaint letter.)

Miami Beach, March 26, 1971

Dear _____:

Good heavens! And to think—I had a bowl of matzo ball soup for lunch.

Schulberg, Roth, and Salinger had better look to their laurels. I haven't read such cheerful vituperation since the German Ministry of Propaganda stopped churning out sneers about sweaty, Semitic skins, interlaced of course with paeans to pale, Nordic complexions.

Since you were smitten with the scene at our pool, I'm sure you noticed some similarity to Thomas Mann's short story, "Blood of the Walsungs," wherein all the Jewish protagonists dance a slow pavane of mutual distaste, held together only by their even greater distaste for the barbaric goyim, represented in this instance, I suppose, by the lounge attendants.

By the way, if the insects you encountered were indeed third generation. I can understand your distress. The third generation of anything is almost always annoying. After your crowd had exhausted the entire national supply of peroxide, carved out a veritable Mount Rushmore of nose jobs, and developed a cardiac condition like you wouldn't believe from tons of bacon and eggs, the third generation made a complete 180-degree turn, grew lovelocks and a beard, changed its name from Reginald to David, and exodused to join the nearest kibbutz, with only an occasional postcard home in, what eise, Hebraic slang.

However, I would be pleased to use a portion of your remittance to arrange a final solution to the problem of the nonregistered guests in room 738. The only trouble is that your remittance was not enclosed. An honest error? A dishonest Arab in your office? Or another in-

dication of inherited racial shrewdness, as undoubtedly
Dr. Goebbels would label it.

Sincerely yours,
James G. Baird
Exec. Assistant Manager

(Authors' Note: Now *that* is an executive assistant
manager.)

San Francisco, May 14, 1971

Mr. James G. Baird
Executive Assistant Manager
Hotel Fontainebleau
Miami Beach, Florida

Dear Mr. Baird:
   Sir, please excuse the delay in following up your letter to me. Besides the unceasing tedium and pressures
of my work-a-day world, I was, I confess, stymied by
the difficult task of providing a proper reply to your very
thoughtful and challenging missive.
   For a period of time I sat, flabbergasted—beside myself with admiration for your incisive intelligence and
wit. At one point I wondered, My God, what is this?
*Did the Fontainebleau hire this man specifically to an-
swer my letter?* Well, Mr. Baird, I will never know. So
all that I am able to do at this point, having found the
time, is to sit down and reply as best I can to what you
have written.
   First of all, may I say you struck me to the quick.
You recognized the ultimate truth about me and about
Jews in General (how's that for a book title?). That is,
among our fleshy rank and file is indeed found the very
quintessence of anti-Semitism. Naturally, it is for genet-
icists and/or psychologists to determine the important
factor behind this quirk. But you and I both realize that

it exists; and that I exist—wandering among grease-glazed bodies, peroxided wigs, Nanette Fabray nose jobs, and hating it all.

But . . . now, and perhaps because of your letter, I have realized that it is time for a change, at least on my part . . . I mean, after all, these poor Jewish people—my God, have they been worked over! Physically and emotionally. In the forties, even the cultural literati began going after them with fangs bared.

Schulberg and Salinger, as you mentioned in your letter, all got in their licks, and then in the late sixties, Roth delivered his near *coup de grâce*. So really, at this point, do they need me, one of their own, attacking them like a pack wolf? Of course not!

And I believe that you should take credit, at least in part, for my realization . . . hereafter, should I appear on the premises of the Fontainebleau ("Land of Milk and Honey"), I will be the epitome of recessitude and good behavior. From my lips will fall nothing but words of sweetness and appreciation. In short, I will behave.

Alright, Mr. Baird, I've stated my position now. May I say that there is something about your letter, actually about you, that I find curious. You mentioned being familiar with the messages of the Minister of Propaganda in Nazi Germany. May I go so far as to ask exactly how you were privy to these messages?

Having, as I now have, assumed this new protective stance, I feel it is vital that I know in detail your connection with Hitler's Germany circa 1940 to the present time. We all fantasize, Mr. Baird, and I must say in connection with my question, I have fantasized with the best of them . . . Knowing as I do that you (because you told me) listened to the "Dr. Goebbels Show," I have imagined that there is the distinct possibility that you were, and perhaps still are, involved in depth with the now scattered but still existent Nazi Party. Is it too monstrous to believe that at this very moment in Miami

Beach, the final Kafka-esque act is being prepared? That in a hotel full of nice, soft Jewish people, there is a basement room—candlelit and secretive—where the plans, the final plans, are now being laid?

And that one bright sunny Florida morning in the future these plans will reach fruition? That suddenly Obergeneral Baird will stride to poolside in a brown shirt! That from the kitchen, where for twenty-five years he has been slicing lox, will come Martin Borman, resplendent in his braided uniform fresh from the Fontainebleau moth locker! That from the cabanas former poolside attendants will appear in their leather boots and steel swastikaed helmets!

Suddenly, the Fontainebleau is in pandemonium! Achtung! Achtung! the headwaiter—General Jodl—is heard over the PA system where a moment ago Dennis Day had crooned. "All guests out of those disgusting bikinis and return to their rooms! We are taking over!"

I hope that this scene will never be played out. But then I suppose I need reaffirmation of some sort.

Please write and certify that nothing of this nature is going on, that my fears are unfounded. Enclosed find my check for the full amount covering my lodging.

Assuming that I will receive confirmation that you are not a member of the S.S., Luftwaffe, or Storm Troopers, I will, in return, display a goodly amount of forbearance toward the Fontainebleau.

> Thank you for your letter.
> Yours truly,
> Signed: _____

(Authors' Note: Now, *that* is a satisfied guest.)

Before the Justice Department demands to know how we came into possession of the Fontainebleau Papers, this addition:

To C. DeWitt Coffman:

Witt, I thought you might get a kick out of reading these. To me, they are prizes.

I've been a bit busy—still looking for a hearing aid a guest complained about. He said a pigeon came in the room and flew away with it. Warmest regards.

Lou Rogers
President, Hotel Fontainebleau

(Authors' Note: Now *that* is a hotel president. As soon as one customer is made happy, another one starts raising hell about the pigeons stealing his hearing aid.)

9

The Humor Roomers

Hotels attract practical jokers. On some harried days, hotel management itself seems like one big practical joke. Only the Imp god of hotels, for instance, knows what would prompt somebody to explode a cherry bomb in a commode.

"We just thought the force of the explosion with the lid shut and all would splash water up and scare people in other rooms," explained the dripping students who bombed the toilet. This was at the Inverurie in Bermuda.

What it did was blow the toilet apart and flood the bathroom.

The guy who sat on the closed lid was right where most people wish all practical jokers would end. Right

114

in the middle of his chuckle he got his aspiration blown up.

"I hated to take their eighty dollars for the replacement," said Conrad Englehardt, president and general manager. "But only because even their money was wet."

The fact is, not too many people are madly in love with practical jokers as a breed. Practical joking would seem to vie with smallpox in popularity. But, like puns, or sin, an awful lot of it happens, for something which gets bad-mouthed so much.

Sometimes immense labor goes into a practical joke. At the Elbow Beach, also in Bermuda, the assistant manager kept getting thick-tongued calls from a guest complaining there was no furniture in his room. "Sure, sure," said the assistant manager, "you just take a nap and we'll send up an entire suite as soon as possible"; then he hung up. Not long after, the same drunk called back.

"I took a lil' nap and there'sh still no furniture."

When the assistant manager went up the guy was asleep on the floor using the telephone as a pillow. The room was bare. His friends had moved the furniture piece by piece into other rooms, after he had passed out. He came to as porters were moving furniture back in. Naturally, he tackled what he assumed were furniture thieves. Then he promptly passed out again.

All the effort was for nothing. When he finally sobered up he didn't remember a single thing about the out-and-in moving transaction. His frustrated friends even brought in the assistant manager as a witness.

"You guys will do anything to make a gag stick, won't you?" he scoffed. "Who the hell believes practical jokers?"

Too many people, that's who. At the Jefferson Hotel in St. Louis some years ago, highly indignant clergymen assembled in convention began to splutter in shock at the management about the Reverend Jones who was welcoming them to the hotel. Management scratched its head and, possibly until now, never quite figured out who the "welcoming preacher" was who was giving the brethren rather unusual directions.

It was the late great reporter, Spencer McCullough, of the St. Louis *Post-Dispatch*—which was near the Jefferson. McCullough, a portly and impressive man, himself a theology school dropout, had been in the hotel covering a Teamsters meeting. A group of visiting preachers, assuming he too was a Man of God by profession, asked him about local cultural matters.

"Ah, yes, I am Brother Jones," said McCullough, shaking hands all around, in the preacher-filled lobby. "I suggest you take in Muny Opera, Shaw's Garden, and our splendid zoo. Also, our riverfront vista is unequaled, we have many historic landmarks and a fine symphony orchestra. Also, let me jot down directions on how to get down around Sixth and Olive."

"What is there, Reverend?" he was asked.

"At the risk of overpraising my own home town," said McCullough solemnly, "it is in this area you will find operating some of the most splendid hustlers this side of Memphis, lovely girls, one and all. Merely say the Reverend Jones sent you."

At which point he left the jaw-sagging, speechless preachers with a hearty, "Bless you, my brothers!"

And at the Royal Orleans in New Orleans, the new night room clerk was stunned when the veddy British female voice on the phone gave her room number and said, "Would you knock me up at seven in the morning? Thank you."

She hung up. The room clerk was still standing gap-jawed when a bellman asked him what the trouble was. The bellman then laughed and explained that that was simply a British term, meaning would you please *wake* me at seven.

"Oh," said the clerk, not sure whether he was relieved or not.

The *next* night—after the British lady had checked out—the same night clerk got a call from what sounded like the same British voice, from outside the hotel.

"I waited for an hour, m'deah," said the sultry voice. "I wore my nicest negligee and even left the door a bit ajar. Are you that bashful, darling, or should I check back in sometime?"

"Check back in!" he said eagerly to the voice—actually a bellhop's girlfriend. "I'm not bashful, sugar . . . it's just that some goddamn fool told me knocked up only meant a time call in England."

The best practical jokes leave no comeback at all, and Bob Benchley, the great humorist, wasn't above going to a lot of work to perfect a situation.

When Frank Case owned and operated the Algonquin in New York, Benchley invited him to dinner at his home in Scarsdale. When Case was shown into the guest room he found the sheets, towels, ash trays, and bathmats were from the Algonquin—at dinner, all the china, glassware, silver, and napery were also from the hotel.

Stolen? Purchased? Both? Case never knew. Benchley had his man pegged—Case felt that as a guest in Benchley's home, it would be bad taste to ask. And equally bad taste when Benchley was at Case's Algonquin.

Plus the fact that with Benchley, nobody was ever *sure* about anything.

Hotelmen themselves sometimes resort to a form of practical joke—deception—when it's truly practical.

Art Bruns, the storied and offbeat owner of the plush Miami Springs Villas, knew just what to do when a house officer said a maddened wife was screeching in a hallway. She said she knew her husband was inside a certain room with a woman, and what kind of an immoral place was this?

"Madam," said Bruns, in his most courtly manner, trying to mollify her in the hall. "You must be mistaken. I am sorry, but I cannot open that room on your say-so. Anyhow, nobody answers the knock, as you see, and—"

"Come out of there, you worm!" the woman screamed. To Bruns she bawled her threats to call police, the newspapers, perhaps the National Guard. At the door she yowled, "I know you're in there with a redhead!"

"Please, please, madam," said Bruns, worriedly, and argued with her at length. When other guests began sticking their heads out their doors to check the racket, he finally sighed and agreed to open the door in question.

"Aha!" squalled the woman. A pajama-clad redhead was seemingly taking a nap. The woman rushed into the bathroom, yanked open the shower stall—and stared in confusion at a nude and soapy stranger.

The woman screamed and left, bug-eyed.

"Thanks, Joe," Art said to the man in the shower. "You can go on back to work. As for you," he turned to the redhead, "get the hell out of here, and tell your boyfriend I said for neither of you to come back."

While Art had stalled the wife, the errant husband had been helped out the ground floor window by a house officer, and a bellman quickly substituted in the room.

"I run a nice place," said Art blandly. "Wives can't kill husbands here—it gets spots on the rugs and stories in the papers."

Now, that's more practical than joke. The true practical joke has no point except the joke itself. The true practical joker uses the materials at hand and does so instantaneously. Consider the lounger in Brooklyn's Hotel St. George, who for the sake of a joke caused part of the French navy to riot.

"I'm sorry, I don't understand," the room clerk was saying to a dozen hand-waving guests, French sailors who spoke no English.

"I speak French," said a man in the lounge, solemnly. "They want to know if you have a steam bath."

"Certainly, certainly," said the clerk, pointing the way through a corridor and downstairs to the steam rooms.

The sailors went in, a bit puzzled; became even more puzzled when attendants made motions for them to disrobe. In almost no time there was a roaring gang fight.

What the sailors had been originally trying to ask was how to find a subway.

The hotel actually had to call the French Consul to mollify the sailors. The St. George hired three cars to take them around town free. The practical joker, of course, had disappeared—leaving a couple of steam room attendants with black eyes, and a dozen French sailors with no telling *what* impression of American men.

Practically all of Miami's sportswriters and announcers, plus what seemed like a good portion of Miami generally, turned out at Miami Springs Villas to honor the late Clure Mosher, offbeat and popular sports commentator whose stock in trade was the verbal needle he used so well.

Publicist Julian Cole dreamed up the joke, again beautiful in its simplicity. Mosher, among his testimonial gifts, was given the most decrepit, swayback horse available, to go with his horse-playing abilities. The testimonial car wasn't a new convertible, but a jalopy. None of this bothered Mosher, of course—he was no mean joker himself. And as each speaker got up to insult him, you could see him waiting to return the darts with interest.

Then . . . they got him . . .

When it finally came time for his farewell address— Clure was moving to a New York station—he got up. He picked up the mike carefully. He looked around at his tormentors, all out before him. He cherished the moment, for he knew each of their weak points and he knew precisely how to slay them verbally. It was his moment! Time to do his thing . . . murder 'em!

He opened his mouth to start talking.

It was the prearranged signal.

As one man, the multitude got up and left the testimonial banquet.

In Chicago, the city editor was big winner in the payday poker game in the traditional hotel room. It was only early evening, but he wanted to quit while ahead. "Cash me in," he finally said.

"Jeez!" said a player. "You going to buck the traffic jam during this snow?"

"Huh?" said the city editor, glancing back over his

shoulder at the snow-covered window. "I'll be damned. Bad traffic, huh? Well, I'll play a few more hands."

Within two hours he lost his winnings, then his paycheck, then what money he could borrow, and, glumly, left. Muttering, he stopped in the lobby and called his wife with what is usually a pretty good reason in any northern metropolitan city. He said, "I'm a little late—damn traffic is awful because of the snow."

"What snow? How drunk are you?" she asked.

It was a cold clear night devoid of snow—except the spray-can variety with which other newspapermen had covered the poker room window. They had wired the can to a stick and held it, valve open, from the window of an adjoining room, covering the panes. The city editor never, never mentioned it.

To play Hotel Tic Tac Toe you need a large hotel and a room with a view of floors of other windows across a courtyard. Sandy Bain and his friends invented it at two o'clock one morning. Sandy is vice-president of marketing for Restaurant Associates. Before that he was in the hotel business. He also used to be a theatrical agent. With that kind of background, perhaps you can't help playing things like Hotel Tic Tac Toe.

The invention may not give him and his friends ranking with Da Vinci and Edison. But it has a certain something. Let us not attempt to define it. Only to explain it.

Bain and his friends were staying at the Stratford Motor Inn in Connecticut. Floors of blank windows faced them across a courtyard in the night, from the room where it is entirely possible they were having a little drink.

All of them were staring silently out the window at the other darkened windows; sleeping niches in the night. "Hmmmmm," said Bain. "Lookit all the dark rooms . . ." And Hotel Tic Tac Toe was born.

Directions

1. Each player in turn tries to guess what room number an opposite room is and dials that room. (It can only be played in hotels where you dial other rooms inside the house direct.)

2. If and when somebody answers, the player says, "This is the hotel engineer. Sorry to bother you but we are having emergency problems. Would you please turn on your lights or at least one lamp so we can check the circuits?"

3. Players take turns. The first player to light three rooms in a row—up, across, or slantwise—wins.

If the hotel people, or complaining sleepy guests, catch you at it . . . you lose.

The fact that the practical joke is associated with Americans, however unjustly or inaccurately, may explain why the management of a Russian hotel never mentioned one peculiar episode.

Neal Mack, longtime general manager of the Mayflower in Washington, D.C., took a trip to Moscow after a Paris convening of the International Hotel Association, of which Mack was president. A group of American hotelier friends met in Mack's room before a sight-seeing trip, and somebody felt a slight lump under the carpet.

The carpet was rolled back and there concealed cleverly, but not cleverly enough for Americans raised on espionage stories, was a wrapped strand of multicolored wires disappearing through a hole in the floor!

To thwart the Communist electronic bugs they cut through the wires . . . and the chandelier in the room below crashed to the floor.

In honesty, what gives Americans the reputation for practical jokes in hotels is, one fears, partly due to Americans in hotels. What is more firmly entrenched in folklore than the American Legionnaire leaning out of a window with a paper bag full of water to drop on an unsuspecting citizen below? That dangerous practice seems to be dead, or sleeping, now, but the cartoons and fables continue. The facts, as usual, were stranger than the fables—as old-timers at the St. Louis Statler know.

So many bags of water were being dropped out of windows during a Legion convention that police were called to keep a watch across the street.

And, still, bleating pedestrians were—ker-splash— soaked with the pin-bombing of a Norden bombsight. The puzzled cops saw nothing. Nobody leaning out of, or looking out of, windows.

What was happening? This. Our ex-boys in the Service had truly reverted to type; put artillery observers in the windows of hotels across the street . . . using surveyor's instruments. The observers—above and behind the watching police and house officers—simply signaled. The triggermen, crouched down behind the Statler sills and peeking out, had only to flick the waterbag out. Blooey! Another clean hit!

If there is one comforting thing about practical jokes, it is the marvelous frequency with which the jokester himself gets a backfire reaction—the biter-bit syndrome.

Sometimes it is mild, the backfire, and in one case produced a beautiful, if confused, punchline for a situation with a cast unequalled this side of *Alice in Wonderland*. No offense to cast members, lovely ladies all and talented: Lady Bird Johnson, Julie Andrews, and Carol Burnett. It was the plot that made it surrealistic.

Carol Burnett and Julie Andrews, in a Washington hotel, had called Director Mike Nichols to come down to their suite for a drink. He said he would be right down.

Carol and Julie decided to shake him up with a gag; trotted down the hall and, when they saw the down elevator stop at Mike's floor, two floors above, stood to one side of the elevator doors. When they opened, Carol and Julie went into a burlesque of passionate embrace.

It wasn't Mike who got off but Lady Bird Johnson. Carol practically dropped Julie and flushed, her mouth working like a grounded ladyfish.

Lady Bird said calmly, "Aren't you Carol Burnett?"

"Yes, ma'am," squealed a red-faced Carol, and then heard herself squeak, "And this is Mary Poppins!"

The practical joker eventually gets his, for what small comfort that is, and, sooner or later, in the degree he deserves. Carol and Julie's prank was harmless—too many practical jokes aren't.

At the same hotel, a genius of a bellman has since gone on, we deeply pray, to better things. Certainly, he deserves them. His revenge on a conventioneering boor of the cruel-joke persuasion is classic. The delegate thought the exploding cigar the finest product of human endeavor; actually shook hands with a buzzer in his palm; squirted evil-smelling perfume from his lapel flower; and reached a new low when he "tipped" this bellman, on a room service call, with a blistering half-dollar he had heated with his cigarette lighter. And he laughed at the pain, with the wotza-matter-can't-you-take-a-joke attitude of a medieval headsman.

He forgot the bellman. The bellman didn't forget him. The bellman made it a point to be on hand when the ho-ho hotshot was checking out.

The bellman—it had all been framed—walked up to the room clerk and, without warning, threw the contents of a vial of ink on the front of the clerk's shirt. Even the departing guest thought that a bit much . . . and the room clerk feigned rage approaching apoplexy.

The clerk screamed, "You silly son of—"

"Wait, calm down, Arthur," said the bellman. "It's disappearing ink. Trick ink. It'll dry right out, without a trace."

"Yeah?" growled the room clerk, looking down at the stain—which had already begun to disappear.

"Sure," said the bellman, holding up another vial. "Good gag, huh?"

"Hey, great!" said the loudmouth, grabbing the full vial. "This'll really shake up the guys!"

He actually gave the bellman an entire dollar—a wild extravagance for him—although this included the tip for carrying his bags out to the crowded airport limousine. The bellman didn't really mind. He got to see our Jovial Hero throw the ink on the white shirt of another delegate, who was speechless with rage.

As the limousine pulled away, the joker was still chorting and saying, "It'll disappear in a minute, it'll disappear in a minute!"

That was in 1968 but one assumes it hasn't disappeared yet . . . the second vial was indelible ink.

Veteran hotelmen, in fact, aren't the best patsies for a practical joke. They have seen too much. The room clerk at the Pick Congress in Chicago was busy registering delegates to the International Livestock Show, the colorful, carnival-like affair that changes the face of Chicago each year with its western atmosphere and hoopla.

The lobby was jammed with cowboys and cowgirls, and the clerk was busy writing forms. A bevy of cowgirls descended on the front desk and asked the room clerk if a friend, scheduled to arrive shortly, could stay overnight with them. He said surely, just make sure the friend registered.

An hour later the girls came in with their friend. His bellow bounced off the walls. The clerk, his back turned, leaped two feet in shock. But when he turned he never changed expression, although he was facing 1200 pounds of shorthorn steer.

"I'm awfully sorry, sir," he said to the steer. "Young ladies are not allowed to have members of the opposite sex in their rooms—house policy."

It was a masterful ad lib and brought lobby applause.

A bartender named George at the Sheraton Mayflower in Akron, Ohio, built practically the whole business of the hotel bar around his personality, or lack of it. Nobody really ever knew if he was joking or not.

He always snarls at customers. "Whaddyawant?"

"Uh, a rum and coke."

"I don't fool with crap like that."

"Er, a Scotch and soda?"

"Look, ding-a-ling, there's twenty-four kinds of Scotch. You think I'm a mind reader?"

On and on. He never smiles, never apologizes, and if people dawdle over their drinks he threatens them with

But when he turned he never changed expression, although he was facing 1200 pounds of shorthorn steer.

a cover charge of two bits per five minutes for taking up
the barstool. The place is jammed. Don Rickles became
famous with the same personality. Who knows why?

(Rickles told one of the authors his own favorite line,
and it was a true ad lib. Frank Sinatra stalked into the
Sands in Las Vegas, with his retinue, when Rickles was
playing there. Naturally, everybody stared at the great
Sinatra. Rickles bawled, "Hi, Frank. Welcome! Come on
in! Be happy. Make yourself at home—*hit somebody!*"
Frank, to his credit, broke up with the rest of the room.)

The absolutely unanswerable line was composed by
two hotelmen, back in the thirties. Franklin Moore of
the Penn Harris in Harrisburg, Leonard Hicks, Sr., of the
Morrison in Chicago, and the head of a hotel chain in
Indiana, all fine after-dinner speakers and humorists, were
fast friends, constantly ribbing each other. Their buddy,
many times married, and quite a ladies' man, died and
was laid to rest with elaborate ceremonies, and a massive
headstone with the usual dignified inscription. The two
surviving friends, feeling something was missing, had the
footstone made.

It bore a simple message: *At last he sleeps alone.*

At the Lincoln Hotel in New York, the switchboard
operator got a call from a guest screeching in panic. He
shouted that he *had* to be in New York City in a matter
of hours—it was his wedding day.

"Get me a plane reservation," he was screaming. "Have
a cab waiting!"

"But you are . . ." Click. He hung up. She called
the assistant manager who raced up. The poor guy, with
his pants on backward, his face ashen, and an awful

hangover, shouted, "Those dirty bastards! Get me a plane reservation! Omigod, how did I get to Cleveland?"

His buddies—hotelmen—had given him a bachelor party the previous evening. After he passed out, they thoughtfully checked him into a downtown Manhattan hotel, after stripping the room of everything bearing New York identification. Then they substituted linen, matches, stationery, and ashtrays they had foresightedly borrowed from the Hollenden Hotel in Cleveland. As a finishing touch they placed a Cleveland phone directory and a couple of Cleveland newspapers in his room.

"How long will it take me to get to New York?" he shouted.

"Exactly sixteen floors, sir."

Cruel? It's not so bad—not when you consider the victim was getting a little poetic justice. In the past he had been one of the group which got another groom-to-be plastered. Literally. *That* victim woke up with a "broken" ankle in a cast, and swore off drinking after that blackout. It's said he started again after limping through a Bermuda honeymoon and then having the cast removed, as per fake instructions left by a nonexistent doctor. His ankle had never been broken.

And that's the danger, for hotelmen. It's the atmosphere of innkeeping that gets you, where hardly anything is exactly as it seems.

Professor Louis Sack teaches hotel management at New York Community College in Brooklyn. He instructed older students by practice as much as by theory. In communications, he had students really call managers with strange requests—the point was to learn how experienced managers cope.

One student called the manager of the Park Sheraton. He claimed to be a UN official who needed accommodations for a group of thirty-seven. He said there were two little things: these were Mohammedans, and dietary laws demanded they have dishes untouched by other humans. Not merely clean plates, mind you, new ones. And, oh yes, all the rooms—quite naturally—must face east.

Other students had different assignments, like the one who told the manager, "I represent fifty theatrical people. They prefer very small rooms, as they tend toward *ouvrezlaphobia,* the opposite of claustrophobia, and they would like a special rate, as they sleep four to a bed, sideways, being midgets."

Students compared notes on managers' reactions. It was educational. Not a manager turned a hair. The conclusion: *Whatever* happens might be a gag, come midgets, Mohammedans, or moo-cows, or any combination. On the other hand, and practically speaking, it might not. Even *ouvrezlaphobic* Mohammedan midgets would be more than welcome, if they don't take cattle of the opposite sex to their rooms or parachute cats from the windows.

After all, rules are rules.

America's greatest authority on the practical joke— H. Allen Smith, who once wrote a whole book about them—comes back repeatedly in his book, at least by illustration through anecdote, to what seems to be a prime rule. The greatest practical jokes are usually simple and . . . this is the fascinating part . . . so often happen to the victim *without him having a clue as to what the hell is going on.*

Let us term it effect without cause—or at least evident

cause. The man whose hat brim is carefully tacked down by office colleagues each day and a quarter-inch shaved off the brim—he does not notice. The brim gets narrower and narrower. He looks more and more like a demented elf when he has his hat on. One day he catches sight of himself in a store window and says, "Why the hell did I buy this ridiculous looking hat?" He throws it away. *The funny part is he never has a clue.*

H. Allen Smith speaks of stark simplicity. The authors of this book favor, for pristine purity, the London jokester who uses only a ball of twine. He stands on the sidewalk, at the corner of a building. A stranger approaches. He says, "I say, sir. I am measuring for construction. Could you do me the great favor of a moment's aid? Please hold the end of this string, while I go around the corner with the ball of measuring twine. When I give a tug on the string, walk slowly around the corner toward me, winding up the string."

"Certainly," says the stranger.

The measuring engineer goes around the corner out of sight; stops the first man coming the *other* way. He says the same thing and hands this stranger the ball of string.

He then goes back to the corner, tugs the string, and disappears into a doorway.

Very slowly, very carefully, the two strangers wind up the string until they meet at the corner.

It is said, being reserved Britishers as they are, they often stand for several minutes, eyeball to eyeball, these strangers, each holding one end of the string. They do not know what to do. *They haven't got a clue.*

So it was with two American television commentators in Paris on a junket in connection with an Air France inaugural flight. Both are deadly with jokes on each other.

Smith hied forth. Meeting two young ladies of the evening, he said he was representing his friend Mr. Brown who was seeking female companionship. He paid them handsomely in American money, sending them to Brown's room number. They were delighted, but said the American money looked a "beet fun-eeee, monsieur."

Smith assured them the five hundred dollars was as solid as the Confederate States of America itself—see there at the top it says that—and, if they didn't believe it, to check before they went up. Smith then departed. The girls went on to the hotel. Being thrifty French and prudent, they did indeed check. They were told, of course, it was indeed funny money.

The point is Brown knew none of this, and it is the convolutions that get you. When two shapely French girls appear at your door ready to hop into bed with you, that is startling enough. When two shapely French girls try, apparently, to sell you five hundred dollars worth of Confederate money *before* they get in bed, *you haven't got a clue.*

Without seeming to praise practical jokers, it must be admitted the hotel world owes something to them. They are a tiny part of the *atmosphere of something unexpected is going to happen.*

The press agent for a stripteaser who used boa constrictors in her act used a hackneyed publicity stunt once too often—going to the local newspapers and saying she had lost her snake which would be purportedly roaming the streets of whatever city. Only the most unwary reporters still fall for that one.

The St. Louis *Post-Dispatch* is not noted for unwary reporters. Some years ago, two of them got sick of the press agent seasonally having his girl "lose" her snakes each time she played the Grand Burleycue. The lack of originality was insulting.

The reporters wangled two snakes from the curator of reptiles at the zoo: a blacksnake and a kingsnake, both fairly good-sized. They put the snakes in a cardboard box. They gift wrapped it. They punched air holes in it. They went to the press agent's hotel and to his floor. One of them went to his door and knocked. The press agent came to the door and looked blankly at the stranger.

Briskly, the reporter said, "Parcel delivery."

The press agent took the box and shut the door. (No tip.) The reporter joined his buddy at the end of the hall. Silently, they leaned on the wall and smoked.

The first scream was a good one. The second was better. The press agent came out the door like a squeezed watermelon seed, took the corridor corner on his right ear, and kept going. The reporters nodded in satisfaction. They went downstairs to the lobby.

One picked up the house phone. When the desk answered, he said, "I want to complain about that awful man in 608 who keeps losing his snakes out of his room."

He hung up. The reporters then strolled out of the hotel. The day seemed brighter, somehow.

10

Motel Business in Japan

(This is the entire content of a letter sent by the president of a Japanese motel concern to exchange notes with his counterparts in America. It has its own fascinating style and viewpoint agree the many motel and hotel men who have passed it around thoughtfully.)

Motel Business in Japan

This new business just rising in Japan.

Its future looks very prosperious under the influence of motorization.

One particular phenemenon of Japanese MOTEL is that people use MOTEL for LOVE AFFAIRS. Especially the young lovers.

With avobe reason, aged people with families hesitate to use MOTEL for stay, with ideas of LOVERS on MOTEL.

Most of the MOTELS are managed by the individuals as their SIDE BUSINESS in small scales. But for account of

One particular phenemenon of Japanese motel is
that people use motel for love affairs.

its increasing popularity, the BIG business (Co/Inc/
Ltd?/Etc.) is to step into this field.

The Basic Condition for Motel Management

1. Cheap land. The location is a little bit away from
the main highway.
2. Increasing demand. The more young couples are
enjoying themselves using car.
3. Saving of lavor cost. For its management very
small lavor is sufficient.

Some Particulars of Japanese Motel

1. Garage with shutter.
2. Devices of the room for young lovers. Moving
bed. The mirrors. Etc.
3. Cheap fares. Bookable by hours.
4. Solidation. Indifference of the employees. No
need of personal service in MOTEL.
3. There are many cases of the "THIEF" behavours.
Some people bring out the furnatures of the room. HOW
THIS CAN BE STOPPED?

The End

(All motel men will agree those are wonderfully *avobe*
reasons.)

11

The Solid Gold Country Boys

WE BUILD A NEW ROOM IN THE TIME IT TAKES
MOST PEOPLE TO FIND ONE. TWENTY-TWO
MINUTES, TO BE EXACT

> (*A current motto of Holiday Inns*)

WE'VE GOT TO CUT DOWN ON THE TIME IT
TAKES TO BUILD THESE ROOMS.

> (*Kemmons Wilson, Founder of Holiday Inns*)

(Holiday Inns form the biggest hotel organization the world
has ever seen. Its enormity is staggering, its growth so swift
it seems eerily alive, and its future eludes even the vast
imagination of those who run it. Run it rather like ruddering a comet, for the motel business moves so swiftly there
is often no precedent to steer by. This one chapter departs
from anecdotal treatment to outline how this phenomenon
got launched.)

137

"If I've got my clothes on," said Kemmons Wilson, chairman of the board of Holiday Inns, Inc., "I've got my measuring tape with me."

He grinned. He pulled the steel tape out of his pants pocket. His suit, if you didn't look closely, could have come off the conservative, medium-price rack. Kemmons himself looks home-town Kiwanian. But the steel tape is the one that took the measure of the lodging business, and there is a certain steel deep in his eyes—or quicksilver—something that glints through. And Kemmons, like quicksilver, moves with magical swiftness without ever seeming to hurry.

"You ever see my magic rabbit trick?" he asked, grinning. Is this the program chairman of the Rotary? He well could be, and happy at it. What he is, however, you remember, sitting in his plush executive offices overlooking seventy-five strange and jam-packed acres of "Holiday City" in suburban Memphis . . . what he is just happens to be founder and ramrod of the biggest y'all-come-see-us operation this planet has ever seen.

"Hold this momma rabbit in your hand," said Kemmons. He produced two little sponge rubber rabbits he carries everywhere. He said gleefully, "I'll hold the daddy rabbit in my hand. First, we'll let 'em kiss. You know how rabbits are."

Kemmons was relaxed. Unhurried. Sofa sprawled. He had just jetted back from France and Yugoslavia. He was fixing to jet to South America. Next morning, early.

"Blow on your hand," said Kemmons, happily. People sat waiting patiently outside his office. They had the ideas; Kemmons had the money. "Now. Open your hand."

Kemmons does not like to be hurried. When the visitor

inside the plush office opened his hand, only the momma rabbit lay there.

"You gotta blow *hard!*" said Kemmons Wilson reprovingly. The visitor felt like a failure. He blew hard on his balled fist with the rabbit in it. Mrs. Sue Todd, secretary, popped in. So-and-so had flown in from New York. Would Kemmons see him? "Sure," he said, "I'll see anybody."

"Open your hand now," he said to his visitor.

The visitor did, finding he now held the momma rabbit *and* the daddy rabbit *and* a whole passel of baby rabbits!

"How the hell do you do that?" the visitor asked.

"People keep asking me that," said Kemmons, picking up a can of candy from a simple-looking desk. Until you looked closely and noticed it cost six week's pay. "They always ask me that." Kemmons grinned. "You want some hard candy? Got peanut butter inside."

He's built an empire with that approach.

"Somewhere in these United States," wrote Sinclair Lewis, back in the 1920s, "there is a young man who is going to become rich. He may be washing milk bottles in a dairy lunch. He is going to start a chain of small, clean, pleasant hotels, standardized and nationally advertised, along every important motor route in the country . . . he is going to have agreeable clerks, good coffee, endurable mattresses and good lighting . . . he will invade every town that doesn't have a good hotel already . . ."

Well, Sinclair was right. Kemmons came up out of Arkansas hardscrabble, and runs the biggest one. Overalls no more. But he didn't get the idea from ole Sinclair.

"I got the idea for Holiday Inns from the most miserable vacation trip I ever took in my life," he said. "The rooms were awful, and everybody wanted two dollars extra per kid. I've got five kids. I thought, well, who's going to do something about motels?"

There are more than 1400 Holiday Inns around the world. They have large rooms, a swimming pool, and a restaurant. They have guest services from free ice to, sometimes, free dog kennels. Younger people now don't know how revolutionary a concept this was back in the early fifties. But it was. And there is no charge for children under twelve . . .

How did he do it? Once *Newsweek* did a story on him titled *"Homely Hints on How to Make $90 Million."* *Newsweek* doesn't even know it didn't really find out how he did it.

The right idea at the right time, is how, combined with the right man. All else is retroactive press releases. Kemmons was certainly the right man. He is part Bible Belt orthodox, part no-limit gambler. He has a mysterious energy; it baffles his friends and possibly sometimes baffles him. The fact that he can go to sleep instantly any time and under practically any conditions doesn't really explain it entirely.

His eyes have humor and he is relaxed. He has a toughness overlaid with Memphis courtly. He grew up poor, but it's not money that makes him go. He lives simply. Kemmons Wilson is that most agreeable of men—all he wants is to do exactly what he wants to do. And that is what he manages to do.

At seventeen in Depression Memphis, he bought a secondhand popcorn machine on time, rented theater lobby space for $2.50 a week, and before long was thrown out when the manager realized the popcorn kid was making more than he was. He sold the popcorn machine and bought five secondhand pinball machines, put the profits into others. He built a $1700 house on a lot he bought, and borrowed $3000 on it— sold the house and lot for $6500. Things like that.

"This guided me toward the building business," grinned Kemmons Wilson. He kept buying houses for ten percent down, then theaters, a Wurlitzer distributorship. When World War II came, he cashed out for $250,-000 and flew Air Transport Command in India. That's multiplying a lot of rabbits right there, since 1913 when he was born.

After the war he went back to Memphis and building. He became one of the town's busiest developers.

"I figured I wouldn't be a success until I owed a million dollars," he said. In 1951 he went on *the* vacation trip and didn't like the motels. So, he changed the motel business.

He built the first motel on borrowed money. He says it had to be successful because he had to meet the notes.

"How did you learn the technical end of building when you were a kid?" he was asked.

"Well, I didn't know too much. But back then an awful lot of carpenters were out of jobs. If you could scrape up a little money, you could always hire somebody good to do those things . . . " He ate some more hard candy, smiling gently; carefully explaining how he did it.

He teamed up with Wallace E. Johnson. Like eggs teamed up with ham. It was an almost molecular welding of forces. Arkansas hardscrabble meet Mississippi cotton patch. Howdy, friend. Want to put up more motels than you can shake a stick at? You know it, good buddy.

Wallace E. Johnson runs the financial establishment out front and Kemmons is in Ireland or Asia selling the pitch. Johnson is flamboyant, loves his backslapping role as the Memphis establishment rajah; Wilson is quieter, grins a little bit sideways. Both know how to count the house; both know exactly where everything is at all times, including the exits; and both share a secret mirth known only to Southern Country Boys. They call Wallace "that prayin' millionaire from Memphis," and he comes on like a tentful of gospel. Kemmons lives almost *unobtrusively,* doing only what *he damn well pleases.* Neither mind is shackled by concern over the improbable. Lots of times things work, if you just try.

Each would be the first to admit he certainly couldn't have done it without the other.

(Both have said separately that one secret of success is finding the right expert when you need him.)

You have to assume that if one hadn't existed the other would have invented him. Together they laid out the plans, called in builders from all over the country, and kicked the motel franchise operation into startled life.

Memphis, descended from the riverboat speculators, built by the high-rolling gamblers called cotton men, looks fondly upon the wheeling-dealing pair who run the biggest industry in Memphis; nods, smiles benevolently. Wallace and Kemmons have really amounted to something. (They're from right around here, too.)

And the Holiday Inn signs keep going up, from somewhere east of Suez to St. Pete across the bay.

THAT PRAYIN' MILLIONAIRE FROM MEMPHIS

Wallace E. Johnson was forty years old and making $37.50 a week when he heard the Lord instruct him to build houses for poor folks. Wallace did.

If there is one thing Wallace Johnson is purely good at (and there are several), it is doing what the Lord tells him. And as a direct result of this, Mr. Johnson is positive, he has risen from an Edinburg, Miss., cotton picker to the man national magazines refer to as "the Henry Ford of the Building Industry."

En route, he has not been reticent in suggesting specifics to the Lord. He prays precisely for what he wants.

"Oh, Lord," went one prayer, quoted in a national magazine, "Let me this week start an office building that we have ready to go in Indianapolis. Let me start the building at Sam Houston Hospital in Texas, too . . . and let me pay the bank that $800,000 that I owe. Amen."

Then Wallace Johnson unfolds his prayerful hands and looks about alertly for ways to make these things come true. It doesn't take long to grasp the effectiveness of this duo.

And it doesn't take long to understand that Wallace Johnson, the self-proclaimed "po' little old peckerwood boy from Mississippi" is a mover and a shaker, Deity assistance notwithstanding.

He is also a Memphis legend and not solely because of his position as vice-chairman of the Holiday Inn board.

He's a man of a thousand anecdotes, a firm believer in jumping in and helping the Lord—seemingly doing everything but drive the bulldozer, and he could do that.

"I love to deal," says Johnson, whose evangelical zeal has been known to convert a 285-pound Irish construction foreman from strong drink to prayer.

"Bomah!" booms Mr. Johnson, disconcerting some visitors. It is his motto, his self-description, and it stands for, he is quick to point out, "Builder of Men and Homes." He has maintained this sort of startling zeal unflaggingly since he was eleven and met his Personal Saviour in a Mississippi piney woods church.

"No praying over me, no pleading, no pressure of any kind," he has recalled. "Just little ol' Wallace Johnson walking down the aisle all by himself to give his heart to Jesus."

He contracted to build his first house when he was eighteen. He lost his hard-earned $1800 capital. He kept coming back; by 1939 borrowed $250 on his old Ford and that year built eighty homes. The next year he built 360. It was the Depression—but he had noted that the government was guaranteeing eighty-five percent on mortgage loans.

He and his wife had five thousand signs painted up saying LET WALLACE E. JOHNSON BUILD YOUR HOME ON THIS LOT. People saw so many Wallace Johnson signs they figured he must really be a volume builder. Actually, he would get twenty-five dollars earnest money, and only when he got a prospective buyer then find who owned the lot and buy it.

He took a correspondence course in architecture. He bought his own lumber mills. He tithed ten percent, right on, as he had when he was a dollar-an-hour carpenter back in Mississippi—and he still tithes ten percent.

Kemmons Wilson leans to sales and promotion, Johnson to watching costs. Brilliant men surround them. William B. Walton, president, himself a legend, heads a platoon of executive talent that combines to make up one of the most efficient corporate brains on earth. Most of the executives come to take for granted that Johnson does have some contract with the Lord.

"I wouldn't be surprised if he sent out a prayer on the Holidex, *and got an immediate answer!*" one executive said.

Johnson has been known to write out "first drafts" of his prayers on legal size pads to make sure he's leaving nothing out. One of these said: "O Lord, make us one of the greatest leaders of the nation in the building of men and homes. Help the city officials of Memphis to understand that this is our goal so they will help us instead of hinder us . . ."

That seems to have been granted.

And a prayer which, in part, urged the Lord to help "make connection with the right kind of banks" concluded with the suggestion that these bankers understand what constituted safe investments "so that we can go on and on and on. Amen."

Indeed, Wallace Johnson has gone on and on and on. If manifold business pressures ever bother him, he doesn't show it—like Wilson he has the gift for instant relaxation and says, "When I turn the light off at night I'm asleep before the room gets dark."

He and his Lord have evidently never exchanged a cross word. What may be more startling is that, to anybody's knowledge, neither have he and Kemmons Wilson. They are two rugged individualists who don't clash, two entities who, when it comes to success, simply go together.

A popular, if ever frustrated, discussion around Memphis establishment circles is which one is the "real" reason for the success of this empire.

It would be easier to decide exactly which was responsible for ham and eggs making it so big.

How did this combination expand Holiday Inns from a concept to reality, aspiration to actuality, from an idea that met initial apathy to worldwide success? What made it grow to an institution which like the wheel, Coca-Cola, the yo-yo, Howard Johnson, and the green park bench, seems now always to have existed?

It was in 1951 that Kemmons had the idea to get away from rather casually run Ma & Pa motels and the hot-pillow philosophy of roadside lodging, and bring mass production to the industry. What did he do?

He decided on a basic 120-room unit, four times larger than the then average. He figured a 120-room unit could be operated without a lot more staff proportionately. His selling points were reliability, economy, and extras. The reaction?

Twenty years ago the "experts" told Wilson that the motel industry was dangerously overbuilt.

"It's the greatest untouched industry in the world," he kept insisting. He built his first one, in 1952, on a main highway into Memphis.

Helped by his mother, the late Mrs. Ruby L. "Doll" Wilson, professional decorator, he furnished the rooms in a style that had warmth and hospitality, qualities largely lacking then. Relatively slowly, he put up three more Inns in Memphis. (Where there are now eleven.)

IT REVOLUTIONIZED
THE MOTEL INDUSTRY

In 1953 he teamed up with Wallace Johnson.

Together, they invited seventy-five builders from all over the United States to discuss their franchise dream.

Sixty-one came. But a year later only three had made any progress in developing Holiday Inns.

What was Holiday Inns—the idea—selling? Essentially, it was "The Great Sign." (The Holiday Inn sign, now an object of great veneration.) Essentially, it still is. But the going was slow.

"I'll tell you how Holiday Inns got its name," said Kemmons. "A draftsman for a Memphis sign company made me up a drawing. At the top he had scribbled 'Holiday Inn.' He had seen the Bing Crosby movie named that, the night before. Pretty good sign. Good name, too. I kept it."

When the professional builders responded too slowly, Wilson and Johnson did the usual, for them: the unexpected. They turned to business and professional men, anybody who understood the Holiday Inn dream—and who had money *and* imagination enough to move.

By the end of 1964, more than five hundred Inns had been operating. By mid-1971 it was up to fourteen hundred and moving fast.

Some foreign cities which need a hotel simply give him land. Nobody else ever thought to ask. Once in Rome, Kemmons, a Memphis Methodist, had an audience with Pope Paul. He said he knelt, kissed the Pope's ring, and to his considerable atonishment heard the Pope say:

"Mr. Wilson, I've heard of the work you've done with Holiday Inns and I understand you're building one in Rome. Could you tell me where it is?"

Kemmons recalls that he was so surprised he couldn't think of the location.

"Later," he says ruefully, "I thought that if I had had

any sense at all, I would have asked the Pope for some land."

The land where Holiday City is now was largely swamp. Now, the seventy-five acre complex of business offices, display areas, and subsidiaries is, in a real sense, its own city; it has its own Post Office and is nerve center for the Holidex computer system.

Holidex reserves a room in any Holiday Inn by push button. If one Inn is full, space is reserved in a Holiday Inn nearby. The computer keeps track of each "Sorry, no room." Wilson, as a result, knows exactly where, and on what road, to start a new Holiday Inn.

It's one reason you will never see a "No Vacancy" sign at a Holiday Inn. Kemmons would rather have potential guests come in and ask. It's not only because another Holiday Inn is almost surely down the road a piece, it's good business.

"I don't know, it's just that a 'No Vacancy' sign is sort of bad manners, I think," said Kemmons. "It makes people think you don't want them."

Find out where business intuition stops and true southern manners take over and you would know more about Kemmons Wilson and Wallace Johnson. Otherwise you will wonder forever where all the rabbits come from.

"DAMNDEST GENERAL STORE I EVER SEEN!"

That is what one small-town Holiday Inn manager said, with exceedingly good cause, after walking wide-eyed through the Institutional Mart of America. That's the supermarket for Holiday Inns, where you can buy a golf ball or a swimming pool or a saloon shaped like a ship.

Franchisers don't have to buy furnishings from the Institutional Mart. But most find it a fine idea. Wallace E. Johnson does the shopping for them that way, and Brother Johnson has a rule: bought low is half sold.

You can buy everything here, plus the kitchen sink. You want a Holiday Inn? Through IMA you can arrange for its design, contract for its building, finance it, furnish it and buy a long-term maintenance and supply deal—and all in the twinkling of an eye. And if it's not a Holiday Inn, but an office building, clinic, whatever—you can still work out most of the details without leaving Holiday City.

Wandering around the giant Holiday Inn supply rooms is a shopper's idea of paradise. It also has a strong tendency to shoot down the lingering thought of mass-produced conformity, which is the "Free Soul's" inherent objection to chain-store living. If this is conformity, it's not unbearably constricting; you can get modern aluminum furniture, yes, but also Mexican handwrought wood furnishings, a cocktail lounge exactly like an old Pullman club car, a bar so exactly like the interior of a sailing ship that it's chief danger is not inebriation but seasickness—or Holiday Inn's own labels of booze to furnish it, Holiday Inn's two-cent lollipops to keep the kiddies bribed while you're having a snort. Paintings to suit every conceivable taste, and some for tastes unborn. (Employees get dandy discounts from the bust-out room: all sorts of art and furnishings which just didn't sell.)

Now that you've bought the swimming pool, Holiday Inn will send a resident astrologer-artist over to paint

the zodiac on the bottom, if you wish, for a scant eight
hundred bucks.

Jerry O'Roark, public relations director, and his assistant, Whit Perry, come up with statistics—they find the
computers almost have a sense of humor.

> *The carpeting in Holiday Inn rooms is sufficent to carpet
> a two-lane highway from New York to Washington, D.C.,
> and to carpet Broadway in New York, Pennsylvania Ave-
> nue in Washington, and Sunset Boulevard in Los Angeles.
> However, in 1966 there was only enough carpet to carpet
> a two-lane highway three-quarters of the way from New
> York to Washington, D.C.*

The longer one reads that over, the longer one ponders
the vagaries of the computer mind.

The visiting writer, from Miami, was also handed this
statistic:

> In one year the soap used in Holiday Inns was sufficient
> to bathe the residents of the City of Miami.

O'Roark denied he had been expecting a Miami hippie-
type writer. ("I just enjoy all the computers here.")

Here are a couple more—accurate, incidentally—statistics for any statistics-lovers who may be in the congre-
gation:

The number of Holiday Inn beds is sufficient to sleep
the population of the entire state of Wyoming.

The supply of drinking glasses used to make all Holiday
Inn rooms ready for check-in in 1971 would be sufficient to
serve all the residents of the United States and Canada at
a tremendous good-neighbor party. [He will run up on re-

quest the number of two-cent lollipops needed for the kids.]
The combined population is 249,000,000; the number of
glasses, 264,819,180.

In 1966, the 67,000,000 cups of coffee served in Holiday
Inns would have provided one-third of the population of
the United States with a cup of coffee. In 1971, the
110,000,000 cups would serve more than half the population.

It won't be long before everybody can have a cup and,
if the Solid Gold Country Boys perform as usual, maybe
three or four.

"WE BUILD A NEW ROOM IN THE TIME IT TAKES MOST
PEOPLE TO FIND ONE," blares the Holiday Inn ad and
motto. "TWENTY-TWO MINUTES, TO BE EXACT."

And Wilson and Johnson ain't just whistling Dixie.

Where will the management people come from?
The Holiday Inn University trains thousands of Innkeepers, year after year. It's an institution in the green woods
of Mississippi near Olive Branch, a few miles from
Memphis.

Holiday Innkeepers receive three weeks of intensive
training, regardless of prior background. Graduates take
immense pride in their "diploma." It's progressively more
co-ed . . . female managers increase in number each
year.

It's a university using every shortcut training device;
computers, closed circuit TV. Graduates leave with five
pounds of printed orientation material. They will, after
all, face four inspections a year when they get back home
—and these inspections are intense.

"Inspectors don't sneak around in disguise," said Whit Perry. "They make themselves known when they arrive, but Innkeepers never know *when* they will arrive."

It's not just in Europe that small towns, particularly, place great store on erection of a Holiday Inn. America is full of Holiday Inns which are focal points for local social and business events. People meet at the lounge; civic clubs have an indigestion-free restaurant at which to meet, sometimes at long last; local Chambers of Commerce have a fighting chance for obtaining small conventions or part of large ones; and, in general, a Holiday Inn becomes a permanent and important part of a community. Standards therefore are set high and sternly maintained.

"It's a tough, white-glove inspection and includes everything from checking the way beds are made to testing the food," explained Perry.

"What happens if an Inn doesn't pass muster?"

"The Innkeeper gets a warning and a certain amount of time to correct the problem."

"If he doesn't?"

"The Holidex and the Great Sign are jerked," said Perry, ominously. "It doesn't happen often—but it happens."

"But the owner still has the Holiday Inn building?"

"He has a *building*," said Perry. "But, without the Great Sign, he doesn't have a Holiday Inn."

He is, this tortured errant, presumably left to wander in a dull Great Sign-less limbo of purgatory forever. If he has studied his lessons, he need not fear.

"Inkeeping is a great career for a young man or woman," aid Carman B. Robinson, a young man who has risen to vice-president of educational facilities. He was manager of a pecan shelling plant in Jonesboro, Ark., when he saw opportunity in Holiday Inns, and Kemmons Wilson saw the right kind of man in him.

Is the picture of an innkeeper (or hotel manager) changing these days?

"You know it," said Robinson. "The stress is on more managerial ability now and less technical skills. The day when a manager did everything, rising through every job, is vanishing. You used to have to apprentice in every specialty. Now we have to compete for bright young people. Young people have too many ways to go. If you're good, you can move fast.

"Opportunity is wide open in the twenty-one to thirty age group. Not limited to that, of course. We work hard, and successfully, at developing talent in the organization —but the way we're growing, we need new people.

"One main change is learning that service fields shouldn't be confused with being servile. Level with people, help people, *serve* people. It has nothing to do with fawning or servility. It's sometimes hard to teach youngsters that and sometimes a damn sight harder to unteach experienced people."

The University couldn't be tradition-bound if it wanted to. The Innkeeper Development Program is so new it has to fly by the seat of its pants, has to use trial and error.

"There's no precedent," said Robinson. "Who would we copy? Where we're going, day to day, nobody's been."

Back in the executive suite, Kemmon was asked to project twenty years. Will computers replace people in the lodging field?

"Not really, not much at all," said Kemmons Wilson. "Matter of fact, I had some experts run me up some research on that. They used computers. The way I figure it, twenty years from now it will be about the same in this business—human beings who know what they are doing. Human beings who know how to make computers work for them."

Any computer who has visions of taking over better be intensely programmed on how to be an old country boy hisself.

12

May I Keep My Lion in My Room?

I DID NOT LIKE THE HOLIDAY INN BECAUSE
THE BED WAS SO COMFORTABLE MY HUSBAND
SLEPT ALL NIGHT.

> (*Guest service form letter received by a Holiday Inn*)

When you've got almost fourteen hundred Inns furnishing a world-wide network of syndicated shelter, what have you got?

You've got the damndest array of documented episodes ever known to the hotel business, for one thing.

Here are a few examples.

In Louisiana at the Holiday Inn of Bossier, a young newlywed couple checked in, obviously more accustomed to the farm. Innkeeper George Dement, who some time previously had equipped his beds with the "Magic Fin-

"Looky here," complained the bridegroom. "How come I cain't get no music? Every time I put a quarter in the slot all it does is make the dern bed shake!"

gers" coin-operated vibrating devices, got a call from the groom four hours later.

"Looky here," complained the bridegroom. "How come I cain't get no music? Every time I put a quarter in the slot all it does is make the dern bed shake!"

In Florida, a little old lady eavesdropped in the lobby; heard an employee say to the front desk, "I've got a girl for Room 306 for eight-thirty and a girl for Room 204 for nine o'clock." She demanded to know what a nice old lady like herself was doing in a place like this; went away red-faced after learning the conversation concerned baby sitters.

In Pine Bluff, Ark., Innkeeper Ray Dwyer smiled tolerantly when he noticed two of Pine Bluff's finest, fishing with rods and reels in the swimming pool, during the annual party of the Pine Bluff Order of Police. It was the bobber going down that got him—the cops had put catfish in the pool.

At the Chattanooga-Downtown, Innkeeper Sidney Hill was host to the World's Richest Tomcat, a part Siamese accompanied by his owners, Mr. and Mrs. Brad Jernigan, who had set up a forty thousand dollar trust fund for Kesil the Cat.

Faye Heard, housekeeper at the Jackson, Mich., Holiday Inn, found an unregistered guest in a room, a billy goat. At the Tennessee-North in Nashville, Frank Jamison of Hughes Aircraft landed in a helicopter by the restaurant, checked in, got back in his chopper, took off, and parked again in front of his room.

At Montego Bay, five hundred guests attended a Hindu wedding. Among those checking in was Abdullah, who bears the title "The Black Jewel and King of the Universe." He says he is four thousand years old. Employees said he didn't act it—he has seventeen children, the youngest a year old.

Innkeeper Ray Zalanka, however, may hold the Free-for-12-or-Under Record set when a scoutmaster and his troop checked in. The scoutmaster paid, but his nine 12-year-old charges, with sleeping bags, stayed in the room with him free (no extra beds, no charge.) In Lincoln, Nebr., Holiday Inn changed its "Drop in Anytime" sign after a driver went up on the six-foot retaining wall.

When Stuart Mullis, assistant restaurant manager at a Holiday Inn in Valdosta, Ga., got a call for room service, he finally figured out it was from another motel. The guest said he didn't like the food he had ordered there, pleading slow starvation. Why not, Mullis decided. The assistant chef got a five dollar tip for taking six sirloin-strip steaks to the party. When the other manager objected, he was told, "You won't feed these people. Somebody has to."

Gentle Ben the Bear was standing up, seven-feet tall, at the registration desk at the Inn-West in Milwaukee, having his picture taken "registering" during the Wisconsin State Fair. "Uh, pardon me," said a solemn guest in the lobby, to an employee. "I hesitate to mention this. But do you see a bear registering over there?" The employee nodded; the guest sighed in relief. At that point in walked Neal, the huge lion from the Daktari show, and also reared up on the desk. The guest said shakily, "Damn good thing I verified the bear."

Dave Case and his cousin Sharon Case of Syracuse, N.Y., stopped at the Chattanooga-Southeast Holiday Inn and told Innkeeper Ron Seddon they liked Holiday Inn because it allowed guests to keep pets in the room. Seddon beamed. Dave and Sharon brought in *their* lion,

Boris, a big rascal, who promptly got up on the bed for a catnap. "What could I do?" said Seddon. "We have to live up to our reputation." Boris liked to ride the elevator up to the third floor room with Dave and Sharon. Porters walked up—for days after.

In Dallas, a guest asked about accommodations for Spot. "You can keep your pet in your room, sir," said the switchboard operator. The caller said, "Honey, you ever tried to sleep with a horse?"

In Memphis, Jerry O'Roark recalls vividly, a young lady with an obviously good figure—she was nude—was taking an evening swim. The Innkeeper walked out and commanded. "You get right out of that pool this minute!"

Slowly, languidly, she climbed out, walked over to the Innkeeper and, stark naked, exhaling martini fragrance, said, "OK, I'm out—now what!?!"

The Innkeeper squeaked. "You get right back in that pool this very minute!"

A bank robber held up Merchants National Bank & Trust in Indianapolis, got $24,000 at gunpoint, and took two bank officials with him as hostages. He took them to the Holiday Inn-South of that city, in fact, calmly went into the lounge with his prisoners and began sipping cocktails.

He kept his gun hidden, but a guest had seen the three men in the parking lot when the bankers had their hands raised, and police had been called. More than two hundred policemen, FBI agents, and deputies converged.

Deputy David L. Warholak, former security guard at the Inn, put on a waiter's red jacket; began serving in the lounge. He and Mrs. Betty Stanforth, a waitress, quietly persuaded guests to leave. As guests left, plainclothesmen replaced them. With the room cleared, Warholak put the tray down, wheeled with drawn gun, and a dozen "customers" leaped on the robber. He had all the money in a briefcase in his lap.

When the Baytown, Tex., court docket got too crowded for the regular court sessions, Justice of the Peace Glenn Vickery used the Holiday Inn auditorium for a courtroom.

In Slidell, La., a guest named W. E. Wood wrote a letter of commendation to Innkeeper Jim Bright. Wood had ordered two grasshoppers. The young employee who finally came to his door said he had looked all over the yard and couldn't find any, but would keep trying. In Detroit, a guest with a broken suitcase handle asked room service for a very small screwdriver. He got a glass of vodka and orange juice, half full. In Houston, two thirsty couples talking in a room ordered four screwdrivers. Finally, a sweating employee appeared with four real screwdrivers and said, "Is it O.K. if one of them is a Phillips?" In New Orleans, a guest asked the waitress if the bartender would make a whiskey sour. The girl said no, she thought it was sour when they bought it.

In Chicago, a caller asked about reservations for the following week in St. Louis; the answer was given so swiftly through Holidex it befuddled him. The clerk heard him say, "Er . . . tell me. Are you a recording?"

Claude Dill, an employee of the Holiday Inn at Concord-Kannapolis, N.C., had been walking around the place chatting with Patrolman Jack Cabe, who had a little boy following him. Sometime later when queried, Dill said, "*My* kid? I thought he was yours!" The frantic phone call came about two thirty that afternoon. A family, en route to Pennsylvania, had checked out that morning and driven for hours until they found only six of their seven children were with them. (Who can tell with that many in a back seat?)

The lodging business has come a long way since Ogg, eh? For one thing, we can run up a composite picture of the traveler.

Nine out of ten guests of Holiday Inn have a family income of more than ten thousand dollars; one out of two is from a metropolitan area; eighty percent make at least one air trip a year; and sixty percent rent a car once a year. Two out of three have used travelers checks in the past five years; three out of five spend more than five hundred dollars on vacation; and seventy-six percent are traveling on business, or say they are.

Favorite sport is golf. Then fishing, bowling, hunting, boating, tennis, water skiing, snow skiing. Favorite booze in order is bourbon, Scotch, gin, vodka, blended whiskey, brandy or cognac, rye, Irish whiskey.

Sixty-three percent of the travelers own their homes; ninety-six percent own one car; fifty-five percent at least two. (In order: Ford, Chevrolet, Pontiac, Buick, Oldsmobile.)

Ninety-four percent own at least one TV set, and sixty percent own two or more. (Seventy percent color TV.)

We could go on with facts of the American traveler. (One out of two entertains friends at home at least once a week; three out of four buy soft drinks; Coke, sixty-five percent; Seven Up, thirty-one percent; Pepsi, twenty-seven percent; and ginger ale, fourteen percent.) Who needs more statistics?

The basic fact remains the same thing that Ogg found out and that no innkeeper better forget.

It's the NEXT guest who is the exception.

People remain unclassified.

To wit:

In Appleton, Wis., some restaurant guests ordered fried bear. The puzzled help finally figured out why. The Great Sign out front that day had this inscription: WELCOME, NATIONAL BOW HUNTING CHAMP—FRED BAER.

Two "women" went into Birmingham-South and produced sawed-off shotguns. Bobbie Chapman, night auditor, and Dot Palmer, the evening bartender, turned over the proceeds from the till; gave police a good description of the robbers. Police radio cars stopped a car fitting the description, down the road. "Who, us?" said the two men in the car, both with wigs in their laps and shotguns in the back seat.

In Indonesia, workers starting a Holiday Inn put up their own Holiday City—moved their entire families to the building site until the job was finished. In Hong Kong, construction men rejected metal scaffolding as an unsound idea; built their own traditional scaffolds . . . of bamboo. At several building sites, metal fences put up to reduce thievery have been stolen. And in Newfoundland, the contractor was in such a rush to finish on schedule that he lost two electricians—they were plastered into a crawl space and had to be cut out.

Those, then, are some of the people in the syndicated shelter business. No predicting them. At the Medical Center Holiday Inn in Memphis, where rooms don't start until fifteen floors in the sky, Innkeeper Malcolm Flake nevertheless had complaints of Peeping Toms shining flashlights into the windows. If anybody knows what to do about heli-peepers, tell Flake.

DOLLY SAYS HELLO . . .

The soft and soothing voice of Dolly Holiday is heard more hours by more millions than any other voice—from midnight to five A.M., seven days a week, she covers the night, nationwide. More than sixty radio stations carry her show, sponsored by Holiday Inns—and the nostalgic pop-classics she plays have made her a friend to insomniacs everywhere, from prisoners to homesick soldiers to the ordinary traveler and to night people everywhere.

Dolly Holiday has talked to more people than any other woman in history. She has a gift of making each listener think she's talking directly to him.

"They'll be taking some of the guys from the county jail in Leavenworth," says one letter, "and before we go, we wonder if on the night of August 3, you could play some Doris Day and Nat King Cole. We're not sure we'll be able to hear you where we're going . . ."

"I'm listening to you while on automatic pilot a thousand miles west of Honolulu . . ." says another letter.

Famous author Erskine Caldwell has written a chapter about her; she receives many proposals of marriage; Merchant Mariners have named her the girl they would most like to take on a cruise to Saigon; little old ladies send her pictures of their cats and poodles. One woman wrote, "I hope your doors are locked, staying up as late as you do."

Her real name is Dotty Abbott, native of Memphis, unmarried, a congenial, no-airs friendly woman who lives with her mother in a big pink house in Memphis. She chooses her selections from a vast library of records, but sticks to about four hundred classics in the pop field. She has an infallible instinct about what people want to hear —and they're mostly of remember-when or Our Song variety.

She and Kemmons Wilson agreed in 1955 that the world of travelers just might need its own voice of the night. That voice is not confined to Holiday Inns, where it comes over the pictureless TV sets after programming is over, but is all over the country—Dolly's voice is an institution; among all of America's great advertising schemes, Dolly Holiday stands unique in one respect. The world of night people is in love with that word-from-the-sponsor, and it's so friendly-intimate you don't realize you're being advertised at.

Torch songs, ballads, memories. Dolly Holiday, herself a professional singer, knows what the night people listen for.

She gets love letters. She gets *like* letters; hundreds of people simply write to tell her how nice it is to tune in and, surprisingly, get "These Foolish Things" or "As Time Goes By" in a 1970s era of rock and raucous.

"Hers is the voice from the night," wrote Robert Johnson, columnist for the Memphis *Press-Scimitar*. "She is the friend in the small hours for those who want someone to talk to them, companion to the lonely, evoker of memories and renewer of pledges for lovers, bringer of hope to the loveless, enchantress of candlelight and wine for the romantic, mistress of moods for the dreamers. She is many things to millions of people, but to each she brings a special warm intimacy."

Dolly is single and gets many letters like one from a prisoner in Walla-Walla who wrote repeatedly saying, "When I get out, I'm going to come get you." At last report his ambition still remained high, though he had thirty-seven years to go on his sentence.

It's strange but a fact that, although she is as much heard as any woman in history, and that includes Martha Mitchell, Dolly has never been heard of by so many others. To day people, she's so often Dolly *who?*

"What's wrong with this TV?" demanded a traveling salesman who checked into a Miami Holiday Inn. "I'm getting good music, but no picture. Best program I ever heard but I can't get anything but sound."

It was explained that all TV channels were off and the sound was Dolly Holiday, who comes over after regular programming.

He called back the next morning and said, "How can I get that music back? All I can get now is the #%# news!"

As for Dolly, she says, "I love doing the show. There's a difference between lonely and lonesome. Lonely, simply being by yourself, is something we all need sometimes. I just pick the records to go with it . . ."

And the night people listen and dream.

CHAPLAIN ON CALL . . .

A clergyman is available at any time to our guests who have a spiritual need. He has both experience and training in counseling and is acquainted with clergymen of other faiths and with other sources of help when referral is needed.

(CHAPLAIN-ON-CALL *card placed in each room of hundreds of Holiday Inns*)

"I have a gun at my head and my finger on the trigger," said the woman who called Rev. Norman Williams, in Everett, Wash. "Tell me why I should live in the face of my hopeless situation, or I pull the trigger."

The minister, at home, shook sleep from his mind and started talking, slowly, matter-of-factly. It's one thing to "talk in" suicides off a window ledge or from other situations all too familiar to hotelmen everywhere. It's another to have a life hanging, literally, by a wire. After a good hour of talking, the woman put the gun down. After two hours, she was willing to accept such statements from Rev. Williams as, "Children run away, adults face the truth."

After five solid hours—dawn was breaking—the woman had seen a way out of her problem. (She had been unfaithful to her husband and couldn't turn to her own pastor back home. He was the one with whom she had been unfaithful.) She later wrote to the Rev. Williams and said she owed her life to him—that it was during that long and agonized conversation she had realized that, of all the alternatives facing her, suicide was the *only* one which would have solved nothing. Williams to this day has never met her. But a stranger gives thanks for him and prays for him every day.

"Just that one case, that one person saved, would be worth all we've put into this Chaplain-On-Call service," said Rev. Charles L. Woodall. "But it's turned out to be a bigger thing than even Dub Nance ever dreamed."

The Reverends W. A. "Dub" Nance and C. L. Woodall head the Holiday Inn Chaplaincy Program.

More than fifty suicides, at a very conservative estimate, have been prevented nationwide by the Chaplain-On-Call Program.

The very concept was enough to evoke cynical remarks
and scornful raised eyebrows when Dub Nance, a Memphis preacher, came up with it in the late sixties. But
no cynicism came from the corporate offices of Holiday
Inns, where, as noted, a strong religious streak runs deep.

"Christian laymen in this corporation had made their
business a means of bearing witness to their faith," said
Reverend W. A. Nance. "The idea of spiritual guidance
for travelers, as well as for employees, got immediate
acceptance."

When this book was written, plans were under way for
additional facets combining religion, in its oldest and most
revered forms, with the newest electronic devices. Dial-a-
devotion: two minutes of inspirational message on tap.
Closed-circuit TV programs of sermons and religious
music. A chapel in each Inn. (Not services: a place of
meditation and prayer.) And the "Open Bible" policy
has been a reality for years—when each room is made
up, the Bible is *left open on top of the desk* by maids, not
tucked away in a drawer.

(And the chaplaincy program files are thick with testi-
monials from travelers who say a glance at the open Bible
changed their lives in some significant way.)

However, for pure drama it's unlikely anything will
ever surpass the results from that Chaplain-On-Call card
printed at the head of this chapter.

More than 750 Inns, at this writing, have inaugurated
the service. It's Rev. C. L. Woodall's job to explain it to
individual Innkeepers . . . who pick their own local
chaplain.

"The chaplains receive no pay, at least not in money,"
said Woodall. "He and his wife are invited to be guests
of the Innkeeper for Sunday dinner, as an expression of
gratitude."

(This goes back to the old Preacher-for-Chicken-on-Sunday tradition of the South. Woodall, grinning a little ruefully, said one franchise Innkeeper had angrily dropped the program. The local minister was bringing his wife and a passel of kids *every* night . . . for the most expensive menu items, and signing the checks with a flourish, *then* repairing to the bar for a decidedly un-Christian snootful. Thinking fast, Woodall gave the Innkeeper a solution, which he followed. Woodall said, "Please don't drop the chaplaincy program. Just drop the freeloading chaplain.")

With zeal—but not overselling—Nance and Woodall explain their program to Innkeepers. It's not a syrupy approach at all; there may be lots of atheists in motel rooms, is what it boils down to, but what of the guests who aren't? Or who need help, and *now?* Hard facts like the following bolster their case.

"Tell my wife why I shot myself, Preacher," said a man who called Dr. Gordon Clarke, American Bible Society, Indianapolis, Ind. Dr. Clarke immediately replied he would be better able to do that after a face-to-face explanation. (It's important to try to get *to* the person and establish a human-to-human contact. It's equally important not to insist.) The man agreed. He was a top executive who had been fired.

Dr. Clarke went to the man's room. After a talk he gave the minister the pistol. When the "suicide" and the preacher went to the man's home, the wife said she was delighted he had been fired because that job had made him, said Dr. Clarke, "pure hell to live with for a long time."

The Reverend Robert E. Gartman, Memorial Christian Church of Midland, Texas, told of a woman who had called him after going to an Inn because of a fight with her husband who was drinking.

"After some venting of feelings, she said it was good to have someone to talk to," said Reverend R. E. Gartman. If she hadn't had somebody to tell what a rat her husband is, evolves the very human moral here, she might have divorced him.

The Reverend Roy Kutz, Saint John's Church, Columbus, Ohio, would have made a good reporter. A man who called him for help did, indeed, need help—but he had repeatedly lied trying to conceal his problem. When Reverend R. Kutz discovered the man had lied about his business affiliation, he pressed for the truth; he found this worthy was recently out of jail, had broken probation, and was seriously considering curing his condition —dead broke—by illegal means.

Reverend R. Kutz got him to (1) call his probation officer in Pennsylvania and report in, (2) get an up-to-date VFW card at the chaplain's expense, (3) borrow enough money from the VFW to tide him over, (4) report to an employment service immediately, and (5) meet Kutz to make sure he had his priorities in order. Not bad service for a stranger in a strange town with "insoluble" worries.

The Reverend Robert F. Smith, Plant City United Methodist Church, Lanett, Ala., had this story to tell: "The guest was drinking and talked of suicide. A daughter was held in Atlanta on drug charges. I called the Atlanta authorities and helped get the matter settled. The parent calmed down."

There may be a novel in those crisp facts.

Dr. T. Newton Wise of the First United Church of Homestead, Fla., recalled: "From the first word the caller said, I knew he was in trouble. I went to his room. He had a supply of poison and all the farewell letters written . . .

"He asked me to have prayer with him before death. I suggested it was also customary to read the Bible. So I read about another man who was ready for suicide and how St. Paul helped him.

"He asked if I thought I could help him untangle a long line of lies he had told. We started making long distance calls. He began to see a ray of hope. He was at our Methodist altar the next Sunday, and made a complete change in his life."

The Reverend C. Anton Danielson, Lord of Life Lutheran Church in Darien, Ill., got a call from a lad who had taken an overdose of sleeping pills. He got medical aid . . . then had the boy released to his custody (he had been in a number of foster homes) and arranged for special schooling. Until legally old enough to work, and with the confidence to do so, he had a home—with the Chaplain-On-Call.

Somehow it tends to take away the cynicism, the quick joke about Instant Dial-A-Prayer, the easy scorn, when you think about the fact that, all over this nation, there are men—big-city ministers of some fame and small-town preachers few ever heard of—who are ready and toughly able to respond to pleas from strangers, torn and despairing. There is a quick raised eyebrow, perhaps, at the Chaplain-On-Call card on the bureau, and the swift sneer sometimes. But there are pregnant girls and despairing

*parents and persons with terminal sickness and those who
are terribly lonesome in the night . . . who were saved by
hard-headed mercy, not easy and too frequent scoffing.*

*Drink it in booze or water or whatever your religion
dictates, but drink a toast to those who minister to wayfaring strangers . . .*

"No, and we're sort of surprised too," said Reverend C.
L. Woodall, in answer to the obvious question. "We just
don't get crank calls or gag calls—hardly ever. I'm not
sure I know why we don't . . . with a number to call in
every room. Let me qualify that a little bit. We *do* get
the occasional call from somebody who just wants to see
if a chaplain is really there. Strangely—not so strangely,
maybe—a lot of these seemingly casual callers turn out to
have problems themselves.

"Drunks? Let's put it this way about our one-too-many
types. The proportion of unmanageable problems does
seem to climb sharply in the hours after the bars close.
But, isn't the drinking itself a problem? We can help with
that, too."

The number of nut calls, in short, is very low. With
an invitation to call a chaplain in every room, that fact
can only be attributed to the fact that chaplains must
have guardian angels working overtime.

Or else the people somehow, deep down, know a sin-
cere good-hearted thing when they see it.

Not always, of course.

On one Chaplain-On-Call card a little P.S. was added
right after where it says, *A clergyman is available at
any time to our guests who have a spiritual need . . .*

It said: *For nonspiritual needs, call Dawn—888-6543.*

Imagine the heartbreak of the bride who had gone on her honeymoon and was promptly abandoned by her new husband, who skipped with every cent of her large inheritance. She couldn't believe it, said Rev. Harlow H. Guiley, Northside Baptist Church of Elkhart, Ind. She was stranded and, of course, the motel bill got larger every day.

"I finally convinced her of the brutal truth, that she had married a con man," said Reverend H. H. Guiley. "She was afraid her parents would have nothing more to do with her. She was desperate. But we got a call through to her father and he sent the money for her bill and transportation."

The story there could have been a suicide note.

Then there was the young couple in the Holiday Inn near Niagara Falls who called the chaplain to marry them. He did.

"I'm always skeptical of this sort of thing," said Rev. Kenneth W. Neal of Cleveland Heights Christian Church, Cheektowaga, N.Y., "but I invited them over to the church. They said they had seen my name on the card on the dresser. My wife took a couple of Polaroid pictures to give the bride and groom. I never accept a fee from church members, and I consider the Holiday Inn an extension of my parish."

The Reverend James R. Rowles, Jr., Penelope Baptist Church, Hickory, N.C., tells a moving story of the stark need for friendship when tragedy strikes.

An elderly couple en route from Florida stopped at an Inn. The husband died of a heart attack, after being hospitalized. The doctor in the case called the chaplain who had to break the news. The old woman was alone in that part of the world . . . except for the great comfort of a friend who came from nowhere: the Chaplain-On-Call. She later wrote him a letter which started, "I was a stranger among strangers . . ."

The stories go on. Each one says something about humanity reaching out in crisis—and finding help.

Dub Nance says, "We have to remember this. We sometimes only get one chance to make a good first impression."

He also says, "We cannot serve God and mammon, it's said. But we can serve God *with* mammon."

That's part of the Holiday Inn story, a story where new chapters come too fast to keep updated.

Let's close with what may be the answer to the best straight line ever given in the lodging industry, at least in the past couple of thousand of years.

"Sure. There is room at the Inn," said Robert Nagel, when a couple registering as Joseph and Mary came into the lobby with their donkey.

It happened in Akron, Ohio, where there is an underground church called—yes—Alice's Restaurant. It had been protesting and dramatizing the commercialization of Christmas.

One underground churchman, named David Bullock, decided to show what would happen to the Holy Family these days in a materialistic society.

In beard and robe, with a young lady in Biblical garb, a donkey following them, Bullock walked into the Downtown Holiday Inn of Akron. He filled out a registration form: Joseph of Nazareth and Wife, from Judea, stating: "I need a room for the night. My wife is heavy with child."

Robert Nagel, night manager, said solemnly, "Well, you've come a long way."

Mr. Nagel handed them the key to 101 and said, "Sure, there's room at the Inn."

"I knew they couldn't pay," he said, "and that something was up. After all, a donkey isn't a normal means of transportation."

"Joseph" Bullock, his faith in the evils of materialism perhaps shot down a bit, was offered a free meal for himself and "Mary." He said they weren't hungry but could use a drink. Nagel had drinks sent to the room.

It was not a publicity stunt but it got a lot of it, and *New Yorker* magazine said:

One would like to shake Mr. Nagel by the hand. We thank him for adding immeasurably to the merriment of our Christmas, and for his exhibition of that unpredictable, shrewd, and sometimes highly inconvenient human generosity that makes sweeping moral judgments so risky— even for the most earnest of moralists—and makes life so richly interesting for the rest of us.

This Joseph and Mary picked the wrong outfit. Even if there *had* been no room at the Inn, another room would have been built in twenty-two minutes. No charge for the donkey.

13

Ogg and Wogg

As previously noted, the first hotel was started by Ogg about 7:45 one evening in 688,188 B.C. on what would have been a Saturday.

And the second hotel was started promptly thereafter when Ogg's fellow tribesman, Wogg, opened his own cave. It was the first hotel competition. (Even then, everybody thought it was easy to run a hotel. Or Ho-cave.)

"That crummy boob!" shouted Ogg in Neanderthal. "He swiped all he knows about the hotel from me! Now he's even cutting prices! He will ruin the industry! We'll be overbuilt! The prehistoric rat!"

"Haven't you heard of the population explosion?" said Mrs. Ogg, trying to comfort her husband. "Why, Wogg is your friend."

"That was last week," muttered Ogg, "now he's the competition!"

Ogg was worried.

Soon, business was off. He knew things would compare badly with last season, if there had been a last season.

Wogg's hotel cave was a half-mile nearer the Expressway exit, which was the trail followed by members of other tribes as they came out of the primeval forest. (Primeval Exit One.)

Wandering members of the distant Tree Tribe, and occasional tourists from the even more distant Cliff Tribe, would rush out of the forest to escape the night demons, looking for a place to stay.

Naturally they stopped at the first hotel they came to. The Wogg Arms. Ogg's hotel—the Ogg Roc—suffered. So did Ogg. He said it was the worst season anybody ever had. (The fact it was the only one was no comfort.)

"This overbuilding is ruining the industry!" Ogg kept moaning to Mrs. Ogg. "The world will not support two hotels! This world used to be a nice casual resort area. My resort area! Now look at it! Overbuilt!"

"Well, you better think of something," said Mrs. Ogg. "I notice Wogg isn't complaining. And *his* wife has a new saber-toothed stole . . ."

Ogg snapped his fingers. He said, "I've got it! I'll advertise and promote!"

Mrs. Ogg said, "What do those words mean?"

"How the hell do I know?" replied Ogg thoughtfully. "I just invented them—all I have to do now is to find out how to make them work!"

He slicked his hair back, put on a loin cloth with a belt in the back, made the world's first attaché case out of alligator skin, and marched forth—the world's first Hotel Promotion Man!

He rolled a big rock down the trail, past the Wogg Arms and nearer the exit. He opened his attaché case. He took out his colored clay. On the rock he painted a picture of the Ogg Roc entrance. He painted a picture of an Ogg Roc bed. Four—count 'em, four!—bison skins!

Tourists who rushed out of the forest to get in out of the night demons took one look at the billboard and sped past the Wogg Arms . . . to the place with the thick beds.

Wogg retaliated. He put up a *rock board* showing a thick steak and a bed with *five* bison skins.

Ogg put up a still bigger rock board showing a thick steak, a bed with six bison skins, and a guest lolling comfortably while having breakfast-in-the-skins.

Wogg gave up. He came back to Ogg sheepishly, and said, "You win. Can I go to work for you?"

"I suppose so," said Ogg, generously. "Experienced help is hard to get. It just so happens I need a man to go on a promotion tour and drum up some convention business. In the hotel business, I've found, you can't wait for business to come to you. You have to go after it."

"Gee, Ogg, sir," said Wogg admiringly. "No wonder you are a typical Neanderthal Success Story!"

Ogg drew up several promotion pamphlets. (Pictures of the Ogg Roc painted on small stones.)

"Go to the Tree Tribe and pass these out," Ogg instructed Wogg. "We'll go after the vacation trade."

"You are a genius, promotion-wise!" cried Wogg and, on expense account, raced toward the home of the Tree Tribe.

The members of the Tree Tribe ate him.

So much for the potential competition, smirked Ogg, and settled back to become comfortably wealthy.

He wasn't comfortable long. Other cave-hotels opened. The owners inaugurated excursion rates. (Most of the bison in prehistoric drawings found these days are simply excursion-rate transportation ads.)

In the long run, Ogg triumphed.

He painted pictures of Ooga, a sexy cavegirl, on his *billrocks*. Ogg had invented the first cheesecake ad!

He painted pictures of Ooga, a sexy cavegirl, on his *billrocks*. Cavegirls wearing only sparrow skins! Ogg had invented the first cheesecake ad!

*   *   *

Of course, hotel promotion and advertising have come a long way since then. Haven't they?

14

The Drumbeaters

LODGING FACILITIES FOR THOSE WHO WISH TO
HAVE EXPERIENCES ON JAPANESE BEDDING

*(A promotional sales message of the
Hotel Fujiya in Miyanoshita, Japan)*

Good publicity fills the hotel. Good promotion fills the hotel. Consequently, the good drumbeater is at a premium. He's the man with the maverick mind who tells the world the best room is at *his* inn.

Today's public relations expert outwardly bears little resemblance to the flamboyant flak of decades past. He would be as out of place as a B-movie reporter, with the upturned hat brim and the hip flask, in *The New York Times* city room; as out of place as the dated gang boss returning from stir with his pinstripe suit and the sub-Tommy in the violin case. He would be an anachronism.

Outwardly, however, is your key word. Inwardly, and no matter the buttoned-up Madison Avenue facade, the good ones often are the same old flaks at heart, marching to the same old drumbeat. That is meant as, and will be accepted by the pros as, praise. You cannot change a press agent's secret heart by painting Environmental Engineer in Charge of Promotion on a frosted glass door . . .

Anyway, the thrust of hotel promotion may not have changed that much, not basically. The co-authors of this book agree on that, after years on opposite sides of the strange game called hotel selling; one of them, as a hotel man, selling publicity, and the other, as a newspaperman, cynically trying not to buy, and often failing dismally. For, as newspapermen know the world over, and as hotel drumbeaters forever point out, the greatest screwball stories come out of hotels.

And if there is a dearth of screwball stories, the drumbeater will bring one out of the dust of nothingness into type-high reality, with pix. Take the cats.

Back in the thirties, the Rennert in Baltimore acquired much of its fame because of its Oyster Bar and also because H. L. Mencken, newspaperman for the ages, made it his unofficial headquarters. Mencken mentioned the Rennert often in his Baltimore *Sun* column, said to have been written on thin asbestos. The Rennert, beer, and oysters were on the very short list of things in this universe which Mencken did not profess to be violently against. (It was said that Mencken was a man of such moderation that he could make one oyster last through ten steins of beer.)

Despite the column plugs, however, the Rennert was in the doldrums in the mid-thirties Depression days. The hotel hired its first promotion man—DeWitt Coffman.

He concentrated on getting big-name bands to stay there; then he went after conventions and meetings of any large groups. He managed to book a four-day cat

show. There was whooping and cheering from management—not only because two hundred cat-lovers would be
in residence as paying guests, but because the newspapers
went big for human interest stories on the cat show.
(Animals top human interest stories, which is why Ogg
gave free mammoth rides to the kiddies.)

It was a great publicity success. Unfortunately, it was
learned too late, four hundred of even your most stylish
tabbies cooped up for four days in an enclosed area have
an aftereffect. The odor permeated draperies, carpets, and
even marble floors. Some months later the hotel was torn
down. The cats may not have caused that directly, but the
odor was certainly no deterrent in the decision. Although
the site is now a parking lot, there are old-timers who
swear that on a damp day the odor of cat urine lingers on.

The moral of this story, however, lies in the so-called
Sophisticated Seventies. At the Playboy Plaza in Miami
Beach. Surely one cannot get more sophisticated than
that, eh? And what was the greatest publicity gimmick
so far devised by publicity purveyors of today? Cats.

"I love good publicity stunts, especially if they're
funny," wrote Jack Roberts in the Miami *News*, himself
a hardened ex-city editor and winner of a National Head-
liner's award for writing the best local column in the
nation. "The arrival here today of alley cats seeking the
title of 'All-American Glamor Kitty' certainly fits that cate-
gory."

Roberts said, in fact, it was "purrfectly absurd." He said
it in a promotion man's dream of nirvana: two columns
down the front page of the local paper.

This is all to say that hotel publicity has changed to
this extent: The cat contest at the Playboy Plaza was
sponsored by "Kitty Litter," an odor-inhibiting substance

you put in a kitty cat's bathroom box. We could not ask for a more cogent parable to epitomize how hotel promotion has changed since the old days:

It's still the great old world of press agent stunts—it's just that these days you cover up the smell.

The good press-agent stunt, no matter how seemingly original, almost always has certain hallmarks. It may deal with a celebrity. (Any celebrity: at this writing there are —truly and literally—publicity men offering plush accommodations to the King of Norway, Willie Sutton, and Flipper the Porpoise. Among others.)

The stunt may tie in with an already newsworthy event, to get the hotel mentioned. It may use animals. In the fifties, hotels vied to play host to Sabu the Elephant Boy and his elephant; later it was Gentle Ben the Bear. Almost always, if you dig deep enough, the successful stunt has elements of the inevitable . . . and with it, the tried and true.

The good press-agent stunt is accepted by the media, one grows to feel, for much the same reason a front office cashier at the big Golden Triangle Motor Hotel in Norfolk was once stuck with four bad checks for one hundred dollars each in the same week *and from the same man.*

This cashier was questioned at length by the general manager, who even suspected the cashier of collusion.

"Why in the hell did you take one check after another from the same fellow?" squalled the boss.

And the cashier said, "Well, he looked so familiar."

P. T. BARNUM IS BACK IN TOWN

That's the title of an article by Martin Judge in *Hospitality,* the lodging industry's magazine, and it deals with some of the great publicity stunts of Marriott Hotels, Inc., which joyously and unabashedly loves a good press-agent gimmick. Judge writes: "Marriott Hotels, Inc., like Barnum the Master Showman, uses extravagant ideas rather than extravagant spending to make the front page."

And Marriott, among the other good maverick-minds, knows further that there isn't enough money to buy the publicity you get free when a publicity stunt works just right.

One Marriott classic was conceived by W. W. "Bud" Grice, marketing director in 1962 when Lt. Col. John Glenn went into historic orbit from Cape Canaveral. As the countdown started in the spacecraft, Grice's mind went into countdown. An estimated sixty million persons were watching on TV. How to get Marriott before that dream of an audience?

"We've only got $100,000 in the budget," said the ad man. At that moment a TV announcer noted that newsmen were gathered at the home of Mrs. Glenn.

"Put two hundred cartons of chicken in one of our panel trucks and send it to me with a driver," said Grice. He went to within a block of the Glenn home, where he said to the driver, "I can't get through with this suit and tie on—but if any officers stop you, just say you're bringing Mrs. Glenn's lunch."

It worked. In went the red-and-black Marriott truck, which Grice had ordered washed spanking clean. As it pulled in, the first unofficial vehicle to appear before the cameras in the area, TV men said to sixty million people, "Well, it looks like Bill Marriott has sent out lunch for Mrs. Glenn."

The press corps, munching Marriott chicken, also wrote about it—and, like most good publicity plans, it had a later benefit. When John Glenn subsequently went to Washington to visit President Kennedy, he was asked where he was staying.

Glenn said, "I'll stay at the Marriott. It took care of my family when I wasn't around."

Before the Glenns got there a sign at the Marriott which had said Presidential Suite was pulled down—another put up which said The John Glenn Suite. Wire services sent out pictures worldwide. That's what separates the pros from the hopefuls in the publicity world . . . knowing how to use the unexpected.

Max Wolkoff was handling publicity for the famed Eden Roc, which had booked an oriental revue. Wolkoff decided to set off the world's longest string of firecrackers in a celebration to attract press notices. And oh, it did.

"We hung a string of firecrackers from the top of Eden Roc," said Max. "Actually, they were just one-inchers—the kind you exploded as a kid.

"What I failed to realize was that firecrackers have a cumulative effect, I guess you would call it. Hell, I was planning on just an interesting little ceremony. I lit the bottom firecracker. God! As the string kept exploding upward, it was like the Normandy beachhead—tiles were flying off the facade for fourteen stories, motorists on Collins Avenue were jamming on brakes and jumping out of their cars, half the people in Miami Beach must have called the fire department."

A dozen pieces of fire equipment raced to the Eden Roc. It caused an incredible traffic jam. Newspaper photographers panted up. The law was not amused. Max and the manager were placed under arrest. It was a *great* story, and got a big play after cameramen raced back with their pictures and made the edition.

Only then did Max Wolkoff say to Rocky Pomerance, the Miami Beach police chief, "Rocky, actually it was *you* who signed the permit—and here's my official permit."

"Well, why in the hell didn't you say so?" roared Rocky at the police station.

"I wanted to wait until the photographers left," said Max quietly, happily, a press agent to the core.

Tom McCarthy is director of the Marriott chain's advertising and public relations. He tries to take the dullness out of groundbreakings and dedications of new sites in the chain.

He has succeeded admirably. To open the Marriott at Dulles International Airport, sky divers plunged 8,500 feet to a small island in the hotel's lake and presented the flags of the United States, Virginia, and the Marriott company to assembled dignitaries. The press covers something like that whether it really wants to or not.

To mark the groundbreaking for the St. Louis Marriott, local big shots and the press boarded an Ozark Air Lines jet. They were greeted by Miss St. Louis and a Dixieland band. Airborne, J. Willard Marriott, board chairman, was handed a mysterious black box by Miss St. Louis while reporters gawked. He pushed a button. The plane banked sharply to the left. He pushed another button.

A few thousand feet below on the hotel site, a burst of colored smoke exploded and billowed skyward with a thousand helium-filled balloons!

Actually, it wasn't remote control—it was done by synchronization of watches with ground control. Who said it *was* remote control? The press, gratified that nobody tried to pull the wool over their eyes, wrote at great length, and kindly, about all the practice runs for the event. The pure goofiness of a good stunt is contagious.

Psychology? Try this on. In introducing its Mexico property, Marriott ran *two* press junkets—one for Mexican newsmen, another for American reporters. Why?

Well, in Mexico Mother's Day is a highly revered institution. So Mexican reporters were invited to bring their mothers to see the Paraiso Marriott; 225 Mexican reporters and mothers came on the all-expense paid visit to Acapulco.

Later, American reporters were invited. It is understood that American reporters also have a deep and abiding love for their mothers, but seldom place them in top priority when thinking in terms of a trip to Acapulco.

The American reporters were simply told to come and relax and *not attend* dull speeches or dedications.

It is difficult to say which group of reporters had the best time, as a comparison boggles the mind, but the publicity was immense.

At the bottom of the publicity business, subtle and sometimes diabolically devious, still lies the basic philosophy exemplified by the story of the famous Tennessee mule trainer. It was said he could talk a mule out of being stubborn and into the paths of cooperation. A despairing farmer brought his mule in for training. The old trainer eyed the mule, picked up a heavy stick, and cracked the mule sharply on the nose. The farmer cried, "I thought you trained mules by *talking* to them!"

"Yep," said the trainer. "I do. But first, I got to get the mule's attention."

That is close to saying it all about press agentry. Loew's Hotels stopped traffic at the opening of Loew's City Squire Motor Inn in westside New York City. Outside the entrance sat Premier Khrushchev and President Kennedy, amicably chatting . . . and rocking in rocking chairs. Two actors in makeup.

It has that something . . . call it gall squared . . . which goes *past* the press's well-founded cynicism toward publicity stunts. Reporters will eye one gala promotion scheme and shrug it off without writing a line. And contrary to most opinions you can't, with very rare exceptions, buy a reporter. You can blow your year's budget on a freeload, but unless it has a readable angle, the reporter couldn't get it in his paper if he tried, and if he's a good reporter he won't even try. Obversely, he'll be the first to go for an obvious publicity gag if it has, well, *macho*.

Les Dill knows this so well he has become that rarity —a newspaperman's publicity hound; one of the most imaginative humanity has known.

He's a tall, hulking, country-looking Ozarkian whose mind is about as countrified as an IBM computer with a dash of Nick the Greek. He's become a millionaire by promoting a hole in the ground—Meramec Caverns on Route 66 near St. Louis, one of the nation's great tourist attractions.

Millions of people a year go through the caves now, and he has motel accomodations on the site. He made it through pure publicity genius. It was Les who sent his son-in-law, Rudy Terrell, to New York City in a tiger-skin. Rudy, huge club over one shoulder, looking precisely like Ogg, blithely walked through Gotham and proceeded to try to climb the Empire State Building. Arrested, he let it be known he was a caveman. From Meramec Caverns, of course. That one even made *Life* magazine. But Dill's greatest feat, to lure tourists and motel guests, was finding Jesse James alive.

Les Dill bought these magnificent caves back during the Depression, and feels that local legend about Meramec Caverns having been the hideout of the James gang might well be true. Anyhow, hundreds of billboards proclaimed it. He took the all-important step further. He went out and found Jesse James still alive in the 1950s. In Kansas City.

"I have found Jesse James!" he proclaimed in press releases to AP, UP, and large newspapers everywhere. "Come to Meramec Caverns and interview him!"

Scores of reporters flocked in.

"How do you know he's Jesse James?" they demanded.

"How do I know?" said Les, shocked at this cynicism. "Hell, he *says* he's Jesse James. You think I'm going to call Jesse James a liar?"

Many reporters set out to prove this old man could not be Jesse James. Oddly, perhaps, several decided they had come up with proof that he was. The controversy raged in print, and the U.S. Mint could not have bought the publicity. Even now, years later, articles still appear.

In 1970, one of the writers of this book, a St. Louis *Post-Dispatch* reporter at the height of the controversy, looked across a glass at Les Dill and demanded, "Les. We're close friends. After all these years, who was that old man?"

"Must of been Jesse James," said Les. "That's what all you reporters wrote when he died. Again."

Another time, Dill was promoting a rock festival for hard hats. Stay at the motel, square dance in the caverns to country music. Everybody got a free rock.

It's true, fortunately or unfortunately, that the hell-for-leather approach to publicity has to a large extent passed. Big business is big business. Selling of accommodations more often now approaches high level diplomacy and, when a big convention is at stake, may well exceed it. The hotel business is full of soft-sell sorts who would be a great comfort in our State Department, but the old hard-sell and hoopla still have a place—if only because the hotel business seems to enjoy it so.

"There are certain flexible rules," said Aaron D. Cushman, the publicist. "We try, for instance, to tie the event we are publicizing as closely to the local environment as possible." (Mexico and Mother's Day.)

Work on publicity stunts is often far from ad lib. Planning may take months. Brainstorming sessions follow. Sometimes there are dress rehearsals. (The remote control box over St. Louis.) And—sometimes—they backfire. Or, at first, seem to.

At the Fontainebleau, the "Dream Wedding" was trumpeted in advance. There was no cost spared for the joining of these young sweethearts, both from financially prominent families.

The bride was to descend a pink staircase. A smoke machine was to send up billows of delicate fog. "I want it to look as if the bride were coming down from heaven," said her mother.

Now none of this, of course, was intended as any crass

The bride began her "descent from heaven" but the
groom got cold feet.

publicity gimmick—but, naturally, the Fontainebleau let the press know it was happening. Interest was relatively mild; it was, at best, a good society page story.

The day came. As on signal at the dress rehearsal, the pink-carpeted stairs were bathed in a golden spotlight and the bride began her "descent from heaven." But no groom appeared. He had gotten cold feet and was on an outbound plane, leaving the bride stranded on her billowing smoke-machine cloud all alone.

That got publicity, for the heavenly marriage had gone to hell.

Good publicity sometimes comes inadvertently. Here is a passage from a guidebook sent out by hotels in the resort area of Riviere du Loup in Canada. It's been unforgettable to those who read it, and has been passed around a lot.

> You will be surprised by all accomodations! Restaurants and cabins, water closet, opportunities for waggons. The park of the Luminois Cross offers an equally panorama. You will never forget the sight of the sun setting across the water and playing poetry.
>
> From that moment if you are slightly a poet it will be ectasy.
>
> There are thousands of frisking trouts.
>
> If you are born tourist, this means that a beautiful scenery does not keep you indifferent. Also the opportunity to get acquainted with St. John River and St. Louis du Ha. Ha.

If you are slightly a poet you will remember that, if only to worry about what opportunities the *waggons* have.

But the first paragraph of an actual letter from a South

American hotel to a prospective guest may top it all. Certainly it has struck a responsive chord in the hotel business, and copies have been passed around the world. We reprint it without knowing whether the writer meant "booked up" or not. We do not want to know. The first paragraph of this otherwise crisp and businesslike letter says:

Dear Mr. and Mrs. _____:

We acknowledge receipt of your letter dated 25th November and hasten to inform you that if our representative asked for a deposit it is only to protect the guests' reservation, as our hotel is always fukked up . . ."

15

Button-Down Ballyhoo, Basically

ICKLE MICKLE BICKLE!

> (*Thought-provoking sign outside the Akron Tower Motor Inn, Akron, Ohio*)

As the morning session of the U.S. Junior Chamber of Commerce convention adjourned at noon, the loud-speaker in the lobby crackled:

"Will everyone please go into the street at once! If you can identify the man on the twelfth floor ledge, tell the nearest policeman! He'll take you to the twelfth floor to try to persuade the man not to jump!"

Everyone rushed out into a street already clogged with throngs gawking upward. Fire engines and police cars screamed up. The man was waving the crowds back so he could jump. (This incident happened shortly after a man had leaped from the top of the Gotham Hotel in New

York, while newsreel and newspaper photographers recorded his death.)

The crowd waited in that strange mixture of dread and delight that only the prospect of deliberate self-destruction seems to bring to the human heart, or lack of it.

Suddenly, the man let fall a 50-foot white banner he had held rolled up behind him. It hung suspended down the side of the building, and the message in huge block letters proclaimed: FALL FOR MINNEAPOLIS NEXT YEAR!

Yeh. A ballyhoo stunt promoting the next convention site. That was about thirty years ago. Have hotel space-grabbers changed?

Yes—outwardly, if not deep down. It's still basically ballyhoo. But with more of a polish to the facade now . . . usually. (Usually, because any given year will produce isolated ballyhoo stunts—this year included—as primitive and happily unashamed as the aforementioned. But, fewer and fewer.)

The straight press-agent stunts of the preceding chapters are melded into and largely overshadowed by more subtle sales techniques of today. And it's usually hard these days to tell where a publicity man ends and a sales executive begins. This is because quite often it's the same man, who, like the hotel industry itself, has grown up fast in a hell-for-leather trade. Just don't be fooled by his outward button-down appearance, or whether he calls himself promotion director or vice-president in charge of sales. There's a maverick mind beneath that Madison Avenue narrow brim, right on, as often as not.

And if selling has now taken on big-business overtones, and it has, the salesmen do what works. But, deep down, selling is but a few ticks in time away from the days of pasting the house ad on the fanny of the best looking stripper in town . . .

The Depression years of the thirties changed the hotel business tremendously. Previously, a hotel manager was primarily a fellow who had more guests than he could handle. Then came 1929. Hotels suddenly had to scrounge for business. Everybody did, of course—but it was new to hotels.

Managers started looking for salesmen to fight for business. There weren't any trained or experienced salesmen. Nobody had needed them. Top hotelmen were usually technicians, principally with a depth of knowledge about the food and beverage side. Usually they had apprenticed their way to the top in a tough field. A college graduate who, back then, told his family he was considering the hotel business would have been considered foolish. Why would anybody with an education want to be a waiter or a clerk?

The Depression began to change that. The industry was dying for that combination of education, charm, and personality which makes up a salesman. The whiz kids began to move in, to go after the big chunks of money. Conventions.

Whatever jolly things conventions meant and mean to conventioneers—another chapter will deal with the go-ings-on at conventions—to hotels conventions meant, in many cases, survival. All large hotels set up sales departments. The larger cities organized convention bureaus.

Among the first strong boys in the convention bureau game were Royal Ryan of New York, Joe Turner of Cincinnati, Al Skean of Atlantic City, Russ Schneider of Washington, D.C., Herb Boning of Kansas City, and Mark Egan of Cleveland. Great hotel salesmen included Neal Lang of the New Yorker, Johnny Schlotterbeck of the Mayflower, Ray Hall of the Baker Hotel in Dallas, John Stubblefield of the Savoy Plaza in New York, Dick Flynn of the Drake in Chicago, John Bowman of the Stevens in Chicago, Bud Fisher of the Plaza in New York, Adrian Phillips of the Chalfonte-Haddon Hall in Atlantic City. The list goes on, but those were the first of the Ballyhoo Boys.

Along came fellows like Danny Amico at the Sherman in Chicago, Tex Carlton at the New Yorker, Dill Parrish at Chalfonte-Haddon Hall in Atlantic City, John Nolan at the Hollenden in Cleveland, Henry Dienna at the Commodore in New York, Bob Quain at the Roosevelt in New York, Rush Strayer at the Greenbrier in West Virginia, Lennie Hicks at the Morrison in Chicago, Bud Smith of the Sheraton chain, Charlie Craddock at the Edgewater Beach in Chicago, and, elbowing along happily in these root-hog-or-die days of no-limit ballyhoo, C. DeWitt Coffman of Washington's Mayflower.

Today's salesmen are a bit more scientific and circumspect, with some exceptions, than they were in the earlier years—if only because most organizations now select future sites by committees instead of by the membership voting in general session. Back then, all was fair in love, war, and convention selling.

Many top conventions met at the Greenbrier in White Sulphur Springs, W. Va. The only way to get there was on the Chesapeake and Ohio Railway sleeper. One year the train went down loaded with New York and Washington ballyhooers. Each was to be allowed to present his sales pitch the next morning.

Strange things happened to the salesmen. Some of them found their berths filled with ice cubes. About every hour somebody pulled the emergency cord, stopping the train and waking everybody. Others were short-sheeted. It went on all night. Nobody got any sleep. At six when the train pulled in, the traveling promotion-boys dragged to their rooms, leaving time calls to make sure they would be up to make their sales pitch before the committee.

Oddly, all the calls were cancelled. The operator later kept saying to the screaming oversleepers, "But, sir, you cancelled it yourself." Only one salesman showed up at the convention committee and got the business for next year . . . He had already checked out when the cursing competition finally woke up to what had happened—and began to form the mob—to lynch Schlotterbeck.

Johnny Schlotterbeck was one of the wildest. One year in Washington, D.C., everybody was after next years' convention business of the Ladies of the Oriental Shrine. But much of their in-lodge business revolved around secret ceremonials. Doors to meetings were locked and guarded—to anybody, particularly males.

At a rite with much pomp and ceremony, the lights in the room dimmed. A bugle call sounded. A spotlight split the room. A color guard of ladies entered in full regalia. The leader of the Oriental Shrine ladies entered.

On her arm was Johnny Schlotterbeck, wearing one of her headdresses and happily drunk as a goat.

He stood weaving and grinning. The Grand Leader led the delegates in song. They sang, "Oh, Johnny, Oh."

Only then did the beefy sergeant-at-arms throw him out.

The other salesmen gave up. Johnny had already gotten the business . . . although, and perhaps coincidentally, he was in the hospital for six days after the convention was over. The diagnosis was exhaustion.

Competitive hotels were not always bound back then

by rigid definition of ethics. Leonard Hicks, now head of the widely known International Hotel Representatives, and the author of books on how hotels get their business, has always been a powerhouse salesman—a postgraduate genius among Ballyhoo Boys.

When Hicks was sales manager of the Morrison in Chicago, he coined the advertising slogan "World's Tallest Hotel."

Bud Smith, one of the Sheraton's drumbeaters, squashed the slogan. He had a subslogan lettered on the bottom of Hicks' "World's Tallest Hotel" billboards along highways. It said, "We Get all the Suicide Trade."

Certain signs say more about the advertising business than perhaps even the advertising business wishes to ponder, as witness some of the work authored by Jon Barnes. Jon has a flair for promotion, and the word "promotion" itself includes a multitude of facets in the lodging business: call it publicity, call it relatively somber sales work, call it uninhibited ballyhoo . . . it's promotion. WE HATE TALL DOGS.

That's promotion, when it's on a motor inn marquee.

What does it mean?

Don't, as the saying goes, ask.

Jon Barnes has managed establishments like the Sheraton Motor Inn in Daytona Beach, the Air Host Inn at Atlanta, and the Akron Tower Inn in Ohio. The goofball sign is his trademark.

"We Hate Tall Dogs" means—actually—nothing; except that everybody who sees it remembers the name of the place they saw it. (Can every high-powered ad agency guarantee as much?)

When the astronauts were first named, Jon put this out: WELCOME, ASTRONAUTS.

Hundreds of calls came in. "Are the astronauts really there?"

The switchboard girls were instructed to answer, "No, but if they come they sure are welcome."

He takes a freewheeling approach. When his Akron Inn put out the sign APPROVED BY HILTON, a raft of calls came in asking if the place were now part of the Hilton chain. Barnes said he had no idea what *that* Hilton thought, but Sam Hilton of Walla Walla had sure liked the joint when he stayed a couple of days last week.

When he put out APPROVED BY SHERATON, he got a call from, among others, the legal department of the Sheraton chain in Boston. They would book no chit-chat about any Irving Sheraton from Dubuque; Jon said, Gee if they felt that way he would take it down. But, of course, the message had registered. Anyhow, Christmas was approaching so he put up: DON'T YOU HO, HO, HO ME, YOU DIRTY OLD MAN!

It's difficult to say how many mental cartoons were thought up by readers of that essentially meaningless caption. At least Jon surely didn't know what it meant. Probably most of the mental cartoons were risqué, if the Liz message is a criterion.

When Elizabeth Taylor ditched Eddie Fisher for Richard Burton, Barnes spelled out DOWN WITH LIZ!

A lot of people including several preachers protested what they immediately deduced was a double entendre. Barnes, in truth, had intended no double meaning. He took it down, saying that an innocent hotelman would be guided by the more sophisticated depth of knowledge of the clergy. Hotelmen lead sheltered lives.

In its place, he put up WELCOME NUDISTS CONVENTION.

One is astonished at how many people are interested

in a nudists convention. Jon had a solemn reply to *this* influx of calls. He said no, the nudists convention wasn't there, but it was welcome, as he had plenty of room. The astronauts had failed to check in yet.

On the Fourth of July, Jon's marquee borders dangerously on making sense. It says, in increasingly larger red letters: f f f f f-ssssss-BAH-WOOOOM!

Which doesn't leave a hell of a lot left unsaid about the Fourth of July. That much logic, however, makes him nervous—his predilection is for the sign which, he says, has evoked the most response of any he has authored. It also heads this chapter. ICKLE MICKLE BICKLE!

Some motorists mull this over and even call back from great distances to see what it means.

It means the lodging industry knows a lot about promotion—is what it means.

For hotel convention salesmen, the prize turkey shoot of all is the convention of convention managers. Bonanza! Some five hundred professional association managers— executive directors of big groups—have their own convention. The hotel Ballyhoo Boys descend in droves, but it's tacitly agreed to lay off the sales pitch right then. Just get chummy, maybe, and do your selling later.

One high-pressure hotel huckster almost killed it for all time. (After all, the association managers don't have to let hotelmen come to their convention.) This hotel salesman docked a hundred-foot yacht at the pier one year at the swank Boca Raton Club in Florida where the American Society of Association Executives was convened. He invited execs aboard, one by one.

They found the yacht was a floating ad pitch for his

hotel—blownup pictures, floor plans, banquet displays, the works.

And the pitchman had girls aboard whose heels were even rounder than the rest of them.

He lost his job over that one.

Moxie is one thing; bad taste another. Ingenuity is the most valued trait. When Mrs. Ida B. Wise Smith was president of the Women's Christian Temperance Union, the sales manager of the Hotel Washington in Washington, D.C., got their coveted world convention by pure ingenuity.

Mrs. Smith was exceedingly enthusiastic about temperance, never missing a chance to convert a person from Evil King Alcohol. The promotion man, hearing out her speeches, hung his head and stated, "Mrs. Smith, I promise you this—sign the convention contract at my hotel and I promise you that I will never take a drink as long as I live."

She signed immediately. She never did find out the promotion man never had taken a drink since he found out he had an allergy to alcohol.

A national manufacturing company representative was being wooed for his convention business by Emmett Bieger, general manager of the Jung Hotel in New Orleans. The 1000-room Jung is famous for its southern hospitality—unfortunately an impolite pigeon, possibly a Yankee, hadn't heard about it.

Jung put the company man in the Presidential Suite. Naturally, there was some partying—and the guest left all the windows open, hoping the fresh air would rejuvenate him. He woke up to find a large grey pigeon perched on the foot of his bed glaring at him. It gave the man a

bad turn—there are certain types of hangovers in which
one thinks in terms of ravens, and doomsday.

He came up shouting. The pigeon went away. His wife
woke up. She made a rude comment about his mixing
Cutty Sark and Old Crow. "Ease off," she said. "You'll
be seeing eagles next." The next morning she was having
coffee in her room. A gray pigeon flew in, perched on
the coffee pot handle, and solemnly did his park-statue
trick—plop, right in her coffee cup.

"Good thing it wasn't an eagle," her husband said.

"A thousand rooms," Jung said, "and that pigeon had to
pick that one."

But Jung got the convention business. Perhaps because
it's not every hotel where a convention director gets such
a great I-told-you-so topper on his wife. Sweet are the
uses of adversity.

*You don't really pick the place you stay in overnight
by accident. Neither do conventions. People are lured to
one place, over another, by promotion. The Ballyhoo
Boys work day and night in devious ways to keep their
place in the spotlight. There are subtle ways and there
are more direct ways, like newspaper ads and billboards.*

*Or the indefinite "word-of-mouth" may have been what
got you. But even that is stimulated by the business promoters. They're relatively new to this age-old trade, at
least in today's carefully planned effectiveness, and they've
become vitally important to success.*

*The Ballyhoo Boys have what may well be the most
interesting and exciting work in the business. They're the
glamor boys, the valiant Warriors of the Word. Spreading
the word—sometimes it's more rudely defined—is their
profession. You're the prize . . . the paying guest.*

A gray pigeon flew in, perched on the coffee pot
handle, and solemnly did his park-statue trick.

CAUTION
NUDIST CAMP CROSSING!

It's a shame there is no prize for gag signs. Nick Bicking, former sales promotion man, owner of the Harbour House in Michigan, would have won it. The idea of a sign in today's high-speed traffic is to get motorists to slow down enough to turn off at a certain motel. It's usually done with a series of expensive signs. But the one above slows traffic to a crawl . . . HAVE YOUR NEXT AFFAIR HERE

The first motel owner to put that on his marquee deserves a prize . . . either for gall or pure innocence. You see that sign spotted around the country now. And, almost always, the operator will say, why-we-mean-banquet-or-convention. Sure.

WOW! That's the billboard message put up outside Atlanta by the Marriott Motor Hotel. What does it refer to? Why, simply what great accommodations lay ahead, or whatever it is that makes you go "Wow!" about a motel. Perhaps the color TV? Right? Sure.

And the hotel promotion mind was responsible for the huge billboards along Florida's Gold Coast to lure tourists across state to the west coast attractions and accommodations. Lying full length, back to camera, and a beautiful back it is from the neck right down to the heels, is a wildly shapely gal in an itsy-bitsy bathing suit. She is peering back over her shoulder at you. The caption is brief. YOU OUGHT TO SEE THE OTHER SIDE

It refers to the map of Florida, right? Sure.

As for newspaper ads, the message is plain. Hotels are equated with glamor. Glamor is bikinis. More and more bikinis with less and less cloth. Look in your local travel section. Look in national travel mags. Look in *The New York Times*.

Ah, the lovelies posed by the pool!

Travel broadens one, is the message, and the broads stop here.

FUN, GLAMOR, EXCITEMENT! says the copy.

And this sloe-eyed dish in the Band-Aid, assets at high port, gazes alluringly from ad after ad.

Thus does Oscar Treadmill put down his newspaper in Far Rockaway and decide it's time he went and got a little, you know, relaxation.

Thus does Mrs. Treadmill, who wasn't born yesterday, go along to make damn sure he doesn't.

Thus, then, and often only then, do they start checking rates, attractions, word-of-mouth recommendation from friends, various seals of approval—and so on.

Ah yes, ah yes, the bikini works, as Ogg, the lodging industry, and the Tennessee mule trainer knew.

First, you got to attract their attention.

Carl Fisher built Miami Beach on a mangrove swamp and 8 x 10 glossies of bathing beauties. Las Vegas hotels are not prudish about displaying lovely ladies. The French Riviera knew what sold even before Bardot took towel-dropping lessons. And it's six, two, and even that the next ad or brochure prepared by hoteldom, be it the Hilton-Harem or the Yeehaw Junction Dew-Drop Inn, is going to utilize a bit of basic fun, glamor, and excitement.

Sort of bring your arms back and up, Miss Fantasia, and inhale—oh, yes, that's it! Click.

TELL YOU WHAT I'M A'GONNA DO

Before leaving the hotel promotional mind to seethe and bubble in its everlasting creative burble, let's take a last look at how that mind works. It doesn't produce by recipe . . . it cooks ad lib and it dishes up everything from nuance-laden potpourri to heavy Mulligan stew. Call it corporate cleverness sometimes, recognize the tripod and keister other times, suffice it that almost always the promotion man has some tribal memory, at least, of selling snake oil off the wagon platform. Thus do the Ballyhoo Boys make the world a little . . . different.

When Frank Berkman was general manager of the City Squire Inn of Loew's Hotels on the edge of Times Square, he got the President of the United States to untangle a convention booking for him. That's class.

When Berkman, to his horror, found he had booked the Mormon Tabernacle Choir in—350 rooms—on dates *before* Shriners checked out during a national convention, he seethed, bubbled. He called the White House, arranged for the choir to stop over in Washington a day for a concert, which prospect delighted the choir. They gave a one-hour concert on the White House lawn. Berkman easily arranged hotel accommodations in summer-deserted Washington. The choir was a smash. How nice of Berkman! Nobody knew it was because a frantic manager had no room at the City Squire Inn, until the following day . . .

Sometimes promotion backfires. Promoters for a Florida city handed out oranges to each delegate at a New

York convention, before anybody noticed they were stamped California Sunkist. The convention went to Los Angeles.

When Howard Heinsius was sales manager of the Berkeley-Carteret in Asbury Park, he insisted the hotel have a complete recreation program to keep guests happy. A vivacious social hostess cooked up an endless variety of entertainment activities. She was relentless about planned recreation. She scheduled guests into a fun-fun-fun "Sport of the Day." It was suggested she ease off a little after she telephoned an important guest and asked, "Mr. Wilson, have you had your Sport of the Day?" Mr. Wilson panted furiously from his room, "I'm trying to have it right now, if you'll quit ringing this goddamn phone!"

A good promotion man instinctively talks good copy in the presence of the press. Ernest Byfield is one of the greats. He gained considerable fame as owner of the Sherman in Chicago, downtown, and the Ambassador East and West, uptown in Chicago, where he instituted, among other things, the world-famous Pump Room. Imaginative, creative, he was a talented showman. When the Tisch Brothers of Loew's Theaters acquired the Ambassadors in the late sixties, they announced a multi-million dollar renovation program—and their advertising was based on this one great line: "Everything new but the Pump Room." Byfield was selling nostalgia before it became popular. And when a syndicated columnist interviewed him, the columnist asked for the secret of his success and prepared for the usual barrage of cliches. But Byfield said:

"Well, it's quite simple. I was standing in the lobby of the Sherman Hotel one morning. My father came down from his upstairs suite in the hotel, which he owned. As my father got off the elevator he saw me, by pure chance, and he took a liking to me."

Hotel salesmen try not to be overeager. They have a horrible example. At the Bull and Bear restaurant of the Waldorf-Astoria, a fresh-out-of-Yale salesman was entertaining a client to within an inch of the client's life. He scared him off finally. When the client put an appetizer in his mouth, the salesman whipped out his Zippo and lighted the prospect's stalk of celery.

To promote its bar, a small Philadelphia hotel offered tape cassettes to its customers. Office noises, traffic noises, whatever. You could call your wife and tell a lie to fit the background noises. The beautiful scheme was dropped after somebody substituted a tape with wild-party noises. ("Hello, dear, my bastard of a boss has got me working late." This does not go well with an orgy overheard in the background.)

In the minds of many, perhaps the finest hotel promotion was done in absolute secrecy—the renovation of the Algonquin. It was done over a period of several years at a cost of several million dollars.

People who love the Algonquin *love* the Algonquin. Its famous Round Table comprised only the best-known circle of greats who have loved it. A certain breed of celebrities love the anonymity—or at least the lack of overt, autograph-grabbing attention—they get at the Algonquin. It is not press agent minded. Asked for unusual happenings, a typically reserved employee told an eager young *Herald-Tribune* feature writer that *nothing* unusual had ever happened at the Algonquin, except one night when Brendan Behan scandalized guests by appearing in the lobby sober.

Algonquin lovers are not wildly progress minded. Management feared they would stampede away in droves if the usual remodeling was done. So, as reported by Arthur Herzog, plumbing, wiring, lobby paneling, and so forth were replaced a little at a time. Chairs were quite literally sneaked out one at a time for recovering in the dead of night. Woodwork was restored when nobody was looking. Rugs were replaced with rugs of the same pattern, which wasn't easy. The bar—called the Blue Room, although it has no blue in it—was restored in Mission Impossible stealth.

The Algonquin believes this axiom: *Bad hotels are all alike, but no two good hotels are the same*.

The Algonquin stayed the same. It still has its own strange and unique customs. (On New Year's Eve busboys march through the lobby, tablecloths over their heads, banging on pots with spoons. "Don't ask why," writes Herzog, "or you will be told that they are exorcising evil spirits, or something equally ridiculous.") The house has its own view of the world and of tradition. When Tallulah Bankhead tried to slip into the dining room in slacks, the Algonquin may have best exemplified its moderation between tradition and flexibility. Where else would Tallulah have been asked to pin a tablecloth skirt-like around herself, to maintain tradition? More important, where else would Tallulah have immediately agreed to do so?

So, in an age when many hotels send out a barrage of press releases to promote the purchase of two new potted palms, the Algonquin spent millions in a secrecy the CIA could envy.

After the renovation was complete—sneaked past many of the sharpest eyes and minds of our time—the management got its reward.

Edna Ferber, novelist and longtime Algonquinite,

checked in and observed, "Why, it looks prettier every time I come here."

The only thing which could have made management happier was for her to say it looked the same.

But it's hoopla. Lasting hoopla. The secret renovation will eventually get more publicity than the best one-shot stunt ever devised, and there have been some dandies.

Jerome B. Temple was president and manager of the Seminole Hotel in Jacksonville when a radiogram arrived from the aircraft carrier U.S.S. *Saipan* on its way home from an around-the-world trip. It stated that the Seminole Indian Princess Matsui was arriving aboard.

Temple, a pride of dignitaries, and 1200 sailors stood at the foot of the gangway after the carrier docked. The ship's band ruffled and flourished. Marching bands awaited.

The princess came ashore, the same sweet girl she had been when she left as mascot of Marine Fighter Squadron 324, except now she wore the four gold stripes of a Navy captain.

The parade through town for the Indian princess attracted considerable press attention. Then Matsui was home, at the Seminole Hotel Bar, from whence she had departed the previous year. You can see her yet. She's the only wooden Indian there.

And the promotion mind was at work when Red Skelton picketed the Marott Hotel in Indianapolis during the Indiana State Fair. A prize black steer had won the blue ribbon at the fair. The hotel bought Blackie and penned him outside the hotel to advertise its great steaks.

Skelton (whose contract called for a percentage of admissions to the fair), picketed the Marott with the help of lots of children carrying signs saying DON'T LET THEM KILL BLACKIE and THIS HOTEL UNFAIR TO STEERS.

Pictures of Red with the steer made the wire services. Red was obviously touched because tears were streaming down his face. A march was made on the governor's office, demanding clemency. The governor granted clemency.

Red purchased the bull back from the hotel. It says here. He gave it back to the lad who raised it.

All this with the greatest solemnity.

All this spelling the hotel's name right.

The moral here is that a good promotion man can do wonders with a hotel and a celebrity. If he's got a lot of bull to go with it.

Red Skelton stipulated that Blackie, in his old age, be put out to pasture and tenderly cared for until he left this life.

It has been suggested the same tender solicitude be shown for hotel promotion men.

But it wouldn't work. They would have a dozen conventions booked into the pasture before the season was out.

In remarking upon the enthusiasm with which sales and promotion people polish the image of their hotels to a glowing sheen, let us make sure their own image is spotless. Perhaps this exchange of letters will suffice.

Orange City, Fla., November 30

American Hotel & Motel Association
221 West 57th Street
N.Y., N.Y., 10019

Dear Sirs:

I have always wanted to open a motel.

But people tell me I shouldn't because of too much illicit love affairs in them.

Is that the biggest problem of operating a motel?
They say it's only salesmen that do it.
Why is it only salesmen that do it?
Wouldn't other kinds of people do it?
I'm a bachelor, who has never been able to get one
girl. So I wonder how salesmen can get a new girl in
every town he comes to.

Yours truly,
Signed: _____

New York, December 16

Mr. _____
Box _____
Orange City, Fla.

Dear Mr. _____:
In reply to your November 30 letter inquiring about
motels, you will find enclosed a selection of materials designed to help those considering the motel business.
With respect to your question about salesmen, I think
this can best be answered by the Hotel Sales Management Association and I have, therefore, referred this
part of your letter to them.

Cordially,
J. S. Fassett
Director, Membership Services

Notation on carbon to Frank W. Berkman:

Dear Frank:

Please take care of that part of the enclosed letter that
relates to the activities of sales personnel.

Jake.

January 2, New York

Mr. _____
Box _____
Orange City, Fla., 32763

Dear Mr. _____:

We are in receipt of a copy of your letter addressed to the American Hotel and Motel Association inquiring about information relating to motels.

In my opinion you have been misadvised regarding the morals of sales people. We have found them to be, for the most part, highly dedicated people.

Traveling sales personnel are the backbone of the hotel industry. These people spend a great many nights in hotels and motels and possibly it just seems that they are the biggest offenders in the matter of the contents of your letter. I am sure I have not answered your question to your satisfaction. However, it is a very difficult question to answer.

Sincerely yours,
Frank W. Berkman

cc: Mr. Jake Fassett

Handwritten notation at top of last letter:

Match up with original and acknowledgements for screwball letter file. Jake F.

16

Take a Wild Guest

> *Guest: Any person who lodges, boards, or receives refreshments, for pay, at a hotel, boardinghouse, restaurant, or the like . . . specif., Law: A traveler who as a visitor takes for pay refreshment for himself or his beasts at an inn or hotel, without reference to the length of his stay so long as he retains his character as a traveler or transient visitor, distinguished from a boarder.*

And tell me, best of princes, who he was
That guested here so late. (Chapman)

(Webster's International Dictionary)

Well, we'll try to tell you, *Webster's International*. But, as you've already found, guests are very difficult to define.

A drunk actually called a lawyer, saying he had been bitten in one of the hotel rooms. The house officer proved he had sat down hard on his own dentures . . .

"There was something about this woman guest that looked familiar," said the woman manager. "I know she had squawked about the price of the room when she checked in the preceding day . . . but it was more than that."

Yes, there was, and the maid discovered it. The woman who had complained about the price had, during her stay, taken the drapes down and made herself a dress of them; the maid found the snippings.

"She wore it when she checked out," said the manager. "Quite a chic sheath dress it was, too—it was the cabbage-rose pattern that looked familiar."

This same woman manager, who with her husband owns and operates several hotels, has asked not to be identified for one outstanding reason. "I don't want these guests to ever remember me," she said. "They might come back." So we'll call her Mrs. Adams.

She has been threatened with litigation. A drunk actually called a lawyer, saying he had been bitten in one of the hotel rooms. The house officer proved he had sat down hard on his own dentures on the bed.

She has been cheated. She has a collection of cheap cardboard suitcases left by guests who, checking in with luggage, throw their clothes out the window; leave a $1.50 hockshop suitcase . . . and an unpaid bill ten times that amount.

She has been baffled. A shapely switchboard operator rushed up to her and said, "Mrs. Adams! That old goat in 402 keeps calling me up and saying he'll give me five thousand dollars to spend one hour with him!"

"Honey," said Mrs. Adams. "Don't worry, if he had said five hundred there's a bare possibility he might mean it. Tell you what. Next time he calls, just say you want the cash in advance . . . that'll shut him up."

The girl grinned and did precisely that the next time the man called. Within ten minutes he sent down an envelope with five thousand dollars in it, cold cash. Well, not cold. (The second suggestion by Mrs. Adams worked better. She sent the money back with a note from the girl saying her husband wouldn't let her. The man tipped the bellman a quarter.)

She has been driven to distraction by drunks. One fell down the basement stairs *three times* trying to get in the elevator. He came back after the third time and shouted, "Goddamnit, I want the *up* elevator!" Another drunk, who had been trying to have a girl sent to his room, kicked open the lobby door, jumped into what he thought was a cab, and asked the driver to find him some action. It was a police car.

She has been shocked—or, at least, as shocked as any hotel manager gets. It became her duty one dawn to wake up a nude man sleeping peacefully on a second floor fire escape exit over a busy street; the calls were pouring in. He, too, had come in loaded, asked specific directions to his room, got them, and followed them. (Get off at the second floor and it's the very last door at the end of the hall. He undressed, used his clothes for a pillow, and went to sleep right over the hotel entrance, outdoors.)

And, shocked, baffled, whatever, she recalls with absolute delight the guests who don't classify.

"I wouldn't want to admit it to them," she said, "but the screwball guests are one of the most fascinating things in this crazy business. Like when my husband was the President of the United States."

A guest, for the second straight night, had been trying repeatedly to telephone President Johnson in Washington. He had a plan he felt the President should hear person-

ally. He kept the switchboard tied up. Finally, Mrs.
Adams called her husband. The guest got his call through
to "President Johnson."

"What's your plan?" said Mr. Adams.

"Top secret," said the guest. "I want to know if I can
come to Washington."

"Certainly," said Mr. Adams.

When last seen, the guest had checked out and was
taking a cab to the airport.

At Las Brisas Hotel in Acapulco, each of the two-
room cottages has its own swimming pool. An assistant
manager was staying in one, a honeymoon couple in the
second. Late at night, after the hotelman was asleep, the
couple had gone skinny-dipping—and locked their key
in the room. The groom knocked on the hotelman's glass
window and asked him to please take his jeep and go to
the main office for an extra key. The hotelman did.

Two nights later, the assistant manager was awakened
again. Same naked guy, same story, same trip.

Four nights after *that,* tap, tap, tap. But, this time, it
was the bride.

"My husband was too embarrassed to wake you up
again," she said demurely, and drippingly, totally nude
in the moonlight.

When Johnny Dolan was general manager of the Bal
Harbour Hotel, he was no stranger to the peculiar ways of
some guests, but when TV sets started disappearing from
the rooms he couldn't figure it.

One day in the lobby he chanced to notice the waiting
luggage of one of the affluent guests who was checking
out. Under the usual golf clubs, tennis rackets, and so
on was a large cardboard box. A bellhop had taken the
empty carton up for the guest to pack books and dirty

clothing in; this was fairly usual. But, on a hunch, Dolan peeked into the carton. Yep, the room TV . . . taking the TV home in a carton (via a struggling bellman) had become fairly usual too. Dolan re-remembered the old hotelman's axiom: a guest's bankroll has nothing to do with his taking ways. When it comes to some guests, it must be the challenge. "Some of these people not only could have bought the TV," said John. "Hell, they could have bought the hotel it came in."

Guests, indeed, have their whims:

—The noted film star who just has to have a tumbler of "special mineral water" served at each meal in the Wedgewood Room of the Chalfonte-Haddon Hall . . . even breakfast. (It's straight vodka but only the head-waiter knows.)

—The celebrities who demand absolute secrecy during their visit to a town, and insist on being treated just like everybody else, and then try to have the manager— and staff—fired for paying no attention to them.

—The somehow enviable calm of the Romeos who sashay in, with a girl, register as man and wife, and have the unbelieveable gall to ask the clerk for a special three-hour rate. (And some guests with broads have been known to register, saying their luggage is en route from the airport; come back down in a couple of hours, disheveled and exhausted, to announce their luggage had been sent to another hotel due to a change in plans, so they wouldn't be needing the room after all.)

At the Lucayan Beach Hotel at Freeport in the Bahamas the bellman brought a gin and tonic to a man in his room and professionally tried to ignore the nude redhead combing her hair at the vanity. The guest said, "Son, bring me a couple more of these—save you some trips." The bellman said, "Yessir, anything for your wife?" The man snapped his fingers and said, "Yes! Bring me a postcard."

You expect the unexpected from people like Buddy Hackett. Once he was playing a foursome at the Concord in the Catskills—hit a screaming drive down the long fifth fairway, but it took a sharp turn into the woods. Buddy disappeared into the undergrowth and was out of sight a couple of minutes. Finally he raced out, buck naked except for his hat and shoes, screaming, "Locusts."

However, the unexpected sometimes seems to come from anybody—when they're caught up in whatever fey spirits seem to haunt even the most prosaic hotel. Some years back, a news commentator famous for his solemn approach to life weaved out of a cocktail lounge in a California hotel and asked the clerk how to get outside.

The clerk pointed toward the exit. The commentator, nauseated, staggered rapidly toward the general area of outside. When he came to a tree, he hung onto it and threw up. Unfortunately, it was a potted palm at the far end of the lobby—

From his book about Johnny Cash (*Winners Got Scars Too*), Christopher S. Wren tells in *Redbook* how hotels used to affect Cash and his troupe.

"Most of their exploits were carried out in hotels," Wren wrote. "In Niagara Falls, their room was directly over the hotel entrance. It was thirty degrees below zero when they poured water from wastebaskets down on arriving guests. Other times they dropped raw eggs.

" 'We did it all as a joke at first,' Cash says, 'and it just snowballed. It got so we were throwing lamps out of windows, just to hear them break.'

"In one hotel they filled the bathtub with hot water and

emptied a case of gelatin into it before checking out. In time, the damage grew more extensive. At one Georgia motel they asked for adjoining rooms. When they found no connecting door, they took the fire axe in the hall and chopped their own entranceway."

And they weren't averse to cherry bombs, either, but there was one thing about Cash and his lads.

When the bills ran up, Cash paid the damage. And that takes a lot of the wayward out of the definition of wayward guest.

It would take another book this size to list the things that have been thrown out of hotel windows, not including humans, but here is a documented list of items flung from windows of *one hotel on one Saturday night*.

An old-fashioned (nonhotel) chamber pot; a pair of crutches tied together (one short and one long); a department store mannequin fully clothed, which flew earthward accompanied by suicidal-sounding female shrieks; a World War II German army helmet, with the head of a male department store dummy in it; the front seat of an automobile, year 1930 (with the word help written in heavy lipstick on it); and a horse collar.

Granted, this followed a story in the local paper of the town—near an Army base—in which the hotel manager made the mistake of saying he would take stern action if any guests threw another fire hose out the window, as they had the preceding Saturday night.

Another example of exceptions outstripping the rules. (A pedestrian once charged angrily into the Roney Plaza in Miami Beach. He had been hit with a large frozen turkey which flew from a window. That's enough to make anybody mad, including the manager, who found kitchen employees on the second floor stealing food by pitching it to accomplices below. The turkey fell short and belted the passerby.

Indeed, a guest can be a wondrous thing. How can a hotelman know what a guest is going to do next? Quite often, it seems, the guest doesn't know what he is going to do next . . . himself.

It was in a Key West motel that a guest raced out of his motel room in the middle of hurricane winds, was blown into the swimming pool, and had to be rescued.

His explanation remains a classic. He had been drinking quite conscientiously for a few days. When he woke up, the radio in his room was announcing the approach of full force of the hurricane, and the tensely calm announcer was saying over and over, "Everyone should seek shelter immediately."

The befuddled guest sat bolt upright, panicked, and dashed from his room.

The wind dumped him right into the pool. After his rescue and considerably more sober, he said sheepishly, "I vaguely remember—I ran outside to seek shelter."

17

Send Up the House Physician, He's Cute

ALL VEGETABLES IN THIS ESTABLISHMENT
HAVE BEEN WASHED IN WATER SPECIALLY
PASSED BY THE MANAGEMENT

> (*Sign under the glass-topped tables of a Ceylon hotel to show sanitary precautions being taken during a fever epidemic*)

The guest awoke with a hangover. A tree went by his second floor window at the Sahara in Las Vegas. He blinked. Another tree went by. *Whoa, boy,* the guest said to himself; *easy, boy.* Three more trees went by. He began to shake. One, two . . . three more trees went by. He leaped up and raced to his window.

He looked out. No trees. Not a tree outside his window . . .

"Send up the house doctor!" he screamed to the switch-

225

board. The doctor came. The "patient" babbled, "I've got the dt's! Give me a shot!"

"You're half shot now," sighed the doctor, prescribing the same old Morning After Miracle Drug—coffee and a calmer outlook. "Take it easy. There goes another tree, see? We both see it, right?"

Large olive trees were being wheeled by on dollies toward a landscaping project around the corner, out of sight.

"Gee, thanks, Doc," said the patient, grabbing his bourbon from the dresser. "Hell, if I haven't got the dt's I might as well start drinking again."

Nobody, including the house officer, sees the guest under more peculiar conditions than the house physician does. The Hippocratic Oath has buried more good stories than all censors since the world was invented. But certain basics emerge.

One is that by some strange quirk in the scheme of things, guests apparently believe that a house physician has some greater obligation to them than an outside doctor would have. Some evidently peg him as a cross between Dr. Kildare and the bellboy.

One guest who painfully zipped himself into the teeth of his trousers zipper screamed for help, as who wouldn't. But after the rescue he was annoyed to find the service wasn't included on the modified American plan.

The house physicians' calls, which are many and varied, are dominated by drunks, followed by nervousness of a wide variety and heart attacks—a few real, many imagined—in about that order.

But, oh, the exceptions . . .

A guest lacerated his head by butting (and shattering)

the screen of the television set in his room, while watching a professional football game.

A guest at a Detroit convention wanted the house doctor to examine him for venereal disease and when asked how long since the possibility of exposure replied, "About an hour and twenty minutes ago."

One doctor for a big motor hotel got a call from a distraught lady guest who said she was sure her husband was dead. The doctor knew from former visits that the husband was a binge boozer, so he tried to reassure the wife. She insisted he was stone cold dead, wouldn't move. The doctor sighed and suggested pricking the sensitive sole of one foot with a needle.

"If that doesn't move him, call me back," he said.

In fifteen minutes she called back. "Come ride over!"

"Didn't the needle punch bring any response?"

"Yed, it did, all ride," she said. "He jubbed up swigging and hid me in the libb." The doctor went over and took three stitches in the helpmate's lip.

Some hotels are parts of huge complexes, with office buildings included, and they house everything from physicians to undertakers—a human could be born, live, and be embalmed or cremated under one roof. The Hotel Dupont in Wilmington, Del., is one of these. People in these complexes have been known to ask for the "house lawyer." One drunk with suicide on his mind said he wouldn't jump until he could get the house lawyer to change his will, leaving everything to his collie. A house physician gave him a tranquilizer, and he didn't remember any of it the next morning.

Hotels cannot ignore the complaints of guests, no matter how screwball or seemingly phony. One reason is the professional "divers," as insurance agents call them. Accident fakers. Their demands run from snagged hosiery to suits for medical compensation with whopping punitive claims. So, in all accidents, real or faked, the hotel must be careful not to aggravate the hurt further. You can't get more sympathy anywhere than you can in a good hotel, and this includes guests who the manager is quite sure put the banana peels there in the first place.

"Some of the divers could have made far more money as professional athletes," said one house doctor. "They can fake a fall down a set of stairs that would kill the average guy, and some of the dives over railings or bannisters would win in the Olympics."

It is the eye of long experience which is cast on "injuries"—a basically jaundiced eye in suspicious cases, and one shared by the hotel manager, the house doc and, most cynical of all, the insurance investigators. The gamut is a tough one to run and most fakers know they're far more likely to be smelled out in hotels than in other places.

All physicians see death. Hotel physicians probably see more than their share of death, which often comes in strange ways.

At the Savoy Plaza in New York, a sheik from a Middle-Eastern nation occupied one entire floor with his entourage of wives, aides, secretaries, and flunkies. He dined exclusively in his suite with his private chef preparing all meals.

One evening the house doctor was summoned on emergency. The bearded ruler was choking on a piece of meat. It couldn't be dislodged. Only a tracheotomy could save him. When the doctor tried to use his scalpel to make the throat incision, the sheik's aides took the scalpel away and threw the doctor to the floor, threatening his life if he again tried to "cut the throat" of their leader. The sheik choked to death with the doctor held powerless.

There are many mystery-shrouded incidents in which a guest leaves a room blood-soaked, without ever calling a physician at all. The hotel always calls the house doctor and the police to report in case there has been foul play.

Usually these cases are those of would-be suicides who slash a wrist, or wrists, then change their mind and decide to live after all. Many doctors have tales of guests who apparently did just that; somehow stopped the bleeding on their own and made their way back to life without any help.

Only occasionally is the mystery of a blood-soaked room cleared up later. But the case of the Valiant Sailor was. He came back, months after his room was found a blood-smeared shambles, and explained . . . and even offered to pay for damages. He said he had left rapidly at the time as, being a regular Navy captain, he was afraid various laws he might have broken might have looked bad on his record—plus the fact he wasn't over-eager to have the Navy know his girl had damn near killed him with a toilet.

The good captain was five foot six. The lady love he smuggled in (this was at the Mayflower) was two inches taller and outweighed him by twenty pounds. They got rip-roaring drunk, among other things, and had a pretty hectic fist fight—the captain said that, at best, it was a draw. The captain quit fighting to go into the bathroom and throw up. The lady did not observe the time-out he called.

While he was on all fours throwing up into the com-mode, she slammed the toilet bowl seat and lid hard on the back of his head, smashing his mouth on the porcelain rim.

He bled all over the room during the rest of the fight.

"I sobered up enough to check out," he explained, "but it seemed useless to try to explain all that at the time—even if I could have talked with a mouthful of re-arranged teeth. You ever get hit with a toilet bowl?"

Keyhole authors have this report from a hotel doctor concerning a malady not unknown to doctors anywhere, but possibly more prevalent in hotels:

> This concerns a call well after midnight. The patient would only say she was suffering. I arrived to find her in what was obviously good shape. Excellent shape, as was apparent by the view offered in a flimsy negligee. She had a bucket of champagne on ice. I asked her the nature of her problem. Patting the bed, she suggested I sit down and she would show me. I explained that her complaint was a condition which could be as easily remedied by a layman as by a physician, and inquired as to why she had called specifically for a doctor. She said her understanding of the Hippocratic Oath was that a doctor never revealed a confidence. It took me a considerable length of time to explain the patient-doctor relationship.

Exactly what the good doctor means by that last sentence will never be known. Confidential, don't you know . . .

One young doctor who services a large hotel, in the medical sense of the word, said after a four-day national secretarial convention that being a physician in a hotel was occasionally like trying to be an intern in a harem. In both places it's the doctor who has to watch out for mouth-to-mouth resuscitation.

In any case, the house physician is in a highly desirable—again no pun intended—position for a young doctor just starting in practice because it does, indeed, give him varied practice and provides a steady income.

And it certainly teaches him to deal with the most widespread ailment in medical annals—hypochondria. In high-rate resort hotels, although certainly not confined to them, there are many wealthy folks whose greatest hobby is imagining sickness. The slightest creak—it may be arthritis or it may be a door hinge—or the first fancy of a palpitation and it's "Quick, the house doctor!"

"Rich people may not imagine more ailments than poor people," said a house doctor, "but they can afford to bore a doctor more often."

And the house physician doesn't have the protection of saying he doesn't make house calls. Every complaint must be investigated because the real troubles range from a scratch to a tumble down a stairwell, and range up to the specters of food poisoning or epidemic disease.

The house physician is usually not on the hotel's payroll except for services such as various immunization shots for the staff or for physical exams. Accident calls are usually paid by insurance. Guest calls are paid by the guest.

So when you feel hung over, or have need for solace or medication of any sort, feel free to call the doc—but don't expect it to be included in the daily rate.

House physician calls are sometimes of a non-medical nature which, while at first seem strange, make a certain sense when you stop to think about it.

A father who was staying at a large hotel with his teen-age boy called the house doctor one afternoon, and when he arrived took the doctor out in the hall and said:

"Go in there and tell my kid everything he should know about precautions against venereal disease, what to do if he gets venereal disease, how to insure that he won't get some poor gal pregnant, and how to act like a man about it if he does. I went through forty hells about all that when I was a kid, but no matter how I've tried I can't really sit down and explain it all to him. I'm going down to the bar and have a couple of drinks."

The doctor agreed, but asked why the father hadn't gotten the family physician to do it. The father said he had meant to, kept putting it off, but had made up his mind that very afternoon to get it over with. The father grinned:

"Junior and I spent three hours at the pool today trying to keep each other from noticing how we were both staring at the bikinis."

One young woman called the house doctor and asked him several questions about sex, explaining she had been ashamed to ask her family doctor. The house doctor answered all her questions. He asked her if she was getting married.

"No," she said, "I'm getting divorced. And I want to make sure I know what I'm doing next time."

At a North Carolina hotel, an excellent German chef named Kurt Hoenigsberg was boning a side of beef when the knife slipped and cut his hand badly. The house physician was called, but Hoenigsberg stood there and sewed up his own wound. "Germans don't like to waste money," he said. But his friends knew he had gone through medical school at Heidelberg, at his parents' insistence, but finally did what he really wanted to do—be a chef.

Guests have been known to smash knuckles when startled by a "burglar" in a darkened room—and hit the "intruder" with a roundhouse punch right in the mirror. One guest somehow sprained a wrist trying to get the cork out of a bottle of Scotch; threw it against the wall where it rebounded and blackened his eye; then stepped on the bottle and fell with a back-jarring thud, en route to the telephone. "Send up the house doctor," he moaned. "And, oh yeah, make sure he brings a corkscrew."

It's in the real emergency that a crack hotel staff becomes a special kind of task force. At the Wilton Hotel in Long Beach, Calif., a frantic mother called the manager to say her son had just called her—and had said he was going to kill himself by jumping from a window.

The manager raced to the front desk information rack. There was no one registered by the name. The switchboard operator—and good ones are a gem in any hotel —came up with total recall; ferreted from her memory the room number that had placed a call to Bakersfield.

She rang the room; no reply. The room clerk was sure the man hadn't left the room. The assistant manager grabbed the master key; the house officer raced after him and found the house physician and they all ran to the room. They just made it—the young man was already poised on the windowsill to jump, having already swallowed an entire bottle of sleeping pills, washing them down with a pint of whiskey. It was a fight to hold him. As the doctor started emergency treatment, the house officer called for oxygen equipment and an ambulance which had already been alerted by the operator. Stomach pumped, he barely pulled through.

Ten years later, well, calm, and happy, he sent his anniversary thanks back to the hotel.

When Earl Duffy was assistant manager in a Boston

The corpse, dramatically flung back on the bed,
gun hanging from one hand in the prescribed Perry
Mason manner, sat up and said, "What the hell
do you guys want?"

hotel, a man called his estranged wife and said he was going to shoot himself. There was the explosion of a shot. When Duffy got upstairs with the house officer and doctor and went into the room, the corpse—dramatically flung back on the bed, gun hanging from one hand in the prescribed Perry Mason manner—sat up and said, "What in the hell do you guys want?"

He said he was expecting his wife, cursed them all out for busting up his sympathy plot, and checked out of the hotel leaving a lobby full of profanity.

"Expecting his wife?" said Duffy. "Hell, as far as I know she never even called back to find when services would be held."

18

Architecture, Design and Decor

ALL YOU CAN EAT FOR $100.00

> (*Sign in a Texas hotel restaurant fre-*
> *quented by the oil-rich*)

Wigwams. Igloos. Castles out of Camelot, forts out of feudal days, emerald apparitions out of Oz. Harem guards for headwaiters, geisha girls to serve you. Spires that point to the sky or sprawling layouts that seem to cover half the county. A swimming pool in each room. Solariums for sun worshippers. Saunas to make a Finn leave his homeland.

Grand and gloriously unexpected, America's inns leap up in every shape and fashion, the architects free of inhibition, the designers not bound by mundane precedent— the birthing of a hotel, for pure wild fantastic imagination, can make an LSD trip look dull.

"The reasons you enjoy a particular hotel are many

and varied," said Morris Lapidus, the imaginative hotel architect whose design extremes have delighted or outraged more building-buffs than anybody else's in America. "The odds, however, are that the physical appearance has a lot to do with your trying the place the first time around. That's architecture. If you felt comfortable and relaxed once you were inside, that's decor. This isn't to minimize the single greatest charm of every hospitality establishment—the people who run it. But architecture and interior design do more to create atmosphere and warmth than any other physical factor."

And to prove it, his creations include New York City's Americana, Florida's Fontainebleau and Eden Roc, and others. Some hotel architects call him magnificent, others blanch in horror . . . it's a field where architecture is as individualistic as hotel architects themselves, and you can't get more individualistic than that. Nationwide.

For instance, it would take another book to describe the hotel world of Las Vegas alone; wild skyline of captured blocks of human imagination, sculptured into places like the Tropicana, Stardust, Sahara, Dunes, Sands, Caesar's Palace, and all the rest. If we ever *are* invaded by visitors from outer space, it's reasonably certain they will land at Las Vegas . . . anybody can tell that's where the action is. Good luck, Martians.

Across the nation, it's America's hotels that to a large part, whether you ever thought of it or not, contribute to that part of the American image which is hell-for-leather, go-for-broke, give-it-a-whirl young and decidedly unafraid.

The booming hotel-industry expansion since 1946 has brought extreme architecture, elaborate decor, way-out innovations, and beneath it all a shrewd knowledge of human nature which boils down to this: in an inn the guest is royalty; ergo, give royalty something to befit a king . . . simultaneously show a profit and meet, or beat, the competition.

The American hotel picture and tradition is young, a whippersnapper compared to the graybeard that is European tradition, but few will argue that the kid has more ideas than his old man. And the ability to make them work.

Given the perspective of time, hotel architectural students of the future may at some distant vantage point decide that American hotels passed the rest of the world in what may be looked back on as the bathtub era.

The Ritz in Barcelona had tubs described as long enough for a swimmer to take two strokes. At the Chabanais in Paris, there was a silver tub in which roués would lounge while girls scrubbed their backs, and lo, the tub would be filled with champagne. The Intourist and Metropol, two large motels in Moscow, have bathtubs which are eight-feet long—in the middle of the bathroom so the bather can slosh and soap up a mess, which drains down the floor. At the Hotel Miramare operated by Carlo Cinque in Positano, Italy, are glass tubs which have a view of the bay over the bather's toes—and over a tank of tropical fish at the end of the tub.

But—America, aha! Now, it can show you an inn with a swimming-pool tub, individual size, inside the room! A full nine by twelve feet, and each pool has its own hydro-massage unit! *Does Europe have tubs where the beauteous back-scrubber could get in with you and do a bit of the Australian crawl if so desired?* One has to say no. And where is this luxury? At the Ramada, in exotic Spokane, Wash.

Does Europe have tubs where the beauteous back-scrubber could get in with you and do a bit of the Australian crawl if so desired?

But let's take a sketchy look at some of the building designs. Not a representative look. Nothing, anymore, is representative of hotel architecture—and the breast-beaters who cry about creeping conformity on the American scene might note at least one small grain of comfort in:

The Christopher in Columbus, Ohio, is shaped like a silo—except the first few floors are parking ramps. The Flying Carpet Motor Inn in Chicago has a main building shaped like an eight-point star wheel, with a towering minaret complete with the muezzin's platform. (Midwestern Muezzins??) In Houston where John Mecom bought a tired old hotel named the Warwick and spent a reported thirteen million dollars fixing it up, the hotel became renowned as a storehouse of treasures: imported crystal chandeliers, Portuguese aurora marble floors, carved paneling from the Parisian palace of Prince Murat, and so on.

And the rate card of the Houston Warwick appeared like this in an advertisement some years back: RATES: *$9.50 to $250.00 a Day*

The Mission Inn in Riverside, Calif., is a faithful reproduction of an ancient Spanish Inn. Florida has a Swiss chalet. Joe Hart built a wild Chinese pagoda-ed motel called "The Castaways," and the Americana in New York is shaped like nothing so much as a boomerang, which financially, it certainly isn't.

The Erawan Garden Hotel in Palm Desert, Calif., is a mixture of Siamese, Chinese, and Thai architecture. And where is Camelot these days, with drawbridges, turrets, moats, and the works? At the Camelot Inn in Tulsa.

Polynesian design and decor is rampant, complete with fire dancers and Tahitian maidens. This is to say that all across the country hotels and motels have made the unexpected almost . . . well, expected.

It's not confined to large towns. Many small towns and hamlets, where the last big building news was dedication of the Acme Laundro-Mat, now take in their Middle America stride the domes, spires, or hanging gardens of the new motel right outside town. And meanwhile— back in the city—you get the revolving restaurant high above beautiful everywhere . . . and you can just about bet your credit cards that the next big hotel will be all out to make the others look dated.

On this theme it may suffice to say that this is the era when you find an oriental world of three hundred rooms of peaked roofs, a lakeside place called the "Tan-Tar-A," when you drive into—Osage Beach, Mo.

Much of the success of a hotel depends on how well the architect and designer do their jobs.

Certainly, the fact that a building is "different" or "creative" doesn't insure success. Just the opposite some- times; there have been impressive flopperoos caused by so-called art simply not working as a functioning opera- tion. The most staggeringly beautiful building is no good unless it can efficiently perform the service it was designed for.

And, certainly, many architects who designed hotels and motor inns during the boom in the late forties and early fifties had never before designed in the field and therefore knew nothing about it. All theory, not fact. A pretty dining room is no good if it turns out the kitchen is out behind the waterfall.

If these architects had only copied successful designs —at least until they got some clue to what they were doing—there might not have been so many architectural monstrosities. One large Philadelphia hotel was completed before it was discovered there *weren't enough elevators*. Rooms had to be ripped out. You would assume somebody would have thought of that . . .

Hotel counselors tell such horror stories. One prospective owner was ready to go ahead with a 20-floor hotel before he learned what the architect had done: the food receiving, preparation, and service areas were scattered over *eight floors*. The wasted time and labor guaranteed that the more food he sold, the faster he would go broke —even his hamburgers were losers the second they were ordered.

A hotel management counselor told *Keyhole,* and he rolled his eyes to the heavens as he said it: "A motel-hotel chain opened a large midwestern operation *without any refrigeration.*"

Horrible examples are literally countless. But a professional architect who really knows what makes a hotel tick can create jewels of mechanical proficiency, which directly affect the ratio of profits, and *also* please the eye esthetically. The workable rule is you can put up the Hanging Towers of Babylon right in downtown Muskogee if you wish . . . but make sure the plumbing works.

Another excellent way to ruin a hotel seems to be treasured by many short-sighted builders. They let their wives do the interior design. Beautiful. There's no quicker way to ruin an operation. You can have a great hotel idea, great space, great location, and put it up in a healthy economic market—and ruin it with inept design. Potential guests come in, take one look, and leave in a hurry. Designing or redesigning is not for amateurs, or managers, or your Aunt Tillie who does wonders with dyed burlap—and certainly not owners' or managers' wives.

The wives may even be *good*. But a designer, even a pro, who may be talented in residential work can be a complete disaster with a hotel.

Hotel design is several multiples removed from home decorating—particularly in such public areas as lobbies, hallways, and foyers.

The strength of colors, size of lamps, the pictures, decor pieces; all these must be more dominant yet not come on too strong; must, in short, fit together the right way. This is almost impossible to do without prior experience.

It's a highly specialized field with people in it like Henry End, Sam Davis of L. B. Herbst, Dorothy Draper (who is two men, neither named Dorothy nor Draper), Carleton Varney, Leon Hegwood, Marilyn Motto, Homer Shrewsbury, Bob Herzog, and other topnotchers. If the next hotel you walk into has a picture of the founder glaring at you from one wall and a stuffed elk looking down from the other, they didn't do it. The manager's brother-in-law did.

All of the architecture, the design, the decor, is, after all, part of a hard-nosed profit-and-loss business and it must work if the establishment is to survive. It was never put better than at the opening of the Golden Triangle Motor Hotel in Norfolk, Va.

This edifice is a glass and chrome high-rise dreamed up by a character straight out of Runyon, Herbie Glassman, a decidedly extroverted comedian-type, but a shrewd businessman and a wealthy one.

There were the dignitaries, the speeches, the color guard, the flag raising, the flapdoodle and hoopla, and then, as one of the owners, Herbie was introduced. It had to that point been all ooh-ing and ahh-ing about the design and decor, but what Herbie said follows:

"Ladies and gemmen, we're happy to have this big

investment in Norfolk and to become part of this wunnerful southern community. We are sure our investment will be profitable here in Norfolk."

There was applause from spectators, and a sigh of relief from those who knew Herbie best. Herbie, however, turned and took a last look at the beauty of this chrome creation, turned back to the mike and bellowed, "If it *ain't* profitable in Norfolk, you'll be able to see the flames all the way to Richmond."

Architecturally, hotels keep breaking ground. Or space. The respected architect William Tabler, who has designed among other buildings many Hilton hotels, says he has already developed plans for a Moon-Hilton. He described it in detail at a graduation ceremony at Cornell University's School of Hotel Administration. And in the famous sci-fi deepthink movie "2001" there were Howard Johnsons from here to Jupiter. And yet, it all goes right back to a version of Ogg, as stated in the "cosmetic architecture" philosophy of Morris Lapidus.

Once he said, "I've been accused of adding too many frills and flourishes. But I think human beings want to have fun, want to dress up the prosaic. With hotel architecture, I do exactly what the first caveman did who looked down into a clear stream, and saw his reflection. He got used to what he saw, after a while. It was OK; but it got a little too familiar. So what did he do? He got some red clay, daubed his face up wildly, and looked back. Now *that* was fun! And basically it's what I feel about hotel design."

Of course, the creative end of hotel inventiveness inevitably runs into the more literal mind of management, and always has; doubtless always will. And the conflict probably balances out to the benefit of all concerned. But

the difference in outlook has left this story, which deserves
reprinting in the author's own words.

The Miracle of Junk That Turned
into Treasure Overnight

By Morris Lapidus

A number of years ago, I was given the title of "The
Saint of Third Avenue." Third Avenue in Manhattan is
the heart of the antique market of the United States. It
probably has more shops selling antiques from the entire
world than any other street in any other city.

Here will be found everything from a Hittite bronze
spearhead to delicately leaded lamp shades from the Tif-
fany glass studios . . . elegant objets d'art vie with primitive objects from Africa and the ruins of the Mayans . . .
magnificent marble sculptures of heroic size . . . jade
carvings . . . Ming vases . . .

I earned the title of "The Saint of Third Avenue" when
I went shopping for the antiques and objets d'art for a
hotel I was designing in another city.

I went shopping on Third Avenue for statues, bronzes,
chandeliers, antique furniture and clocks. The present demand by decorators for antiques had not yet begun. The
decorators at that particular time had gone "modern" and
the antique market was in the doldrums. I was able to buy
beautiful antiques for a song. Marbles and bronzes with
the signatures of 18th and 19th century sculptors were
bought by me for a tenth or twentieth of what they would
bring in today's market. I was having a ball—and my
client was getting treasures of art and antiquity at a
tremendous bargain.

My client and his wife had gotten culture in a big way.

They wanted their hotel to breathe "art" and "luxury." I was using the antiques in my decorative scheme to enhance a contemporary interior that I had designed for the hotel's lobbies and public spaces.

As I shopped, I was literally pulled off the street into the stores by dealers, to examine their wares. Word had gotten around that Lapidus was in the market buying art, furniture, statuary and antiques . . .

I directed that my purchases be held until the time came to ship the entire cargo of art and beauty to the distant hotel. It was then carefully crated and sent to the distant city by van.

I was in my New York office when the cargo arrived at the almost completed hotel, and the owner furiously called long distance.

Without any preliminaries he shouted, "There is a trailer load of junk in front of the hotel!"

I was so upset it took me a little time to realize he was referring to the shipment of antiques.

He simply refused to let the men unload the truck.

"My grandmother *threw out* better looking stuff than the junk you bought for me," he shouted.

I tried to reason with him and begged him to let the movers unload. He finally consented after I assured him I would pay for reloading and shipping all the "junk" back to New York. This was agreeable to him just as long as I could assure him that he would not be "blowing a bundle." I promised I would take a plane that night to his city, rather than argue over the phone.

That afternoon, and en route that night, I kept going over again and again in my mind what arguments I would use to convince my client that what he called junk would be a tremendous asset to his elegant hotel.

I carried on an all-night debate with myself, trying first one attack, then another.

I arrived at the hotel about midmorning. I was all ready with my most persuasive arguments.

My client was waiting for me in the lobby.

Before I could say a word, he put his arm around my shoulder and said, "Morris, I'm sorry I made you make the trip. Don't you think I know the value of the beautiful treasures that you had delivered? Yesterday, I just wasn't myself."

I was speechless.

Yesterday, "junk." Today, "treasures."

It took me a few days to piece the story together. I finally found out what had happened. As the truck was being unloaded, my client, far from the silent type, was giving vent to his feelings in the nearly completed lobby.

As each piece of "junk" was brought in he pointed to it and in a loud voice let the world at large—the mechanics, painters and hotel employees—know in detail what he thought of his eccentric architect.

The entire van load was deposited in a jumbled mass in the middle of the huge lobby. He told the job superintendent to let the men work around it, because the whole mess would be out of there *the very next day*.

That night my client and his wife brought a charming couple to the hotel for dinner. They were well-traveled, cultured people. When they came to the unbelievable stack of marbles, bronzes and statuary, they gasped in wonder, "This is a treasure trove of the most beautiful things we have ever seen in one place outside of a museum . . ."

They were ecstatic and couldn't stop admiring.

My client said nothing.

But early the next morning, before my arrival, I learned, my client came in to find:

Marble busts being used for sawhorses.

Statues as resting places for cigar butts.

Beautifully carved and polished art works being used by plumbers for work benches.

My client exploded: "YOU IGNORANT IDIOTS! DON'T YOU KNOW THESE ARE ART TREASURES?"

Yesterday, junk; today, treasures—and of course the

workmen were confused. He instructed them to build an enclosure around this great treasure and post a 24-hour guard.

It was shortly after that I arrived.

My profession has never grown dull.

19

The Bust Trusters Go to Hotel Land

One hundred and twenty Playboy bunnies (Count 'Em,
240!) live, work, and wiggle at the remarkable Playboy
Club-Hotel at Lake Geneva, Wis. They reside in a dorm
somewhere on the spacious grounds. Members of the
Chicago Bears football team, while checked into the resort, were aware of this.

The knowledge had a tendency to prey on the minds

of the footballers. So, late one night, a carload of these stalwarts set out to find the bunnies.

They drove. And drove. Ever seeking, in the dark. But the resort encompasses one thousand acres.

In the dark, the driver made one last wrong turn. No road. The front wheels hung over a ditch and the engine stalled. Security guards arrived, shone flashlights on the seekers.

"Have you seen 120 chicks with cute little tails around here?" asked the driver.

"Actually," said a security man, "you're trying to drive up the ski slope."

"Goddamnit!" growled a backseat Bear, glaring at the driver. "That's what we get for letting a quarterback drive."

Bunnies 120—Chicago Bears 0.

In fairness, however, any bunny hutch is a hard place to score—and in Lake Geneva it's even hard to find.

"The road to the bunny dorm is marked only with a sign saying 'Employees Entrance,' " said Lee Gottlieb, a Playboy vice-president. "In certain cases it doesn't pay to advertise."

But, oh, in other cases it does. And the vast Playboy empire went into the hotel business with enough hoopla to satisfy Barnum. And whatever guardian angel guides Hugh Hefner on his careening but cool trajectory along life's bobsled run has done it again. Hefner and his key executives—what a Chicago newspaper called the Bust Trust—have triumphed in the resort business, an alluring but often deadly vehicle which has left more bankrupt-bleached bones behind it than did the Conestoga wagon.

And how Playboy hotels have gone after and gotten

not only the swinging set but the family trade is a study in mysterious duality which will drive commonsense-seeming logic right up the wall. (And in Playboy hotels, even the wall has wall-to-wall carpeting. In burnt orange.)

"A *Playboy* hotel?" muttered Middle America, at first. "Why, isn't that the name of that shocking magazine with the s*xy pictures?"

You bet your last G-string it is, Aunt Clara. And sexier than ever, too. The parent—if you will excuse the expression—organization is built on a philosophy that was antibra before Women's Lib realized bras were repressive. And one of the strangest (and until now unreported) stories in America is how Playboy is hauling the PTA-type trade by the droves into its decidedly unusual resort hotels. What's Somewhat-Upper Middle America doing in a place like this? Having a blast, that's what, from Jamaica to New Jersey.

Hefner has tapped the greatest natural resource outside nudity: puritanical schizophrenia. This is one of our most revered institutions. Nowhere has it been more concisely exemplified—at least to a *Keyhole* author—than on a warm Chicago evening in August 1971.

A new Italian restaurant was being opened at the Playboy Towers hotel in Chicago. Top Playboy executives and companions were gathered for a preview and a little pasta and vino. The lobby was writhing with girls in hot pants; girls a regiment of Foreign Legion could never forget. A bunny stood by a huge wine cask, meditating; occasionally flicking her tail.

By the shapely smiling bunny stood a somber monk in flowing robes. Their life styles, to the writer, seemed to clash; the bunny's mini-mini, the holy man's maxi-maxi.

And it was the monk who was passing out wine to all.

Playboy's attracting the family trade.

It seemed surrealistic. Why was this monk at the Playboy party?

Was he doing some special penance in an order given to celibacy? Was it to see if, surrounded by hot pants and bunnies, he would choke in the clutch? Was he taking his Eagle Monk test? What?

And a tourist lady in the lobby said to her goggle-eyed husband, "Do you suppose that is a real priest or friar or whatever he is, standing next to that girl?"

"Where?" said the husband, eyes riveted on the bunny.

"Let's get your father out of here, kids," said the lady, and, smiling, a study in togetherness, the couple and their two kids went toward the elevators and their rooms . . . in the Playboy Towers.

"Are you a real monk?" the writer asked the solemn man.

"I'm a Playboy waiter named Mario," he replied. "Want some wine?"

"You *are* a bunny?" the writer asked the girl.

"A bunny, yes," she said primly. "I am saving up to teach school."

Hubbub in the lobby! Hef was here! He disembarked from a long black Mercedes-Benz of the kind usually seen driving through the American Dream. His license number is HH 1340: his initials and the address of the fabled mansion on Dearborn, that legendary palace where faithful make-out artists are said to go when they die.

With him, among others, was Shel Silverstein, the wildly talented cartoonist, writer and lyricist. The crowd parted. The crowd was dressed up—Chicago mod, sharp Edwardian, and the wide necktie. But Shel had on his blue jeans and a faded shirt; even his beard was rumpled, and Hef had on bell-bottoms and a green pullover, open at the neck; dark shaggy hair down over the back of his collar. They looked like two ranch hands walking into a board meeting. To dress like that and avoid a vagrancy rap, you have to own the joint.

Hefner, reserved but friendly and deeply courteous, is unflappable. He moves easy, like Wyatt Earp. Chicago plays sophisticated—the habitués of the Playboy Towers do not bug him for autographs or anything so gauche. But, oh, they know Hugh Hefner is there!

Here he is, Hefner, the enigma, who owns the whole shebang. Completely unaffected, just like Elvis and the gang when they go to the skating rink—Hugh Hefner, no longer hauled into court on charges that Playboy's nudes (tsk!) have no clothes on, but now a one-man institution and a philosopher; dressed like a hitchhiker on the Interstate, yes, but owning the whole damn thing . . . the J. Paul Getty of the street people in appearance; the empire builder in fact. Who knows Hefner? Nobody, nobody at all, for he is one of a kind and only he truly knows how he does the rabbit trick, over and over and over. And makes it work each time.

"Looks good," he says of the party to one of his key executives, Arnold Morton. And Hef nods to Chicago lined three-deep at his bar; he smiles at Mario the Monk who dispenses his wine; he is friendly with the visiting writer and helpful—knowing he won't be understood anyhow—and when his strolling Italian singer wants a picture taken shaking his hand, why Hef has his photographer take several. He sits at his table with his friends and the artists he likes, and when, later, the vast black Mercedes-Benz pulls away down Walton and into Michigan, past the great towers of Hugh Hefner which point the Chicago sky, a no-limit sky, he is relaxed against the luxurious cushion. As he rides along the streets of Chicago the buzz behind him says *that's Hefner, that's Hefner, that's Hefner* . . .

"What did you know about the hotel business," he was once asked, "when you started?"

"Very little," he said.

(Kemmons, meet Hugh—the other rabbit trick.)

One is inclined to stop the other questions stillborn and not ask how he runs hotels and swank resorts when he never had a clue about the hotel business. One remembers that he had never published a magazine before, either . . .

And the trap of "explaining Hefner" is not for a hotel book; let more in-depth scribes continue to fail at that. It remained for a Playboy doorman to tell us all we need to know, and far more than we've read in all the background articles.

The doorman's name is Casey. He has been a doorman twenty-four years and has never driven a car. He says, "Mr. Hefner has got to be the best boss I ever saw, you know? He never comes near the damn place. I've seen him maybe six, eight times. That's all. So I know things got to be running smooth."

Casey points his finger, without looking up, at the spire of the Playboy building.

"All those offices full of people working for him," said Casey admiringly, "and he's so organized he can stay at home. I admire that in a man. Hefner's got his philosophy, I got my philosophy—and we see eye to eye. The guy who can make a hard job look easy, that's the guy who knows what he's doing."

He unsnarled two delivery trucks; outshouted a cab-driver good-naturedly; joshed with several girl-gawking boy scouts from Idaho; appreciatively eyed the girls in hot pants going in and out of the Playboy building; stood there beneath the large Playboy rabbits painted on the building's facade, dodging hard hats bringing in lumber in the incessant remodeling. The entrance to the Playboy building is one of Chicago's greatest shows. Casey, the doorman who won't drive, is known to Playboy people who speak of his "Irish wit and charm."

Charm and wit he has aplenty, yes, but it gives an out-of-towner a certain satisfaction to break a scoop to the land of the Rabbit Trick.

Casey's last name is Stryganek. *Nothing* at Playboy is easy to explain.

What is the fascination of the rabbit emblem?

"All I know is we've found out that people will swipe *anything* with that rabbit printed on it," said one executive, who told of the Fancy French Phone.

It was in the VIP room of Playboy Towers, an ornate French phone with the rabbit emblem. A highly respectable dowager, there for a business conference, was seen literally jerking it from the wall—and tucking it into her purse. The assistant manager, who saw her do it and head for the elevator, called downstairs and gave quick instructions.

As she came out of the elevator, the clerk called her and said courteously, "Madam, there is a call for you. Would you care to take it on the house phone or the one in your purse?"

Her mouth flew open, she gulped, opened her purse, handed the clerk the phone and fled.

In many instances, Playboy hotels shrug off "theft". The ashtrays bearing the rabbit emblem are taken as a matter of course. But the expensive towels bear no rabbit. Maids are often called for more envelopes of bath-oil beads. (with the rabbit emblem). But the expensive bedspreads are leather and rabbit-less, and you would need an extra suitcase to swipe one. The most swiped item is the "Do Not Disturb" sign.

The "Do Not Disturb" side shows a drawing of a nude young lady flat on her back and kicking her heels enthusiastically in the air.

The "Please Make Up Room" side shows her seated, much more demurely. She looks less restless.

At Lake Geneva, flag thefts were running into important money. The Playboy rabbit flags—three of them— are huge, each fluttering on a separate staff high above the resort entrance. They were, somehow, stolen with regularity and at considerable expense. (The expense was increased by the fact that flag thieves had a way of climbing up and swaying back and forth until they bent the metal pole.)

It presented a considerable dilemma until one of the security guards, an ex-cop from Chicago, came up with the solution. Instead of assigning a full-time guard to watch three rabbit flags, he had a kid shimmy up the poles once a day to grease them. No flag thefts since.

Bunny emblems are everywhere.

When Mayor Edward Snook of McAfee, New Jersey, allowed the city fire department to put the bunny emblem on its red American LaFrance fire truck—the town is near Playboy's Great Gorge Club-Hotel—it prompted a puzzled letter from a man named A. K. Weiner.

"I have seen what appears to be a Playboy fire truck," he wrote. "Am I losing my mind? Or has Playboy decided to put out fires instead of kindling them?"

So far the bunny-emblem fire truck hasn't been stolen, but, souvenir hunters being what they are, it's not past possibility.

This bunny-emblem thing, on a basic business level, is about as playful as—oh, let's say a Holiday Inn sign, and at least as relentlessly promoted, although in the strange duality of Playboyland even reporters who should know better must repeatedly wrench themselves back to that fact. Playboy's hotels, when you get right down to it, *started* in part from a picture of a rabbit; a fact the organization's top hotel executive will make clear in the next couple of pages. (Although we have the strong hunch that Kemmons Wilson of Holiday Inns and Hugh M. Hefner would hit it off great, we resist any temptation to draw comparison of similarities. After all, Hugh was raised Methodist; Kemmons, Presbyterian. That they *both* end up with an inexplicable rabbit trick we will put down to a whim of the Gods of Laughter.)

This rabbit may be the most recognized ad since the barber pole. Bristol, England, delightfully noted in the media that a detour sign's map on the outskirts of town looks exactly like the Playboy rabbit. Whee!

If you wish to learn about advertising, consider that the emblem is sold in decal-packs for a buck, and that Playboy merchandises rabbit garment bags, rabbit golf balls, rabbit chopping blocks, rabbit cheese knives, rabbit everythings—and that Hef's airplane, like Hef himself an effective advertisement, cost $5,500,000 and is called —what else —"The Big Bunny."

Madness in this Methodist? Yeah, sure. He's as wild

and untrammeled as the New York Stock Exchange. A chain of palatial hotels, resorts, and clubs built on a rabbit emblem? Built, in turn, in the early fifties on a basic mammary gland display, followed in 1971 by national acceptance of pictures of fuzzy bunnies? (That is when pubic hair went public in *Playboy,* seemingly with no objection except perhaps from airbrush artists thrown out of work.) None of those happenings indicate anything but a very keen, bold business awareness—and intuition —at work.

Well, there is this about Hefner. It makes little difference if he is so complicated nobody follows his reasoning or so simplistic he blinds lesser minds with the obvious. He certainly does get to the bottom of things. (We know, but to say "to the heart of the matter" is just as bad.)

He was regarded at first by self-styled moralists as some kind of a pornographer, but they all seem to have been drowned out after he grossed the first few thousand million, or whatever it comes to. From tempter to tycoon, this hip-cool lad, this literate ageless scholar; nothing dictates mores like success. The part we like is how he put the pictures of all those naked ladies in the magazine and, almost in passing, now rents rooms to the once-outraged Decency Freaks. It's somehow appropriate that he turned to the strange world of hotels, no stranger itself, that world, to sharp clefts in the human outlook.

There's a bunny on the jet's rudder, too. For sure, some airplane. "The most mind-boggling display of sensual opulence ever assembled in a flying machine," googooed a typical press report from, Midwestern Muezzins help us all, a hardened Chicago *Sun-Times* man. And the story told of how Hefner's "already famous elliptical bed in the sky is upholstered in black Himalayan goat leather and covered with a spread of Tasmanian opposum pelts . . . in the photos, at right, dancers swing in the discotheque area . . . at left, Hefner talks with "jet bunnies" . . . center, members of the press relax on hassocks at the liquor dispensers . . . " (lots and *lots* of photos.)

Uh huh. And the usually staid *Chicago Tribune* said, "What a Way to Go!"

Go where? Why, to exotic lands, like Baltimore and Philadelphia, where the local burghers enjoy being served by curvy-cheeked, breast-billowing, tender-thighed bunnies.

For with seventeen clubs and five huge hotels the rabbit empire is multiplying like . . .

. . . is expanding rapidly.

And—once more, please, grasp the point—it was done on this beautiful duality, this truly schizoid puritanical outlook. Let's mull over another example: Bunnies in Playboy operations in Chicago, Lake Geneva, and Los Angeles "hutches" had a little contest "to see how observant keyholders were." (This is from *"VIP,"* Playboy's magazine to keyholders, which has a wide-eyed innocent style about the damndest things—sort of as if the Casbah beat was being covered by Martha Mitchell.)

What was the contest? To see how many customers recognized the working bunnies as former "Playmates." In short, how many guys who had seen pictures of them naked would know them with some semblance of clothing on? The quotes are great.

An ex-Playmate named Cynthia Hall said, "Many people . . . asked me how I liked my visit to Dartmouth that was mentioned in the story." (See how chatty it all is?)

Lieko English said, "Most people seem surprised to see me in Chicago . . . "

And Avis Miller (also a "jet bunny") reported, "It's funny—not many keyholders connect me with the Playmate. But you always have that not-too-original fellow who does, and asks me if the staples hurt."

(This is from the ubiquitous story where the guy says, "Hm. I always thought women had staples in their navels.")

And Gwen Wong said a customer looked at her and blurted, "Hey, I have your picture in my golf locker!"

So it goes. You have this mind-bending picture of lusciousness falling out of her clothes, and the caption says, "She admires Rod McKuen—'for his soul'—and appreciates people with a sense of humor."

Surely, Hugh H. Hefner *must* have a sense of humor.

And what of the hotels the bunnies built? The bunnies —invented by an enigmatic young capitalist with the ability to choose executive talent so absolutely right that even the doorman is impressed . . .

He hired the right men, Hef did.

Arnold J. Morton came out of the 83rd Infantry after World War II, operated Chicago key clubs, applied knowledge about business and restaurants learned from his restaurant-family background and college, managed the Chicago Playboy Club after going with Hefner, and now sits in the Playboy building as director of Playboy Enterprises and says:

"Hotels? We backed in. Playboy, the name, meant and means entertainment. We did it the opposite way; we had the potential guests . . . keyholders . . . so we decided to go into the hotel business."

He makes it all sound easy, somehow. As one of the

firm's half-dozen or so top men—the real Bust Trusters —he can back off enough to be detached and casual about staggering statistics. For instance, he says:

"We weren't—aren't, really—thinking in terms of a huge hotel empire. Seven or eight hotels grossing a hundred million or so, that's about all we have in mind. But, then, who knows? This total-living concept of resort fascinates us . . . resorts an hour or two from a jammed metropolis, that's turning out to be really something."

Idly, he flips through designs for "total living"— which means *everything* is at the resort—and recalls when the "Jamaica World"—the Playboy Club-Hotel on, what else, Bunny Bay in Ocho Rios was just another distressed hotel with eighteen percent occupancy when Playboy took it over. Occupancy of ninety-seven percent in 1971 with champagne breakfasts, parrots, crocodile hunts; anything to make folks happy.)

There is the Lake Geneva World, with everything including its own airport. The Great Gorge World in New Jersey, not too far from Manhattan. All the others . . . and then, the plans for Los Angeles; the trips to Spain; the good news from London where Victor Lownes III, himself seemingly invented for a Playboy layout, runs matters with that mixture of cool flamboyance and computerized business sense which permeates the big Money Machine.

Morton's eyes light up more over the crack team of convention salesmen he has assembled than they do over bunnies and window dressing. Not basically a hotelman, he can spot talent in hotelmen—and in those mysterious and complex beings called convention salesmen. Where does he get good people?

"Three ways," he said. "Train 'em, buy 'em, and pirate 'em. Where else?" Affable, quick with decisions, unhurried, down-to-earth, Arnold Morton doesn't talk in the glowing terms of the keyholder magazine, *VIP*, which oohs:

> Playboy isn't stopping here. Hotel scouts are searching the world over for new sites, When Hugh Hefner, aboard the Big Bunny, toured Europe and Africa he visited several prospective locations for new Playboy resorts: Spain, Morocco, and Great Britain. Also under consideration are Mexico and various Caribbean islands.
>
> It used to be said that the sun never set on the British Empire; before long, keyholders may be able to make the same boast about the territories over which the rabbit banner flies.

Morton didn't refer to the "bunny empire" a single time. He just builds it.

Staid? Seemingly.

But Morton is the guy who was going to buy the Queen Mary for Playboy, but decided to hold off a little while on floating gambling casinos.

"We're interested more in apartment buildings for singles and young marrieds," he said. "You know, there's a lot to this room-renting business."

—At Lake Geneva a potential trapshooter (total living includes a firing range, of course) asked if skeet were among the birds becoming extinct; he didn't want to upset the ecology.

—At Miami's Playboy Plaza, lady guests are encouraged to enter the tiniest bikini contest.

—Club prizefighting—part of total living—went over

well at the Wisconsin convention center; a bunny parades around the fight ring holding up round-number placards between rounds. She also bears printed decision news of such in-trade terms as TKO. Total living brings you quotes like this from fighter Ernie Terrell: "And something else that pleases me is that you don't hear the kind of gutter language associated with the Madison Square Garden type of event." (Fighter George Foreman said he was pleased by "no drafty smelly locker rooms" and that "I had my prefight rubdown in a round bed.")

—Jamaica guests who wish to go crocodile hunting have four guides made available to them to increase their probability of getting back. Total living!

—Available for charter among the seagoing vessels listed by Playboy Limousine, Inc., is John Wayne's 140-foot converted air-sea rescue ship. It is named the Wild Goose. (Thatsa old total living, Duke, boy! Move out!)

—In London, cocktails, hors d'oeuvres, soup, fish, and sherbet are served *before* the main course. Bunnies keep an eye on guests who get up to leave after the sherbet and inform them dinner isn't even there yet. At Lake Geneva, a huge "Hunt Breakfast" is served. Nobody ever seems to ask what is being hunted. (It ain't the wild, wary skeet. It's total living, good buddy.)

—Are you getting the pitch about total living?

Probably not, not like Hugh, anyhow.

When Hugh and his girlfriend, Barbi Benton, took a little vacation—pardon the deviation from hotels; you've *got* to know about total living—they left the villa in Spain and after a little moonlight gondola-ing in Venice cruised around the Greek islands awhile before stopping in Paris, then later for some brew and schnapps in a Bavarian beer garden. Then they went over to Rome; thence to Africa. (Hugh watched—while in Paris—the

Club Lido nudie show. Talk about your busman's holiday!)

Well, in Africa they looked at elephants and went to Mt. Kenya, and Hugh and Barbi had their pictures taken with some Watusi warriors. Hugh came out against animal slaughter and for synthetic fur.

One press report noted that, while in Athens, Hugh and Barbi visited "one of the most typically Greek sections in town." Evidently Hugh does something to the press worldwide. Get this next sentence: "From the untamed splendors of Africa, the guests repaired to the Athens Hilton."

None of this is the high point.

The high point was not even in Tangier ("beautiful city of intrigue") but in Rabat, of all places. His Majesty King Hassan II of Morocco, who is no slouch at pitching a wingding, pitched one for Hef.

Here is the high point:

"It was a scene straight out of the Arabian Nights," reported John Dante, field service manager for Playboy Clubs International. "There were acres of Persian carpets covering the beach as far as you could see . . .

"Great piles of cushions were heaped up in huge tapestry-lined tents.

"There must have been forty or fifty dancers, entertaining for five or six hours, and all the while, a mounted guard of seventy-five to one hundred Berber horsemen, each with a long rifle, its barrel filigreed with silver, kept charging up and down the beach, firing tracer bullets into the sky . . . "

Now *that's* total living.

Withal, it's not—not exactly—what an executive like Arnold J. Morton means when he says total living. He means a place in the country but near the city where a guy, a gal, or a family can get away from it all for awhile and check into a resort where all services are provided. It sounds so obvious. But how many do you know of?

It sounds obvious, also, to take the cumbersome desk out of hotel rooms and put the drawer space in the bedside tables which have to be there anyhow. But it hadn't been done until Morton approved the design to do it. And Hefner, like any other businessman—not that all things considered he *is* like any other businessman— knows his formula. Show a profit on a service people want.

What Playboy hotels want is convention business and what can only be called family approval. They certainly are getting both. The convention success is understandable.

"But how are you getting family-trade approval of a chain based, starkly, on a breast-and-behind emblem?" The question was put in various forms, all up and down the Playboy Chain of Command.

The answers ranged from oversimplistic—"we provide such excellent service"—to near psychiatric jargon—"puritanical schizophrenia"—to frank puzzlement. ("Hell," said one executive, "I've never even figured out if I should hide *Playboy* magazine from my teen-age son or not.")

We have a partial answer; one cruel truth.

The American wife, intuitively, has reached a highly accurate conclusion. Her husband's philandering inclination, the urge to make firm new friendships with other ladies, has less chance for success in Bunnyland than in lots of more prosaic-seeming places.

It's a look-don't-touch world. And some of the most subtle minds in Hotel Land are working day and night to keep old John Q. Hopeful pure as the driven snow. At least on the premises.

Q: Do you know why? Why with bare-tailed bunnies here and bare-topped pictures there and bare-everywhere girls in the floor show . . . why Hopeful Harry is left with his whining appetites as confused as those of a near-sighted dog in a smokehouse?

A: *Because, and quite naturally, a hotel with scantily-clad or unclad girls all over the place is the last one in the world to allow hanky-panky.*

It would reflect badly on the image.

It remains a peculiar image; confusing to the bemused observer caught up in our transitional era, the 20-year period from censoring the word "virgin" on America's movie screens to nearly forgetting what the word means.

Walk into the Playboy Plaza.

Six beautifully lighted pictures of nudes on the wall. In the pool area, barefoot bikinis with cheeks of tan. In the nightclub act, Minsky's burlesque with strippers worthy of the name.

And you haven't even been upstairs yet . . .

Upstairs?

Upstairs—hundreds of square dancers, from the nation over, in assembly gathered, hoop skirts and overalls, Mom and Pop from Kansas City . . . having a ball at the Playboy Plaza, twirl your girl and away we go!

Just how sinful can you get when they're all hollering do-se-do at the Playboy Plaza?

"Turn and roll away, now sashay!" shouts the caller, and Middle America, with the middles to prove it, leaps about, "Boys, run on around that girl, slide! Circulate! Back around and promenade, a trip around and a do-se-do!"

. . . Do-se-do . . .

Where now, houris of lustful dreams? Where the blithe-some bikinis?, the sex objects when you need them? What gives here with the git-fiddle, as American Gothic meets Black Silk Stockings and French Perfume?

Where are the bunnies of our wishful hopes?

Well, two of them are square dancing with somebody's kindly uncle. The rest are downstairs being trained by Mother.

There is a "Bunny Mother" at every Playboy operation.

Beverly Russell is bunny mother at the Playboy Plaza. That's really what they're called. Bunny mothers.

"Bunny mother," says Beverly, when she answers the phone. She has seventy bunnies to mother. She is some young lady; tall, lovely, intuitive, and with a great sense of humor. She's been a bunny mother for six years; was a Patricia Stevens model before that. She looks a lot more like a bunny than a mother.

She is dead serious about her job. The job of bunny mother is passing strange, when one stops to think about it—but, somehow, when you're *around* Playboy people you're inclined to forget the duality of it all. But the bunny duality is the mystery and, as they say, the story: here is a hotel empire which puts beauties in crotch-hugging bust-revealing scanties, trains them not to be sexy, and comes up accepted, somehow; only a step removed from a girl scout cookie sale, in the wholesome-ness area.

"How do you people *do* that?" Beverly was asked. "*Why* is the family-trade image booming so? What do those square-dancing matrons upstairs think when the bunnies bounce by? Do you understand this?"

Her answer, after long discussion, came up in the

our-girls-are-good-girls classification. And their girls
doubtless *are* good girls, but it is not the answer; not
really.

And Beverly was too diplomatic to say that explaining
all this was hardly her job. Her job is to pick bunnies,
train them and supervise them for the best possible service. She is highly skillful at doing this.

There is a lot of interest shown in bunnies and their
place in the scheme of things. Beverly, as part of her job,
speaks to such upstanding groups as Kiwanians and
Lions and has wall plaques from them for this service.

"Do civic leaders ever make passes at a bunny mother?" she was asked.

"Why, isn't that nice of you?" she beamed. See? She's
a diplomat. She didn't answer.

Some sidelights on bunnies are needed to explain Playboy hotels. All hotels are basically alike, of course—the
conventioneers changing room numbers, the guests who
hide money and forget where, all the strange things—
but Playboy hotels *train* temptresses to be wholesome,
and in the institution of the bunny Playboy hotels are
different. They also exemplify America's changing mores,
at least as applied to the trade name Playboy.

"Only two or three years ago we would advertise for
bunny applicants and I would sit in the office all day
with only two or three girls coming in," said Beverly,
"and back then you could tell *they* were a little jumpy
about it all. Goodness knows what they thought—they
had all heard the silly rumors about what a girl has to do
to be a bunny."

Now she is overwhelmed with applicants.

"Sometimes I interview as many as fifty girls without
finding a bunny I want," she said. "The job has taken on

more glamor and lost *all* the ridiculous lurid aspects it used to have."

She showed a typical letter which started:

> Dear Miss Russell:
>   I am telling you the truth when I say I have wanted to be a bunny since I was twelve years old, and—

She showed pictures of the applicants who had already been in that day. If they get past the verbal interview, they're asked to pose in a bunny suit. All rejections are gentle and painless—the girls now know competition is terrific and everybody can't get a job.

"That really pleases me, not ever having to make a direct turndown," said Beverly, who has a lot of natural compassion and never forgets her own terrible embarrassment on her first job. Never herself a bunny—most bunny mothers have been—she was a Patricia Stevens model and her first assignment was a nightmare.

"I walked out past the buyers, tripped, and fell flat," she said, still wincing.

A firm rule: unmarried girls living with their family *have* to prove that their father and mother know about their bunny ambitions.

It has happened that an occasional irate father has raised a storm after finding out his daughter's chosen career. The bunny mother said, "Why, when I took the job as bunny mother, my own father—I grew up on a farm in Kansas—demanded to know if I had to wear one of those terrible little suits. I told him there weren't any bunny mother suits. He was still suspicious . . . but now he's proud of my job and really likes the girls."

Does she lose many bunnies to matrimony? She

laughed. "Everybody wonders that. Nobody seems to know we don't care if a bunny is married when we hire her or gets married later. Probably a third of all bunnies are already married, and many have children."

Hm. The ignorant bliss was better.

Other notes: a girl using only mild profanity during the job interview is mentally rejected right at that point. Too much makeup is a demerit. So is slouching. Trying too hard to be a sexpot is liable to rule out a prospective bunny. And, of course, so does the general demeanor of the girl who lets it be known that she would do *just anything* to get the job. And Beverly Russell is hard to fool —a good bunny mother has to have more intuition than most people.

"I *do* get fooled, occasionally," she admitted, "but not for reasons having to do with, ah, deportment. Not long ago I chose a girl who was beautiful, cultured, and had a college degree, as many of the girls do. I had to let her go—she couldn't add. She could talk to you about English literature, but give her a check with two martinis to total and she was completey, utterly baffled."

No matter how beautiful otherwise, a girl can't exude the wrong kind of come-on sex but, and this is trickier, she can't look too innocent.

"Some beautiful girls with wonderful figures just look *too innocent* when they get in a bunny costume," Beverly said. "This may be hard to explain to a man. Do you understand?"

The writer replied, "Recently on the beach I was staring with great interest at the rear view of a girl in a bikini. Magnificent. She turned. She looked somehow like a girl scout, despite everything else. I did not know whether to be fatherly or lecherous."

"You understand," smiled Miss Russell. "And then,

we infrequently get a girl who just can't stand the pressure of customers staring at her.

"Most girls—all of them actually—are nervous, at first, when they go on the floor to serve drinks. One week of the training period is given over to wearing the suit only in the training area—they get accustomed to it enough to get through the first couple of days in public, then everything gets to be O.K. But one trainee—she was a school teacher who had quit teaching so she could be a bunny long enough to save up enough money to get her master's degree . . . this girl, after all the training, served *one* drink.

"She took the order, got the drink from the bar, walked across the room, put the drink *and* tray in front of the customer, and disappeared. She went downstairs to change. I never saw her again."

Beverly said, "The nervousness is helped by assurances, and mirrors, showing that the costume fits properly around the ah, well, you can imagine. And new girls often have the feeling they have fallen out of the top part. They keep looking down. The costume pushes up, you know—well, you don't know—well, I guess you do know—"

"I know, I know."

" . . . so it *feels* like one might be exposed."

"*Do* girls ever fall out at the top?"

"Once in a while," she said.

"Can they tell when they have fallen out?"

"Not always," admitted Miss Russell. "Of course, somebody usually notices."

"Yes."

A bunny mother hates to fire a girl for dating a customer but the rule is absolutely inflexible.

"It may really be true love," said Beverly. "Sometimes

it is—a girl meets her dream prince and takes the chance of dating him. But, if we find out . . . she's discharged.

Beverly Russell, then, is one reason the institution called Playboy has bypassed or at least largely silenced the most strident and straitlaced forces. These forces, in fact, unable to defeat all this revealed, shapely but pure-minded outlook have more or less joined it.

Bunnies on the sundeck, square dances on the mezzanine! Flick that pretty cotton-tail and a do-se-do! The mind bends in paradox.

What we have here in America is a sex-dream with a chaperone.

Miss Russell added, "When a bunny becomes a Playmate it has no effect one way or the other on her job. It neither helps her nor hurts her."

She walked across her office, wearing a very well-tailored pants suit, to get her cigarettes.

"Has a bunny *mother* ever been a Playmate?"

She said, "You are so complimentary."

She smiled dazzlingly. Hefner, this supervising chaperone needs a chaperone.

Paradox is everywhere in Playboy's empire.

SiSi Manix, a beautiful red-haired bunny with freckles, who looks like the typical girl next door, if you happen to live in Paradise, is a door-bunny at the Playboy Plaza. She stands at the main entrance and welcomes people. She was a journalism and advertising student in college. A writer recently stood behind her staring and testing his newfound technical knowledge about bunny costumes. (If a bunny costume does not fit exactly right around the upper thighs, a bunny's legs will go to sleep because the weight of the cottontail pulling on the rear tends to cut off circulation. Readers now have the benefit of a valuable tip: a reason for staring at bunnies—to make sure their legs aren't turning blue. SiSi's weren't.)

"Hi, there!" she said brightly, turning suddenly.

"Uh, Hi. I, uh, was just seeing if the circulation in your —actually, I wanted to ask your opinion on something. Playboy's image is changing with women, you know? Why do you think this is?"

SiSi laughed. "Changing? Maybe. Changed. No. You should see some of the ladies who come in with their husbands. I speak and the man smiles but the wife glares, sniffs, and won't even answer me sometimes. Sweeps right on by."

"I don't know what people thought about Playboy hotels; maybe that they were some kind of brothel," said Henri Lorenzi, the hotelman who runs all the Playboy hotels, shrugging, dismissing the question. "I do know it was a stupid notion then and disappearing now. Anyhow, I'm a hotelman, not a psychologist. I consider hotel work a profession. Look at the convention sheet—we're booming while others are dropping. Look here . . . we've got outfits like Prudential, John Hancock—what can be more conservative than that?"

'Why doesn't Playboy go after a Women's Liberation convention?"

Henri Lorenzi dropped his continental suavity for a moment, grinned, clapped his hand to his forehead and said, "You think we're foolish enough to tangle with *them?*"

Lorenzi is, indeed, a hotelman. His reputation in the trade is outstanding; son of a hotel family with great traditions in Europe, manager of big ones in various countries, an old-school, young-looking French-American who did his apprenticeships in every aspect of the business, he is now a key executive with Playboy and *the* hotel expert. He's the kind of hotelman who can handle purchasing for a chain with his left hand, know the profit on every hamburger, entertain royalty and while he's talking to the king notice the fray on the elevator carpet. Lorenzi is a pro in a field where old-school pros are becoming scarce.

He was working for Loew's when Hefner reached out and got him, only a couple of years ago; other executives said, off-the-record, that Lorenzi may be the only professional hotelman ever to come into a chain where he was the *only* professional hotelman. That's substantially true.

"Club managers were trying to be hotel managers," he said. "Good men in their own field, but it was a disaster."

He loves his profession. Professionally, he is saddened —and not even resigned—to what "progress" has done to hotel tradition. He is realistic about this age of cookie-cutter conformity, but he doesn't like it. He just does the best he can in it . . . and other hotel executives testify his best is the best there is.

"Listen," he said. "It is hard in this business to be one who *knows the difference.* I know what some great hotels were. I also know the daily rate would have to be—I am not kidding—at least $250.00 a day to give that kind of service now. Realistically, my job is to give the best and most pleasurable living for a reasonable rate—and that's what we'll do. And we're winning."

One mark of a certain breed of hotelman is the absolute inability to keep from recounting wild happenings in the hotel world. Lorenzi *tried* to steer clear of anecdotes; his desk-top phones were ringing wildly, people were in to see him from the Jamaica operation. It was a pressure-ridden time there in his Chicago offices. (On the thirteenth floor, which wouldn't have happened in the old days.)

But the anecdotes came anyhow.

When he was managing a hotel in the Dominican Republic a 21-member delegation from the French government came to see Trujillo.

Lorenzi explained to the local help that it was a European custom for guests to put shoes outside the door, for shining, at night.

He didn't run into the same kind of trouble recounted earlier in this book where, at the Mayflower, porters forgot to chalk room numbers on shoes and dignitaries had to plow through piles of shoes in the lobby.

"No," Lorenzi sighed. "That would have been far better. After I said these gentlemen would be leaving their shoes in the hall, they were picked up, all right—and never seen again. Every pair was stolen. If you ever try to deal with twenty-one hell-raising, barefooted Frenchmen with their shoes stolen, you will learn a bit about the hotel business."

He was managing a hotel in Paris when the naked baron chased the naked prince through the main dining room.

"I will not use their names," he said. "This would embarrass them."

What had happened? The basic cause of the acrimony is unknown. Suffice it that the prince had in some manner offended the baron.

"They came running down a long staircase, the naked baron right behind the naked prince and the baron was screaming, 'I'll kill him, I'll kill him!' and the prince was, as I recall it, not screaming . . . but saving his breath to run."

Around the lobby, through the dining room, back up the stairs, back down—when employees finally grabbed them and, trying to drape these worthies in tablecloths, herded them back upstairs.

It is the mark of a true hotelman that he would withhold names. One does not embarrass a naked prince and a naked baron.

"In Acapulco we had an educational convention," he said. "A great many deans. We also had a famous and beautiful movie star staying with us. That night she started screaming. One of the oldest deans—the dean of deans—had managed to break into her room and when the security people arrived was chasing her around the bedroom with his intent obvious."

Lorenzi, in the true French tradition, did not recall this with anger but with admiration.

"The old fellow was well into his seventies," said Lorenzi. "The house officer said the mystery to him was how he managed to break the lock. I told the house officer that this was not the most fascinating mystery . . . "

Lorenzi said softly, "I was just thinking. All good hotelmen are a little crazy. We have to be, I guess."

At that point he had been telling of the guest at Lake Geneva who brought a 14-piece band to his room with him from somewhere; slipped them in the sliding glass picture window-door, and began a concert at three in the morning. (The guest was annoyed at repressive regulations which said you can't have a 14-piece band in your rooms.)

Computerized and standardized business operations may bring a bit of factory sameness to hotel operations, yes—but it seems unlikely that guests will ever conform or be predictable.

One odd thing about Playboy hotels is that, with some exceptions, managerial people are a bit more reluctant than other hotelmen to tell anecdotes that happen in their own hotels if they think it will "reflect" on the hotel. They are *very* careful of what they consider the image.

Playboy, the magazine, colors every thought about Playboy, the hotel world.

As Arnold Morton put it, Playboy is a huge *entertainment* dynasty; hotels were more or less an afterthought, no matter how successful now.

To Lorenzi, hotels are everything and if Playboy also wants to put out a magazine or whatever, fine—but *he is a hotelman.*

"Sure, we're going after family trade and we're going after conventions and we're getting both," he said. "Look—here's a note where two waitresses—bunnies, I mean—were discharged in New York for dating customers."

He said, "My friend, how many other hotels do you know where waitresses get fired for even *dating* customers?"

(A letter to *VIP*)

FUN, FAMILY STYLE

My wife and I, our teen-age daughter and her girlfriend recently spent a relaxing and enjoyable weekend

at your Lake Geneva Club-Hotel. Although many keyholders might question taking the family to such a
swinging resort, I can assure them that the Club-Hotel
provides a wide diversity of entertainment and recreation, both day and night, for all members of the
family . . .

Live it up and take the kids along before they leave
the nest for good. Mother and Dad may even feel they've
narrowed the so-called generation gap!

(Signed by a guest from Des Plaines, Ill.)

Ah, yes. They grow up so soon, don't they?

"Personally," said Joseph Marotta, chief of security
at the Playboy Plaza, "I wouldn't be surprised to see
them make *women* Playboys. Keyholders, I mean—let
women be members. Why not? Women are catching on
that the word Playboy doesn't mean what they think.
Things are changing fast. Wives used to think we were
running some kind of cathouse, so help me—one of those
call girl services or something. We're not—you can take
my word for that."

Joseph Marotta has the kind of word you take immediately. He's debonair in his light blue suit and visiting-
businessman garb, but when he starts talking out comes
the direct-from-experience sound of what he is: a retired
career cop from New Jersey who now, as house security-
chief at a Miami Beach hotel, knows more than a bit
about the human race.

He had been pondering the reaction of a gent who had
insisted his wallet with seventy dollars in it had been
stolen along with his credit cards. This guest had gone
home to Ohio before Marotta finally found it—although

house officers had, as a matter of course, searched his room previously.

Marotta explained that some guests get more paranoid with every drink and hide valuables when they start to think about their plans: to get loaded in a strange town. (He recently found five hundred dollars for a "robbery victim" who had hidden it inside his pillowcase.)

"Finally found it after he left," said Marotta. "This guy froze his money worse than Nixon did. He hid his wallet *behind* the ice cube trays in his refrigerator. I called him up and told him we had found it there."

The diplomatic part was trying to talk around the fact that a now sternly-sober businessman might have had a drink or so which caused him to freeze his wallet.

"I was trying to ignore it," said Marotta, "which made it hard to tell this guy he hadn't lost seventy dollars . . . there were one hundred and thirty dollars in the wallet."

Marotta said he was all for equal rights for everybody but nobody should abuse them.

"One guest kept bringing in barroom pick-ups two and three at a time, right to the room, and even got mad when I said that was a bad practice," the security officer said. "I mean, the pick-ups being brought in were real bums."

"Did you have to ask him to leave?"

"Him?" said Marotta. "This was a woman. She kept bringing in these barroom jerks and I spent half my time keeping her from being robbed."

It does seem, Women's Lib or no Women's Lib, that females would be discreet enough to *sneak* unregistered guests into rooms like men do.

But the times, as the saying goes, are a'changing.

American hotels remain individualistic. At least, we

have yet to reach the day when either Holiday Inns or Playboy have a Bunny-Chaplain.

But it's possible that the only reason we haven't is that nobody has thought of it yet.

To some people, hotels are Hefner's strangest and most impressive accomplishment. Bringing Mommy, Junior, and Sis along with Dear Old Dad to Bunnyland borders, to these observers, on the surrealistic.

Bunny mother Beverly Russell spoke to members of the Sandy Springs, Ga. Baptist Church, and they *loved* her for bringing the bunny message to the dinner-on-the-grounds belt. This, to some, is dreamlike strange, for something in America has spoken to us in the night. A rabbit with hardly anything on . . .

When Hefner, *Esquire* ex-salesman, broke, said he would start a magazine, and did so, some were not impressed. When he got away with nude pictures, they were not impressed particularly; when he pulled in name writers, so what; when his shoestring turned to a money lasso, they were not that impressed.

He built a dynasty; they were not impressed. Key-club to conglomerate-think to financial empire to club-resort success? Yawn.

But when Hefner pulls the family trade to the Playboy bunny, everybody has *got* to be impressed; nobody is so blasé he can fail to be overwhelmed by what Hugh Hefner has done to the picture of America's Heartland.

He has made it a portrait in a figurative collaboration to be long remembered.

Hefner and his hotels are a collaboration of Norman Rockwell and Vargas.

Now, *that's* impressive.

20

Keynotes, Bellmen and Ding-a-lings

Reluctantly leaving our hotel signs behind after this concluding chapter, let us classify these last three as representative of *many* hotel signs everywhere. They fall into (1) signs which are quite coherent but mean exactly the opposite of what the writer intended; (2) signs which *should* be incoherent but say precisely what the writer intended; and (3) signs which mean *nothing to the mortal mind* but which make the world a richer place.

(1) GENTLEMEN ARE REQUESTED NOT TO OVERLOOK THE LADIES BATHING PLACE

(Hotel in Portsmouth, England)

(2) DIRECTION RESERVE TO ITSELF REEMBOURSING THE PRICE OF ANY PERSON TICKET WHOSE ATTITUDE IS UNDEARING FOR THE OTHER PLAYERS AND TO ORDER THOSE UNDEARING PERSONS TO QUIT THE GAME

(*Regulation on the Tom Thumb Golf Course at the Hotel Grand Palais, Ostend, Norway*)

(3) EVERY SUNDAY GREAT KOCKS FIGHT AT CA'N VETA JURT IN FRONT THE ANCIENT BASE HORSES!

(*Hotel in Palma de Mallorca*)

At the beginning we said you really can't run hotels with signs. But hotelmen must try; must, indeed, and sometimes desperately, try with every weapon at their disposal in a gloriously kooky, kinky, unpredictable *business*.

Business remains the key word—but even the keys are, from a *business* standpoint, a strange business. They disappear like mad and although the losses run up into the thousands in today's larger city-within-city hotels, nobody has come up with a solution to stop it.

Large hotels have a machine—usually down in the engine room—to cut their own keys.

There are individual room keys, of course. There are area keys for housekeepers and maids, for doors in certain sections or on certain floors.

"And there have been lovesick maids swept off their feet by beachboy types who weren't after what the maids thought," said one manager. "They were after her key."

There are master keys, kept under close guard. In most hotels only the general manager and the chief engineer carry them, or the security chief. The master key is the thief's idea of heaven on earth.

There are "lock-out keys" for in-arrears or suspicious guests. (Your door won't open and you have to go to the office.)

There is the "dead key." It's called that for exactly that reason—it's to open a door even when the door is locked from the inside. (Sometimes they're dead; sometimes just dead drunk, for inordinately long times. Any hotel manager knows a drunk can go without food longer than medical science thinks.)

And, to top it, locks must be changed at regular intervals (at several bucks per lock) to protect guests—and keep insurance rates bearable.

In return for all the protection guests, of course, take the keys.

In return for all the meticulous work to avoid mix-ups, the mix-ups happen; like this manager's nightmare reported in 1971 in *Time* magazine:

> The room in the Dayton hotel was supposed to have been vacant. So it was assigned to Zsa Zsa Gabor, in town for a summer theatre production. But when Zsa Zsa walked in and switched on the lights, she discovered that the room was occupied by a couple of stark-naked men. "I was petrified," she said. "It was scary." The outraged Zsa Zsa checked into a rival hotel and refused to be mollified when the manager of the first hotel had the message "Zsa Zsa, We Love You" emblazoned on his marquee and sent her a bouquet. "He's worse than an ex-husband," said she. "He sent me white mums, which are for dead people."

Like almost everything about the hotel business, key mix-ups would make a book in themselves. The good stories in hotels always have that added strange dimension, such as the plot of the Furious Stewardess.

This girl was on an Air Canada crew grounded at JFK in New York by bad weather. The crew was sent to a nearby airport hotel. She was carrying her overnight belongings in her over-the-shoulder bag, and the clerk merely gave her the key directly instead of to a bellman.

She went up to the assigned room, opened the door, and walked in. A large, hairy, nude male, a beer can on his chest, was watching TV. "Oops, sorry," she blurted.

"S'okay," the man grunted. The girl went downstairs and fumed at the clerk. The other stewardesses told her to calm down; that anybody could make a mistake.

"Why did you blow up at that poor clerk like that?" one stewardess asked.

She calmed down and actually apologized to the clerk.

"Actually," she said, "I was really mad because that big naked clod just glanced at me, and *went right back to watching the damn television again!*"

And, despite all precautions, every hotel is resigned to the frequent guest who leaves and doesn't even click his door shut . . . one reason house officers eat a lot of Tums.

It's not to make you nervous—only realistic—that it is herewith pointed out that a hotel manager's *own* living quarters in almost every hotel has enough bolts and special locks to stop a tank.

You can draw your own moral from this:

"I've been in the hotel business twenty-four years," said Jack MacDonald of Atlantic City, "and I've noticed one fact about a lot of hotelmen. When we travel, we not only lock, bolt, and chain the door. We prop a straight chair under the doorknob."

Bellmen could fill another book, for they are a unique breed whose members contain perhaps more of the damndest individuals than any other branch of hotel work.

New York cabdrivers get the publicity for philosophy, but bellmen as a tribe can spot them cards and the first ten anecdotes.

Edwin P. Shaunessy, general manager of the Park Plaza Hotel in Toronto, remembers a bellman named Joe Schwartz who was working at the Knights of Columbus Hotel in Atlantic City when 150 Roman Catholic nuns checked in for an educational meeting.

Joe Schwartz cheerfully staggered back and forth with baggage. After the nuns were settled in, Shaunessy asked Schwartz how he had done in the tip line.

"I got forty-two God Bless You's, twenty-nine miraculous medals, and three dimes," said Joe philosophically, "and please call me O'Schwartz until I see if these things work."

The bell captain in the Voyager Motor Inn in Durham, N.C., got a call from outside the motel.

"This is Mr. Brown, room 221, and I'm at the airport. I can't seem to reach my wife in our room—please get word to her that I had to fly back on business and will call her later today."

The bell captain went to the room, knocked, got the passkey, and entered. Mrs. Brown, fully clad, was gagged and spread-eagled on the bed, tied down with ropes on both wrists and both ankles. Rape? Robbery? *Nope.* A husband who had a direct cure for nagging.

The minute the gag came loose she screeched, "That dirty son of a bitch did this to me last year in Springfield when I complained about his drinking! I didn't think he would do it again just because I nagged him about his goddamn stinking cigars!"

Bellmen are the ones who get requests for every conceivable illicit service.

"This one guy wanted *four* women," one bellman told *Keyhole.* "Naturally, I told him I couldn't help him."

(Naturally. It is a well-known fact that no bellman in America has ever bootlegged, touted, pimped, or done a single unseemly thing. Ask them.)

At any rate, this man, the spendthrift son of a very famous family, somehow *got* four girls. The bellman saw them leave that night—and it is a matter of record, without identifying the hotel, that the house physician the same night sent this ambitious chap to the hospital with a coronary. (His eyes were evidently bigger than his arteries.)

The good bellman has perfected the blank-eyed stare; seems to see or hear nothing; eyeballs as emotionless as two ball bearings. But he sees everything as he travels the hotel and is the house detective's greatest ally—the non-hustling racketeer bellman, that is. And, as stated, all bellmen are pure and innocent. Also, he can hear currency rustle around a corridor corner, four floors away . . .

He enters more hotel guest rooms more times than any other employee. He is errand boy, messenger, and—were it not for his notoriously puritanical morals and perhaps a sharp-eyed manager—procurer. He is also, more often than not, quite nervous around people writing books of an unknown nature.

"Don'tquoteme," is his favorite big word.

"Don'tquoteme," a bell captain told *Keyhole* in San Francisco, "and I will give you the Bellman's Oath."

"Trustworthy, brave, clean, reverent?"

He grinned. "Nah, lissen. I made this up, A bellman is fast, alert, neat, dependable, deaf, dumb, blind and sexless. Great, huh?"

"Sexless?"

"Man, you *gotta* be! F'rinstance, there's those two rich broads, see, who call me up to the room and—don't-quoteme, but the one on the bed was wearing nothing but, get this, *boots* with spurs *and a mask,* well—"

We won't quote him.

But if any of the approximate 23,000 bellmen in America currently threatening to write their own book ever do, we give them the best possible title: DON'TQUOTEME

Meantime, they remain guys who see more of life in a month than the average person does in a lifetime. And regardless of what he sees, he must never show his surprise, interest, or—certainly—a desire to participate in the events he sees: and he must avoid any flicker of recognition forever after.

The peddler of everything from booze to dope to girls immediately realizes the bellman would be the ideal hustler on the retail level. And, to skip the bellman's traditional poker-faced protestations of innocence in all matters vile, there is one great testimonial to his sense of survival and his discreetness: how many times have you read of a bellman being sent to jail for something?

This doesn't mean he's always moral, not at all. But it does mean he's always thinking . . .

He has a lot to think about.

At the Marco Polo in Hollywood, Fla., a bellman took champagne to the room of a well-known actress. He was gone four hours. Eventually returning, he answered the leering questions well.

"I like to of never got the cork out of that champagne bottle," he said, straight-faced.

At the Conrad Hilton in Chicago a bell captain looked with vast approval on a new bellman and said, "Now, there's the kind of bellman you can trust. He won't even tell *me* the truth."

Like a lot of today's executives, Bob Cournoyer, who runs the Whiteface Inn at Lake Placid, worked his way up to managing director—of the Hotel Hershey in Hershey, Pa.—after starting as a bellboy. He was eighteen, working in a New Hampshire summer resort, when a ravishing Swedish beauty checked in. Later that day, she ordered a beer from room service.

Young Bob took it up. Miss Sweden, on the balcony, was clad only in sunglasses. She asked him to pour the beer and bring it to her.

"I told myself to stop shaking and act like I didn't even notice," Cournoyer recalled years later. And he said he demonstrated remarkable *savoir faire* for an 18-year-old, spilling only about half the beer as he poured it into the glass. It would have worked even better if he hadn't handed her the empty bottle instead of the beer-filled stein.

Years and experience cure that.

Leo Graves, then night manager at the Mayflower in Washington, D.C., looked over his glasses at the oh-so-shy and giggling bride who, checking in with her aging and proudly pompous groom, was squealing and blushing, giggling at the worldly wonder of it all.

As she walked away, hanging for dear life onto the arm of her love-blinded swain, the old night manager watched her wiggle into the elevator and he uttered a line that says it all. "Yeah," he said, "she's about as innocent as a bellhop."

There are, of course, many fine upstanding, clean-living bellmen. Good family men. But bellmen do live in a far out world where daily they run the gamut of every temptation known to man.

Hotel maids are something else. Quite literally. Stop and consider the universal fear of the intrusive maid, who wakes you up when you're asleep or walks in on you under odd circumstances . . . consider that this is a well-founded fear, for it happens just about everywhere.

The maid, in fact, stands tall in American folklore as she is instantly recognizable everywhere, and it's almost awe-inspiring what ominous respect she has managed to command with little more than that broom-cart and a loud knock.

While there are many truly first-class hotels and motor hotels, like the Century Plaza in Los Angeles and the Marriotts, there are also plenty of second- and third-rate clunkers.

To make a point, let's put together a composite of an unhappy hypothetical visit to one of those second-raters—not only because this book is not intended as unqualified praise for the hotel industry, which it would be the first to announce it doesn't deserve, but to make a point about hotel maids.

You arrive. The doorman is leaning on a lamppost chatting and your cab can't get to the entrance. You struggle across the lobby with heavy bags, set them down, and *then* bellmen swoop on them like cawing crows.

You stand waiting at the desk while everybody ignores you. A *truly* supercilious clerk deigns to speak to you. Your reservation can't be found. Eventually it is, but obviously you've caused a lot of trouble—coming into a hotel like that.

The bellman dumps your bag; looks down his nose at whatever the size of the tip. No ice. Twenty-five minutes later a second bellman brings the ice, for another tip. The room TV gets a one-channel view dimly of what appears to be a blizzard in Juneau. The guy who comes up and fails to fix the TV isn't the same guy who is unable to fix the air conditioning or heat—he's another specialist in futility.

The radio won't go very loud but the walls do. You start rooting that the guy in the next room will lose his argument based on his contention that how will she know she doesn't like it if she doesn't try it.

The bed is O.K. if you stay off the petrified wood lump right across the middle. About midnight you actually begin to get lulled by whatever strange sound this sort of hotel *always* has somewhere. (Gnomes in the woodwork? Air in the plumbing? Wolfman in the closet? She's finally trying whatever it is? The ghost of Christmas past? A cuckoo-clock tester from the Black Forest? You can never tell what the noise is or *where* it is. Accept it. Acceptance is the beginning of wisdom.)

And, weak and weary—a raven? The wind, only that and nothing more?—you go exhausted to sleep very, very late.

WHOOM WHAM BLAM BLOOEY!

Wha? Wha wha wha wha?

You sit bolt upright. Doomsday? No.

"You wan' maid-serfs?"

No. Maid service is not what you want—and you scream this or say it tightly, crisply (so you won't start screaming) as your temperament dictates.

It is somewhat after cockcrow. You have your choice of arising to face the Bright New Day, lying there and worrying about various matters, or waiting for the next knock.

Should you sleep she will knock, rest assured.

Should you arise, and dally about with such nonessen-

tial matters as dressing, she will enter while you are
unclad with your posterior in the air looking for the other
cufflink. She will *not* be startled, regardless of what she
finds in the room *she knows full well is occupied.* She's
as innocent as a bellhop.

The reason no hotel maid has written a book is nobody
would believe her. That, or else she doesn't want to get
writer's cramp in her knocking hand.

She will always, however, on her little surprise visit say
the same thing. It is: "You doan wan'na room made up
t'day?" (The dialect is not race-oriented: all maids,
white, black, blotchy, Eskimo, Yankee, Georgia, whatever,
come to say the same sentence the same way. A *Chinese*
maid in any part of America will say, as she walks gum-
chewingly into the bathroom and looks dully at you over
the top of your sports page: "You doan wan'na room
made up t'day?" It is the closest we have to universal
language.)

People have been asked this under all conditions:
while standing on a chair looking over their shoulder in
the mirror to see if the boil on their fanny is better;
while leaping about buck naked doing the side-straddle
hop part of the Air Force exercise; at the moment she
has finally decided to try it if it means that much to you;
while packing the hotel towels into the suitcase; and,
presumably, while standing on the bureau trying to remember if you put the correct number of loops in the
hangman's knot.

"You doan wan'na room made up t'day?"

"No. I was just jumping off the bureau here, soon as I
figure out the knot."

"You ain't checking out today?"

She goes on back out in the hall to roll her shriek-wheel cart, in case anybody—a barbiturate overdose, perhaps—is still asleep. These carts are used only by hotel maids, and are carefully tuned at the factory to sound as if they are forever running over an unusually loud cat.

The composite visit to the far-from-mythical hotel concludes. You try to wash with the practical-joke soap (*Coated with Shellac: Fool Your Friends!*) and cope with bathroom tissue evidently containing a high cellophane-count. (The writer William Price Fox once wrote a description of this kind of toilet tissue in *Holiday* magazine. One of America's best humor writers anyhow, Fox should be immortalized for one sentence alone! It said: "The toilet paper had the quality and consistency of a Clark Bar wrapper.")

One last fight with the plumbing, a bout with the telephone-booth closet, failure to get help with your bags, and you are downstairs where you find that the mail you were waiting for was in the wrong slot and returned by a Mr. Kslocliewrst whose name is much like yours, and you find the snotty room clerk gone. He has been replaced by two silent-order monks in mufti, neither of whom will speak to you.

Eventually, you are curtly motioned toward the cashier, a domineering prison-guard type seated in a cage, who for twenty minutes argues with another guest over his phone bill. (It is Mr. Kslocliewrst vainly denying that he called your wife in Atlanta twice.)

When your turn comes, finally, there is a bit of trouble about the check: she doesn't care if you *are* the governor of South Dakota, the rules say three major credit cards. You barely get out without calling Traveler's Aid.

Now the point is this.

Some version of a few of those incidents has happened to some of us some of the time.

But the hotel maid has happened to us all of the time!

Ladies, we write this not in rancor—but in solemn tribute.

Hotel maids, you are wondrous and you have intimidated America!

Never have so few infuriated so many with so little to work with!

Our hats are off to you!

And, as of course you already knew, so are our pants.

A coauthor of this book, doing research, stayed overnight at an airport hotel in a southern city. It is advertised far and wide as—while in the airport hotel—absolutely soundproof. The greatest jet causes not a whisper of sound from the outside.

This is true.

But early:

WHAM BAM BLOOEY WHOP!

And, through the closed door: "You wan' maid-serfs?"

Tending toward the apoplectic school of thought, the guest leaped out of bed and shouted, "Can't you see the Do Not Disturb sign?"

No answer.

He cracked the door.

The maid said primly, from the door she was pounding on *across the hall:* "You doan wan'na room made up t'day?"

In some fine hotels there are maids who tippy-toe around, and don't bang on doors, and are practically invisible. There are even some hotels where maids don't come on duty until 10 A.M., instead of 8 A.M., so that sleeping guests can sleep a little longer. May their tribe increase.

It may be that all the talk about computerized hotels of the future has a flaw hotelmen have failed to realize. And it is this.

Hotel maids are something else. Quite literally. In an entire huge industry based on getting you *into* a certain hotel, the maid's greatest goal in life is to get you the hell out so she can clean up the room.

She could win.

In which case, everybody else around hotels will be proven to be in the wrong business.

INDUSTRY WITHOUT A SMOKESTACK

Hotels are the basis of conventions. Conventions are a multimillion dollar business affecting us all. The International Association of Convention Bureaus calls conventions "The Industry Without a Smokestack."

The wild and whoop-de-doo side we know.

Professional convention men insist all the Merry Andrew hell-raising the word "convention" brings to mind is over-emphasized. They better hope nobody believes them because whatever else conventions may be—business to businessmen, the herd-instinct to psychologists, a study in crowd reaction to the behavioral scientists—they are, foremost, fun.

This is a light and anecdotal book which refuses to get heavy and significant at the end. But just one listing can show why towns and cities go so hard after conventions—because they affect us all. (In fairness, note the placement of the whoop-de-doo delegate-dollar expenditure, and how far down it is on the list.)

Conventions are, indeed, much more than fun and games and funny-hat ho-ho and a place a man can be with compatible old friends and make lots of new ones.*

Convention delegates pump all those millions into the economy each month and the money, in this order, is spent for:

1. Hotels: rooms, incidentals.
2. Hotels: restaurants.
3. Other restaurants.
4. Beverages.
5. Retail stores.
6. Local transportation.
7. Sightseeing.
8. Theaters.
9. Night clubs, sports, etc.
10. Cars: oil and gas service.
11. Other items.

In this wildly growing smokestackless industry, hotels hustle in a competitive business. When America gets together it goes to a hotel—and a jam-packed hotel, any hotel, could . . . any one of them . . . be the basis of a book or movie, or any number of them.

If there is a drawback in collecting hotel stories, which the authors of *Keyhole* will continue to do, it was best expressed by Toronto's Ed Shaunessy who said:

(* For a short story concerning a lonely man who did nothing but go to conventions, and who in curing his loneliness became an Expert on Everything, see the back of this book.)

"I'm afraid most of my own experiences in the hotel business are either too obscene for publication or too prosaic for humor . . . or maybe just too unbelievable."

And that's a hotel.

Put another way, a hotel is long stretches of the prosaic slammed wide open by the unbelievable.

And from minute to minute you don't know which to expect.

As the hotelman said, "A man doesn't own a hotel. It owns him. It's a fascinating, deceiving, hypnotizing bitch. You find yourself a hundred times swearing to get out of the idiotic business, but there isn't a chance . . ."

OGG, RIGHT ON . . .

Mrs. Ogg adjusted her saber-toothed wrap and said to her husband, "I'm glad you sold the cave you called the —what? I never can remember that word."

"Hotel, dammit!" snarled Ogg. "After all the time I was in the hotel business you could at least remember the word."

"You're so irritable since you quit," said Mrs. Ogg. "You were so happy when you sold the—when you quit."

"Yeah," said Ogg, and as he grinned wickedly a glint of the old light came back to the eyes of the world's first hotelman. "Yeah, what a deal I got from that idiotic Ook. You know, it's funny. There wasn't any such thing as a hotel business until I started it a few cold snaps ago, and now *everybody* thinks they can run one."

"Yes, dear," she said, abstractedly. "Now if you'll help me pack, we can finally take our vacation."

"Uh, actually, dear," said Ogg. "We'll have to put it off a little while."

"What?" she shouted. "Are you going back in that crazy business?"

"Oh, no, dear," he said. She relaxed. He said, "Not exactly. I *did* get a good buy on a couple of caves out on the trail at the long hill. Now, don't get mad—but some guy has invented this round thing and . . ."

"This *what?*" she shouted.

"He calls it a wheel," said Ogg, "and—look, lemme show you these locations, honey, we can't miss if—"

The End

ACKNOWLEDGMENTS

The following leaders of the hotel industry, authors, ad men, publicists, and others have contributed to the writing of this book through anecdotes or direct assistance. We thank them all.

Paul Ames, Director of Marketing, Treadway Inns, Paterson, New Jersey; Danny Amico, Vice-President, The Sherman, Chicago, Illinois; Richard Arey, General Manager, Plaza Inn, Kansas City, Missouri; Lysle Aschaffenburg, President, The Pontchartrain, New Orleans, Louisiana; John Astarita, Vice-President and General Manager, The Drake, New York, New York;

Henry Ogden Barbour, Intercontinental Hotels, New York, New York; Jon Barnes, Innkeeper, Treadway Inn, Newport, Rhode Island; Victor E. Barrett, American Express Company, New York, New York; Jim Bearce, Robert Warner Hotel Representatives, New York, New York; Robert Beck, Dean, School of Hotel Administration, Cornell University, Ithaca, New York; Frank Berkman, Executive Vice-President, Hotel Sales Management Association, New York, New York; Nick Bicking, President, Harbor House Hotel, Michigan; Emmett Bieger, General Manager, The Jung Hotel, New Orleans, Louisiana; Charlie Bird, Director of Sales, Sheraton Biltmore,

Atlanta, Georgia; Collins Bird, General Manager, Georgetown Inn, Washington, D.C.; Ralph Breshears, hotel consultant, Raleigh, North Carolina; Joseph Brosnan, Vice-President, Treadway Inns and Resorts, Paterson, New Jersey; Art Bruns, Miami Springs Villas, Miami, Florida; J. Bryan III, author, Brook Hill, Richmond, Virginia; William Buckley * Director of Sales, Commodore, New York, New York; Knox Burger, literary agent, New York, New York;

D. W. Carlton, Director of Sales, Hotel McAlpin, New York, New York; Lloyd Carswell, Vice-President and General Manager, Sheraton Four Seasons, Toronto, Canada; Robert C. Christenberry, Fort Lauderdale, Florida; Suzanne Coffman, International Hotel Management Company, Coral Gables, Florida; Michael Coffman, Convention Sales Manager, The Deauville, Miami Beach, Florida; William J. Conner, Director of Education, American Hotel and Motel Association, New York, New York; Robert Cournoyer, General Manager, Whiteface Inn, Lake Placid, New York; Joseph Crocy, General Manager, Dinkler Plaza, Atlanta, Georgia; James Crothers, owner, Nassau Beach Hotel, Nassau, Bahamas; George Thomas Cullen, Vice-President, International Hotel Management Company, Newport, Rhode Island;

George K. Dahl, General Manager, Institute of Newspaper Controllers and Finance Officers, Fairhaven, New Jersey; Sam Davis, William P. Herbst Company, Chicago, Illinois; Howard L. Dayton, Dayton Enterprises, Sanibel, Florida; George De Kornfeld, General Manager, Carlton Tower, London, England; Henry Dienna, General Manager, Ambassador Hotel, Los Angeles, California; Carling Dinkler, President, Palm Bay Club, Miami, Florida; Pete Di Tullio, Vice-President, Hyatt International, Chicago, Illinois; David Dorf, Hotel Sales Management Association, New York, New York; Earl Duffy, Vice-President

* Deceased

and General Manager, Royal Sonesta, New Orleans, Louisiana; John C. Egan, General Manager, National Hotel and Motel Educational Exposition, New York; Norman Eldredge, Pompano Beach, Florida; Reuel Elton, Executive Vice-President emeritus, American Society of Association Executives, Fort Lauderdale, Florida;

Jacob Fassett, Director of Research, American Hotel and Motel Association, New York, New York; Karl Fischer, Resident Manager, Essex House, New York, New York; Arthur Flynn, General Manager, Albert Pick Motor Inn, Greensboro, North Carolina; Tom Flynn, Publisher, *Southern Host,* Fort Lauderdale, Florida; Mel Freeman, Pennsylvania Hotel Association, Harrisburg, Pennsylvania; Robert Freeman, Editor and Publisher, *Hotel Management and Innkeeping,* Chicago, Illinois; Sig Front, Vice-President, Sales and Marketing, The Sahara, Las Vegas, Nevada;

Ledyard Gardner, Vice-President and General Manager, The Colony, Palm Beach, Florida; Allan C. George, partner, Harris, Kerr, Forster and Company, Fort Lauderdale, Florida; Milan V. Glumidge, General Manager, Bluebeard's Castle, St. Thomas, Virgin Islands; W. W. "Bud" Grice, Vice-President Marketing, Marriott Hotels, Inc., Washington, D.C.; Charles V. Grigsby, General Manager, Carnival Motor Inn, Daytona Beach, Florida; Paul Grossinger, Grossinger's, Grossinger, New York;

Raymond F. Hall, Six Flags over Texas, Fort Worth, Texas; Scott Hardy, Texas Hotel and Motel Association, San Antonio, Texas; Philip Harrison, Publisher, *Sales Meetings,* Philadelphia, Pennsylvania; Eugene Hegy, First General Resources, New York, New York; Howard Heinsius, President, Needham and Grohmann, New York, New York; Ernest Henderson III, former President, Sheraton Hotels, Boston, Massachusetts; Everett Hetland, President, Hetland and Stevens, Miami, Florida; Daniel C. Hickey, President, Knott Hotels, New York, New York;

Leonard Hicks, Chairman, Leonard Hicks, Miami, Florida; Ralph Hitz, Jr., General Manager, Sheraton Biltmore, Atlanta, Georgia; Gene Hogan, The Deauville, Miami Beach, Florida; Creighton D. Holden, past President, American Hotel and Motel Association, St. Claire Inn, Michigan; Eugene Hosmer, Executive Director, Philadelphia Convention and Visitors Bureau, Philadelphia, Pennsylvania; William Howell, Vice-President, Treadway Inns, Rochester, New York;

Earl M. Johnson, past President, American Hotel and Motel Association, Johnson's Rustic Resort, Houghton Lake, Michigan; Martin Judge, Editor, *Hospitality,* Chicago, Illinois;

Margery Keasler, authoress, Key Biscayne, Miami, Florida; Richard B. Keeley, General Manager, The Americano Motel, Virginia Beach, Virginia; Harry Keenan, Howard Johnson Motor Lodges, Toronto, Canada; Arnold Keithlin, Director of Sales, The Carillon, Miami Beach, Florida; John Kennedy, Hyatt Houses, Chicago, Illinois; John Kinerk, Executive Secretary, New York State Hotel Association, New York, New York; Randolph Kirkley, General Manager, Miami International Airport Hotel, Miami, Florida; Al Koehl,* Koehl, Landis and Landan, New York, New York; Albert Kudrle, American Hotel and Motel Association, New York, New York;

Olaf Lambert, hotel consultant, New Orleans, Louisiana; John S. Lanahan, President, Flagler Hotels, Palm Beach, Florida; Neal Lang, General Manager, Xanadu Club, Freeport, Grand Bahama; Alan Lapidus, architect, New York, New York; Morris Lapidus, architect, Miami and New York; Thomas J. Lennon, President, The Homestead, Hot Springs, Virginia;

C. J. Mack, past President, American Hotel and Motel Association, Vice-President and Managing Director, The Mayflower, Washington, D.C.; Paul W. Mangan, Convention Manager, ITT

* Deceased

Sheraton, Washington, D.C.; Donald B. Martin, General Manager, Martha Washington Hotel, New York, New York; Reginald Martine, Jr., Norwegian-American Lines, Miami, Florida; Albert L. McDermott, American Hotel and Motel Association, Washington, D.C.; Joseph McDonnell, Chalfonte-Haddon Hall, Atlantic City, New Jersey; James T. McFate, past President, American Hotel and Motel Association, General Manager, Hanover Inn, Hanover, New Hampshire; Michael T. McGarry, General Manager, The Claridge, Atlantic City, New Jersey; Hank Meyer, President, Hank Meyer Associates, Miami, Florida; Robert F. Meyer, owner and President, Yankee Silversmith Inn, Wallingford, Connecticut; Fred Mino, * partner, Laventhol, Krekstein, Horwath and Horwath, New York, New York; John Monahan, President, The Marco Polo, Miami Beach, Florida; Gardner Moore, President, Bedford Springs Hotel, Bedford, Pennsylvania; Stuart L. Moore, General Manager, The Oceanus, Freeport, Grand Bahama; William Morton, Vice-President, Director of Marketing, ITT Sheraton, Boston, Massachusetts; Harry Mullikin, Senior Vice-President, Western International Hotels, Seattle, Washington;

Reginald Nefzger, hotel consultant, Houston, Texas;

Leonard Oakes, General Manager, Hotel Sales Management Association, New York, New York; Lawson Odde, Executive Vice-President, American Hotel and Motel Association, New York, New York; Arch J. Oliver, Vice-President and General Manager, Galt Ocean Mile, Fort Lauderdale, Florida;

Porter Parris, General Manager, Conrad Hilton, Chicago, Illinois; Dill Parrish, Vice-President, Chalfonte-Haddon Hall, Atlantic City, New Jersey; Wallace Patterson, Publisher, *Hospitality,* Chicago, Illinois; Sterling Peck, General Manager, Bel Air Sands, Hollywood, California; Howard C. Pereira, Director of Sales, Hotel Lexington, New York, New York; Whit Perry,

* Deceased

Director of Public Relations, Holiday Inns, Memphis, Tennessee; Adrian Phillips, Executive Vice-President emeritus, Hotel Sales Management Association, Absecon, New Jersey; Phillip Pistilli, President, Alameda Plaza Inc., Kansas City, Missouri; George Podd, partner, Laventhol, Krekstein, Horwath and Horwath, Chicago, Illinois; George W. Powell, European General Manager, Canadian Travel Bureau, London, England; W. Fred Puffer, General Manager, The La Salle, Chicago, Illinois;

Robert Quain, Senior Vice-President, Hilton Hotels, New York, New York; John H. Quarty, President, San Marcos Hotel, Chandler, Arizona;

Murray Rappaport,* partner, Harris, Kerr, Forster and Company, New York, New York; Helen Recknagel, Professor, School of Hotel Administration, Cornell University, Ithaca, New York; Robert A. Reidel, Southern Inns, Incorporated, Tallahassee, Florida; Richard Regan, General Manager, Arlington Towers, Chicago, Illinois; Anthony Rey, General Manager, Chalfonte-Haddon Hall, Atlantic City, New Jersey; Robert L. Richards, General Manager, American Hotel and Motel Association, New York, New York; Louis Rogers, President, The Fontainebleau, Miami Beach, Florida; Gilbert Rosenbrier, General Manager, O'Hare Inn, Chicago, Illinois;

Mark Schmidt, Vice-President and General Manager, The Sheraton Cadillac, Detroit, Michigan; William Scholz, Director of Public Relations, American Hotel and Motel Association, New York, New York; Ralph Schwartzberg, The Flying Carpet, Chicago, Illinois; Danny Shaw, hotel consultant, Fort Lauderdale Florida; E. C. "Buzz" Sherry, General Manager, The Commodore, New York, New York; Larry Shupnick, Los Angeles, California; Jack M. Slone, Diners-Fugazy, Atlanta,

* Deceased

Georgia; James Barker Smith, President, Wentworth-by-the-Sea, Wentworth, New Hampshire; H. M. "Bud" Smith, Sheraton Hotels, Honolulu, Hawaii; Sheridan Smith, Sales Manager, The Roosevelt, New York, New York; Roger Sonnabend, President, Hotel Corporation of America (Sonesta), Boston, Massachusetts; Bob Stein, partner, Gardner, Stein and Frank, Chicago, Illinois; George J. Stobie, President, Castle Harbour, Bermuda; Steve Styron, Georgia Hotel and Motel Association, Atlanta, Georgia; Jean Suits, General Manager, Doral Beach and Doral C. C., Miami, Florida; Frank Swadley, General Manager, Dupont Plaza Hotel, Washington, D.C.; Edgar A. Sweet, Sales Manager, St. Moritz, New York, New York;

J. B. Temple, Senior Vice-President, Holiday Inns, Memphis, Tennessee; Robert Thurston, Vice-President, Hertz Skycenters, Huntsville, Alabama; Robert Preston Tisch, President, Loew's Hotels, New York, New York; John Tyler, Director of Sales, The Deauville, Miami Beach, Florida;

Dorothy Walton, Assistant to the President, The Diplomat, Hollywood, Florida; Roy Watson, past President, American Hotel and Motel Association, President, Kahler Hotels, Rochester, Minnesota; Seymour Weiss,* President, The Roosevelt, New Orleans, Louisiana; Robert Whalen, Director of Sales, Playboy Hotels, Chicago, Illinois; Kemmons Wilson, Chairman, Holiday Inns, Memphis, Tennessee;

Bud Young, Innkeeper, Holiday Inn, Airport, Atlanta, Georgia.

* Deceased